AFRICAN WOMEN
AND CHILDREN

AFRICAN WOMEN AND CHILDREN

Crisis and Response

EDITED BY
Apollo Rwomire

Westport, Connecticut
London

Library of Congress Cataloging-in-Publication Data

African women and children : crisis and response / edited by Apollo Rwomire.
     p.   cm.
   Includes bibliographical references and index.
   ISBN 0–275–96218–0 (alk. paper)
   1. Women—Africa—Social conditions.   2. Children—Africa—Social conditions.
   I. Rwomire, Apollo, 1945–
   HQ1787.A3715   2001
   305.4'096—dc21   00–027435

British Library Cataloguing in Publication Data is available.

Library of Congress Catalog Card Number: 00–027435
ISBN: 0–275–96218–0

First published in 2001

Praeger Publishers, 88 Post Road West, Westport, CT 06881
An imprint of Greenwood Publishing Group, Inc.
www.praeger.com

Printed in the United States of America

The paper used in this book complies with the
Permanent Paper Standard issued by the National
Information Standards Organization (Z39.48–1984).

10 9 8 7 6 5 4 3 2 1

Contents

Acknowledgments

I would like to thank the contributors to this volume, without whose effort and commitment its completion would not have been possible. I was very fortunate to work with several colleagues who provided valuable comments and constructive criticism on individual sections of the book. I am particularly grateful to the following reviewers for their helpful suggestions and corrections that helped to improve the style and content of the book: Arnon Bar-On (Israel), Dorothy Brandon (United States), Anthony Hopkin (United Kingdom), Logong Raditlhokwa (Botswana), and Peter Mwikisa (Zambia).

Thanks also go to the Research and Publications Committee of the Faculty of Social Sciences, University of Botswana, for its offer of a grant which enabled me to prepare the manuscript for publication.

Introduction

Dorothy Brandon and Apollo Rwomire

Although women constitute at least 50 percent of the world's population and perform two-thirds of the world's work, they earn only 10 percent of the world's income and own only 1 percent of the world's property (Rowbotham, 1992). Put more simply, women throughout the world live in severe conditions of poverty. Yet even though they are generally disadvantaged in comparison to men, it seems that African women are poorer than women are elsewhere. It is estimated that in Africa, women comprise 80 percent of the poor, as compared to 70 percent and 45 percent in Asia and Latin America, respectively (Olusi, 1997). The case studies in this book clearly demonstrate the extent to which African women are exploited and oppressed in various spheres of their lives. In the home they are overburdened with domestic tasks, sexually abused, battered, and at times murdered—largely because they are female. In the workplace, they are overworked, underpaid, and exploited in other ways.

Like women, Africa's children suffer various forms of abuse, neglect, and exploitation, including physical violence, sexual abuse, emotional abuse, and economic exploitation. Child abuse and neglect come in various shapes and sizes. In the African context, sexual abuse includes female genital mutilation (FGM), teenage pregnancy, rape, and incest. Emotional and psychological abuse is manifested in mental disorders, aggression, promiscuity, poor self-image, drug abuse, suicide, and poor academic performance. Physical abuse includes assaults, burns, cuts, and other life-threatening injuries. Child exploitation is reflected in child labor, pornography, and prostitution. Other types of abuse and neglect are malnutrition, educational deprivation, and medical neglect. Reports indicate that AIDS has orphaned millions of children in sub-Saharan Africa, and many children are themselves infected with the HIV virus. Tens of thousands under the age of 18 are participating in Africa's armed conflicts. And millions of African children (and women) have been displaced by the continent's perennial wars.

Comparing the status of African women and children to the status of women and children in the majority of other parts of the world, or comparing their current status to their own status 10 years ago, it would appear that there has been a considerable decline in their welfare. This suggests that women and children are still not full beneficiaries of many of the development programs that have been instituted in Africa; instead, they are the victims (Karl, 1995).

This chapter provides a comprehensive overview of the status of women and children in Africa by looking at factors that contribute to the overall status of both groups. The contributing factors to this status are interlinked and mutually reinforcing. They include the exploitation of poverty; child labor; social, economic, and political inequalities; limited access to education and health care; and various types of violence. Although many of these factors affect both groups, how and to what extent these groups are affected differ. These factors, however, seem to have more serious repercussions on the lives of women and children in Africa than in most other parts of the world. The following analysis focuses on Africa, yet the problems examined are neither culture specific nor limited to Africa.

EXPLOITATION OF POVERTY

Economic programs, such as structural adjustment programs, have reversed many of Africa's accomplishments. Instead of reducing poverty, they seem to be perpetuating it. In sub-Saharan Africa, the number of people living in poverty is increasing. Between 1985 and 1990 the number of people living in poverty increased by 32 million, and it was projected to increase by 84 million by the year 2000 (UNECA and UNICEF, 1996). In addition, the depth of this poverty has fallen below the poverty line more than elsewhere (World Bank, 1995). According to the 1997 Human Development Report, by the year 2000 half the population of sub-Saharan Africa would be in poverty. With population growth surpassing economic growth, Africa was projected to be 22 percent poorer than it was 23 years ago (APIC, 1998a).

Although poverty affects men, women, and children, there appears to be a stronger link between women and poverty. The number of women living in poverty makes up an overwhelming majority of more than 70 percent of the world's poor. Women living in Africa are among the poorest of the poor. The extent of both "human poverty," defined as "deprivation in terms of short lives, illiteracy, and lack of basic services," and "income poverty" among African women is usually higher (UNDP, 1997). Both types of poverty for women in most countries in sub-Saharan Africa have and still are increasing.

Poverty among women is substantially linked to the "feminization of poverty." This concept means that poverty is largely concentrated among female-headed households. Studies have shown that female-headed households are poorer than those headed by males or by both males and females. On average, females head 35 percent of the households in sub-Saharan Africa (Neft and Levine, 1997). They head 25 percent of the households in Ghana, Malawi, Rwanda, and Zambia and 45 percent of the households in Botswana (UNECA and UNICEF, 1996). Children are no exception to the level of poverty confronting women: Their overall level of poverty is intertwined with that of females, making their poverty status much the same as that of women. Moreover, there seems to be a correlation between poverty and child labor.

CHILD LABOR

The exploitation of poverty is cited as "the most powerful force driving children into hazardous, debilitating labor" (UNICEF, 1997: 27). Because children are paid far less, and they are less likely to question authority, they are employed more quickly than adults are. For poor families, employment of children is unavoidable.

Because of the worsening economic situation in Africa, the number of child laborers is increasing. According to Ashagire (1993), of the world's 79 million children who are economically active, 17 million are in Africa, with a participation rate of 22 percent of all children between the ages of 10 and 14. Nearly 33 percent of the children in Eastern Africa and 24 percent in Western Africa in the same age category are in the labor force.

The exploitation of children in the commercial sector is prevalent in many African countries. For example, the International Labor Organization (ILO, 1996) reported that in Kenya approximately 20 to 30 percent of the casual labor force on all types of plantations were composed of children. This report further noted that 30 percent of the coffee pickers during peak harvest season were below 15 years of age and that on some rice plantations up to 90 percent of the transplanters were children. In Zimbabwe it was reported that children working on large cotton and coffee plantations for 60 hours a week earned about $1 a day (UNICEF, 1997).

Linked with poverty is the commercial sexual exploitation of children. It is estimated that at least 1 million girls worldwide are lured or forced into sex work each year (UNICEF, 1997). This sexual exploitation of children is not exclusive to girls; boys, too, are victims. Although this type of exploitation seems greatest in Asia, Africa is not excluded. Because of the illegal and clandestine nature of this type of labor, there is little reliable data. However, there is no denying the existence of the phenomenon in Africa. According to Mupedziswa (1997: 43), in Zimbabwe:

Some children engage in this "trade" [prostitution] to realize some income. Other female children are forced into prostitution, while a good number enter into forced marriages, all because their parents can no longer afford to look after them. A local magazine recently reported of a 13-year-old girl who was being forced by her own mother to sleep with older men for money. One client is reported to have paid Z$300 for sexual favors, and from this the girl was given Z$100 while the mother pocketed the rest. The matter only surfaced when the child contracted a sexually transmitted disease.

In a report by UNICEF, *The State of the World's Children 1997*, streetwork, work for the family, and girl work were also described as exploitation of child labor. These three types, together with the aforementioned types of child labor, all impact very negatively on the physical, social, and psychological well-being of children's lives. The majority of these jobs place children in hazardous working conditions that jeopardize their lives.

SOCIAL, ECONOMIC, AND POLITICAL INEQUALITIES

Gender inequality is one of the major contributors to the low status of women and the disproportionate representation of women living in poverty. In no part of the world is women's quality of life equal to that of their male counterparts. In terms of access to education, health, employment, and freedom, it is evident that African women have a long way to go in order to balance out the disparities between the genders.

Compared to men, women in most African countries have far less political, legal, and economic power. In some countries, women are reported to have absolutely no rights to political, legal, social, and economic equality. Such unequal access to power in these aspects of life has had and still is having devastating effects on the lives of women. For example, African women work approximately 13 hours per week more than men do, and their work accounts for nearly 80 percent of the food production in Africa. Yet they are not entitled to agricultural credit and extension services, nor do they benefit much from government or international programs favoring cash crops (APIC, 1998b; UNDP, 1996).

Women's participation in the labor force in Africa suggests another gender imbalance in the economic aspect of women's lives. In sub-Saharan Africa, only 34 percent of the working women participated in the workforce in 1990, and in countries such as Benin, Chad, Mali, Nigeria, Namibia, Egypt, Morocco, and Algeria, less than 25 percent of the women were employed in the labor force. Moreover, women who work for pay are concentrated in very low-paying jobs with little opportunity for promotion (UNDP, 1995).

In addition, the unequal representation of women in the political decision-making process is noticeable in the low participation of African women in government. As of July 1998, data from the Inter-Parliamentary Union indicated that of more than 40 African countries assessed, less than 1 percent had at least 25 percent of women in parliament.

LIMITED ACCESS TO EDUCATION

Although the number of literate women worldwide has increased significantly in the past 10 to 20 years, women still make up an overwhelming two-thirds of the world's illiterate population (UNDP, 1993). Many of these women live in Africa. According to data compiled by Demographic and Health Surveys (1994), a large percentage of women in many African countries have never attended school. For example, of 21 sub-Saharan African countries surveyed in the Demographic and Health Surveys' report, nearly half (9) indicated that between 57 and 89 percent of their female population between the ages of 15 and 49 had no formal education. Comparatively, almost 65 percent of the women in Africa over the age of 15 are illiterate, as compared to only about 40 percent of the males. In addition to Africa's adult female literacy rate being the lowest in the world, the number of African women who are illiterate was projected to increase by 14.5 million by the year 2000 (UNDP, 1994).

Limited access to education has implications not only for women, but also for the well-being and development of their children and families, as well as the socioeconomic well-being of the nation itself. According to the Inter-Parliamentary Union and UNESCO (1996), when women without schooling are compared to those with a primary education, the latter tend to have lower fertility rates. Furthermore, they are also more likely to protect the health of their children through immunization and other health measures, and to ensure that their children—girls as well as boys—attend and complete school. Clearly, a major way of empowering women is to offer them education. Educated women are more likely to marry at a later age, and have fewer and healthier children. They tend to be more productive at work and make substantial contributions to national economic and political development.

The Girl Child

Access to basic education in Africa has made tremendous progress over the past decades. This is especially true of primary education. More than 80 percent of the children in Africa are enrolled in grade one, and the number of girls enrolled is almost equal that of boys at this level. However, it appears that as the grade level increases so does the gap between the gender relative to enrollment. According to UNECA and UNICEF (1996), 1 in 3 children in Africa drop out of school before finishing grade four, and nearly two-thirds of the students who drop out are girls (Neft and Levine, 1997). UNDP (1995) describes Africa's education system as pyramidal, with a high concentration of females at the base, or primary level, and only a very few at the apex of the pyramid, or tertiary level. It was noted that only 23 percent of the female primary school graduates enter secondary schools, and less than 3 percent of those who leave secondary school enter tertiary levels.

Girls' access to and completion of basic education, as stated by UNICEF, is limited through attitudes, practices, knowledge, and behavior. These factors create obstacles that contribute to the disproportionate number of girls who have no access to, drop out of, or have low performance in school. Obstacles identified by UNICEF include time-consuming chores; complications from pregnancy; school perceived as a low priority for girls; high cost of education; too few or overcrowded schools; discriminatory attitudes, practices, and behavior by teachers, parents, and community members; and a lack of female role models. Others are gender bias in curricula; teaching methodologies, textbooks, and materials; long distances between home and schools; teenage pregnancy; and early marriage.

Most African countries will face "severe and persistent crises in the education sector" in the coming years (UNDP, 1995). This is due in part to declining enrollment and increasing dropout rates, especially among girls. In addition, the demand for schooling in Africa is declining. This can be seen in Africa's overall 2.3 increase in enrollment during 1990–1995, which was less than the overall increase in population. In Zimbabwe, for example, Gwarinda (1994) outlines several emerging trends that tend to indicate the severity of the situation. The trends are described as follows:

- The objective of universal education is being negated, as fewer people are able to afford sending their children through various levels of education.
- Given that Zimbabwean society is patriarchal, many girl children will fail to acquire formal education, for some families will be forced to maximize the education of boys who are regarded as social insurance for their parents.
- The pre-independence elitist model of education, under which a tiny minority of the people who went to school ever acquired tertiary education, is resurfacing.
- A rigid capitalist class reproduction will emerge, and only the middle and upper classes will be able to afford secondary education for their children.

Hence the objective of enhancing prosperity for the people as a whole will be negated.

- With a shrinking economy, education qualifications will continue to be devalued as various jobs will require higher and higher qualifications, which may not be necessary for the jobs.

- A shrinking economy will intensify racism, sexism, regionalism, and ethnicism as different social groups try to maximize their advantages to earn means of subsistence.

LACK OF ACCESS TO HEALTH SERVICES

Africa has made many significant strides toward improving the health status of its people. Nonetheless, 50 percent of all Africans still have no access to basic health care, life expectancy is 20 years behind that of industrialized countries, and sub-Saharan Africa is home to 70 percent of the world's adults with AIDS. In addition, 40 percent of the population in the region goes hungry (UNDP, 1996; UNAIDS and UNICEF, 1996). Although the overall health status of Africans is alarming, the status of African women is even more appalling. According to the World Health Organization (WHO, 1998), limited information, ideas, and options; poor quality of interaction with health care providers; and unequal power relations that constrain women's decision-making ability, physical mobility, and access to material resources are but a few of the many barriers preventing women from achieving good health.

As reported by Neft and Levine (1997), approximately 580,000 women die yearly in developing countries due to pregnancy-related causes. The average maternal mortality rate for women in Africa is 980 deaths per 100,000 live births and 980 for sub-Saharan Africa compared to 9 for the United Kingdom and 12 for the United States. In countries such as Angola, Chad, Mozambique, Guinea, Somalia, and Sierra Leone, the maternal mortality rate is as high as 1,500 to 1,800 deaths per 100,000 live births. One in 20 African women die during pregnancy or childbirth compared to 1 in 10,000 in developed countries (UNDP, 1994).

During 1995 it was estimated that 13 million (65%) of the world's total population of adults living with HIV/AIDS were in sub-Saharan Africa. The projection for the year 2000 is that this number will increase to between 18 million and 24 million (UNAIDS, 1996). The epidemic poses a serious threat to the health status of African women and children. Of the 13 million people living with AIDS in sub-Saharan Africa, 6 million are females.

According to some researchers, young females are especially vulnerable to HIV/AIDS (WHO, 1997; Neft and Levine, 1997). In 1997, approximately 3 million people between 15 and 24 years of age were infected with the virus, and nearly two-thirds were females (UNICEF,

1998). In Uganda, the ratio of girls infected to boys infected is 6 to 1, and in Malawi and Zambia it is 5 to 1 (Neft and Levine, 1997).

Child Malnutrition

Concerns about child malnutrition in Africa are not new. Concerts, campaigns, and many other efforts have been used to draw national as well as international attention to the problem of visible malnutrition, which is usually caused by conflicts or famine. This type of malnutrition affects 3 to 4 percent of the children in Africa (UNECA and UNICEF, 1996). However, invisible malnutrition affects the lives of far more children. UNICEF (1998) describes invisible malnutrition as a "silent emergency" because it is more difficult to detect. Invisible malnutrition affects 1 in every 3 African children, and 55 percent of children's deaths in Africa are either directly or indirectly the effects of malnutrition-related illnesses (UNICEF, 1998). Malnutrition, visible or invisible, significantly decreases a child's chance of survival. Children with severe malnutrition and those who are moderately or mildly malnourished are 8, 5, and 2 times, respectively, more likely to die than well-nourished children (UNECA and UNICEF, 1996). In sub-Saharan Africa, 42 percent of the children under 5 years of age are moderately or severely stunted in height largely due to malnutrition.

Although immediate malnutrition can be corrected, its long-term damage often cannot be corrected. Children who do not receive an adequate amount of iodine, vitamin A, or iron can suffer from mental, cognitive, and physical damage. In Africa, more than 30,000 children a year are blinded, and millions others are susceptible to diarrhoeal disease, measles, and pneumonia due to vitamin A deficiency (UNECA and UNICEF, 1995).

VIOLENCE AGAINST WOMEN

Around the world millions of women each year are killed or seriously injured due to violence. Violent acts such as rape, female battering, sexual exploitation, sexual harassment, incest, and abuse are but a few of the multiple forms of violence confronting women. According to the World Bank, many of these violent acts "are a significant cause of disability among women" (1995: 1). These forms of violence cause not only physical harm, but psychological, social, and mental suffering as well. The literature on women in development shows that little attention has been paid to the negative impact violence against women has on the human rights of women as well as the development of a country.

As a global effort to prevent and control worldwide violence against women, in 1993 the United Nations General Assembly adopted the Declaration on the Elimination of Violence against Women. According to this declaration, violence against women is any violent act that results in physical, sexual, or psychological harm or suffering to women (UN, 1995). Although 34 countries in Africa have signed the declaration, little to nothing has been done in most African countries to prevent violence against women. According to the African Policy Information Center, South Africa is "the only African country that has enacted legislation outlawing domestic violence and rape" (APIC, 1998b: 1). Likewise, of 28 African countries surveyed by UNICEF (1996), Ghana is the only country that has specific laws that prohibit violence against women in the form of female genital mutilation.

Because of certain religious, traditional, and cultural beliefs, such as having to discipline a wife, much of the male violence against women in Africa is either ignored or condoned. Although domestic violence in Africa is not well reported, it is very high (APIC, 1998b). Pronk (1994) found that violence against women, especially domestic violence and rape, poses a very serious problem in Kenya, Uganda, Zambia, Sudan, Mali, and Senegal. For example, in one district of Uganda only 10 to 20 percent of domestic violence cases were reported to the police (UN, 1989). Not just in Uganda, but throughout Africa many women do not report such cases out of fear of their husbands, shame, or community ostracism—or simply because they have been conditioned to see violence as an acceptable component of the female-male relationship. Examples of this silence or avoidance can be seen in the multitude of African women who are raped by soldiers or guerrillas during times of war. Millions are forced to perform sexual favors in return for staying in refugee camps, and millions are battered or sexually harassed at work and/ or at home. In addition, 2 million African girls are sexually mutilated each year. In many countries in Africa, traditional practices and customs also perpetuate violent acts against women and girls. Practices such as female circumcision, *trokosi,* and restrictions regarding land and inheritance rights violate women's and girls' human rights as well as cause physical and psychological suffering.

In most African countries, violence against women is on the rise. For example, the Panafrican News Agency cites incidents of extreme insecurity in the streets of Zimbabwean towns. It also reports cases of violence on college campuses, where female students have been stripped naked because they were allegedly not dressed decently. Violence against women is pervasive in the home, in the workplace, as well as on the streets. Surprisingly, it is also found in government. For instance, in 1998 a former army chief of staff had to be physically restrained from physically attacking a female member of parliament during a war of words. In another incident, the mayor of Harare refused to settle a matter with a female member of parliament, saying he wanted to talk to her husband instead.

SUMMARY OF THE CONTRIBUTIONS

This book explores various facets of the status of women and children in contemporary Africa. It provides a multidisciplinary and comparative analysis of the nature, origins, and consequences of social problems facing African women and children. It also reviews social policies and programs designed to address the problems.

The contributors to this volume include academics, researchers, and policy makers from a diversity of academic backgrounds, national origins, and theoretical and philosophical orientations. Drawing on their substantial experiences, they provide rich and up-to-date research on the subordination and oppression of women and children in Africa.

The socioeconomic, political, and educational status of women in Southern and Eastern Africa is explored by Anthony Hopkin (Chapter 1) in a comparative context. First, a broad descriptive analysis of the status of women is undertaken, and selected gender issues in the "developed" world and in some Islamic countries are explored. The focus then moves to sub-Saharan Africa and, lastly, to Eastern and Southern Africa. The principal findings of 13 gender- and education-oriented research projects reported by the Educational Research Network in Eastern and Southern Africa (ERNESA) are then considered and evaluated from a regional and comparative perspective. In the final discussion, attention is drawn to the disadvantaged socioeconomic, political, and educational status of women in sub-Saharan Africa in general, and in the region in particular, when considered in a comparative and world context.

As a result of increasing divorce rates in both developed and developing countries, the issue of how divorce and marital separation affects children has been the subject of increasing academic interest. Tapologo Maundeni, in Chapter 2, examines the dynamics as well as the impact of marital separation and divorce on children, with special reference to Southern Africa. She focuses on conflict and violence between parents, decline in family standards of living following divorce, lack of communication between divorcees and children, and loss of supportive networks. Maundeni emphasizes that these experiences cause a tremendous amount of stress to children. She then explores several policy and practice issues that need to be addressed in order to reduce the high level of stress affecting child victims of parental separation and divorce.

In Chapter 3, Norma Romm and Apollo Rwomire provide a global view of the nature, origins, and consequences of various types of child abuse, including physical and emotional. They review the major theoretical approaches that sociologists have employed to explain this complex and controversial issue, and they show the interlinkages between child abuse and certain causal social and psychological factors. The theories covered include strain theory, control theory, cultural transmission theory, neutralization theory, social learning theory, and symbolic interactionism. Various ways of reducing child abuse are suggested.

In Chapter 4, Abdul-Mumin Sa'ad examines the relationship between traditional institutions (economic, political, legal, religious, family) and the seemingly endemic nature of women's oppression and exploitation in Africa. He points out that women's oppression is deeply rooted in excessive traditional social and cultural control, especially in rural areas. He begins with a broad overview of what human rights means and whether women's rights are human rights. Then he examines the nature and extent of oppression of women as embedded in Africa's traditional institutions with special reference to Nigeria. Finally, he takes a critical look at the various policies in Africa (and in Nigeria in particular) that seek to safeguard women's human rights, with a view to evolving strategies that could more effectively further and guarantee women's human rights.

Chapter 5, by Nana Boaten, focuses on the *trokosi*, a traditional religious practice that involves giving young virgins to fetish priests to atone for the sins supposedly committed by senior relatives. While in bondage, the young women are transformed into sex objects and laborers for the priests, who are the main beneficiaries of the practice. The children born to the priests are often abused and neglected by their fathers. It is estimated that there are about 20,000 *trokosis* in the West African states of Ghana, Benin, and Togo. Boaten discusses the social implications of the *trokosi* as well as the legal measures that statutory and nongovernmental organizations have taken to liberate and rehabilitate the captive women.

Chapter 6, by Gwen Lesetedi, is concerned with the feminization of poverty, a situation whereby female-headed families are disproportionately represented among the poorer economic strata. Although Botswana (the case study at hand) has enjoyed a remarkable economic performance over the past two decades, the country continues to experience unacceptably high levels of poverty and inequality. During this period, the proportion of households headed by women has increased dramatically. These women and their dependent children are especially prone to poverty as manifested in low incomes, hunger and malnutrition, and high rates of morbidity and mortality. They are poor because of the lack of economic resources, limited access to education and training, inadequate participation in decision making, and gender-based discrimination in various spheres of life. In order to reduce the incidence of poverty, the government of Botswana has initiated a number of policies and interventions. Lesetedi critically evaluates one of these programs, the Arable

Lands Development Program (ALDEP). Her overall conclusion is that ALDEP has not fulfilled its intended objectives and may even have aggravated the plight of female-headed households in certain respects.

In Chapter 7, Ishmael Magaisa investigates the socioeconomic and psychological aspects of prostitution in the context of Zimbabwe. Based on empirical evidence derived mainly from interviews with Zimbabwean prostitutes, the analysis demonstrates that the so-called oldest profession is a manifestation of gender inequality and conflict. Magaisa argues that prostitution is a reflection of the prostitutes' struggle for the right to economic independence and sexual determination, as well as their refusal to be exploited and controlled, especially in marriage.

Chapter 8, by Roseline Onah, shows that women in Nigeria live in poverty largely because of their limited access to economic opportunities and political power. She asserts that the Nigerian economy and society are so structured that women lack access to capital, credit, land, and education. Gender-based inequalities mean that women, particularly those who live in rural areas, are unable to improve their standards of living. Onah critically reviews policies and programs that various regimes in Nigeria have enunciated and tried to implement in order to promote gender equality and enhance women's access to economic and political power. The strategies covered include the establishment of training centers for women, political and economic awareness creation programs, political education, and adult literacy programs. It is argued that the said programs have not yielded the intended results because they have been essentially elitist. They have not benefited the rural women who constitute the majority of Nigerian women.

Bertha Osei-Hwedie, in Chapter 9, discusses the participation of Zambian women in politics and describes the obstacles to such participation by comparing the First, Second, and Third Republics. She argues that since political liberalization was introduced in Zambia in the 1990s, it has not radically improved the role of women in politics and in some instances has worsened their political situation. Factors such as the patriarchal culture, lack of resources, the character of the state, and lack of commitment and proper strategy on the part of women's nongovernmental organizations, all in an interlinked manner, have constrained the participation of Zambian women in politics since independence.

In Chapter 10, Arnon Bar-On examines the controversial issue of *child streetism*. Street children might not be securely lodged in the life-patterns that the middle class imposes on children, but their reward for trying to maintain a minimum standard of living that their parents and governments are unable to provide them is infinitely preferable to living in the absolute poverty that surrounds them. Bar-On's argument is based mainly on research from several African countries and on a critique of current knowledge about the maturation of children that is informed primarily by Northern mores and by "scientific" proofs. He seeks to explain why, in spite of the aforementioned fact, members of the caring professions find *child streetism* so abhorrent. He further questions why it is taken for granted that certain norms can, and should, prevail in Africa just because they are found in Northern societies.

Faustin Kalabamu (Chapter 11), with special reference to Botswana, shows that despite vigorous pursuit of gender-neutral policies for over 30 years, the housing conditions of male- and female-headed households still differ. Taking the town of Lobatse as a case study, he explains that the differences are due to continued adherence to legal, institutional, and philosophical patriarchal beliefs and structures. He also contends that unless everyday actions, attitudes, perceptions, obligations, and requirements that define women's and men's roles, relations, and expectations are deconstructed, gender-neutral policies, however consistently observed, will not eliminate gender inequalities.

According to Mark Chingono (Chapter 12), change in the relationship between women and the environment is being accelerated by the massive expansion in scientific and technological knowledge worldwide. With reference to African women, Chingono explores the dialectic between women and the environment, and pays particular attention to the role of knowledge and power in shaping it. The analysis necessarily becomes a project of deconstruction and reconstruction, of myths and possibilities, respectively. Chingono questions the myths about the presumed relationship between women and the environment and those that celebrate patriarchal ideology and other hegemonic discourses. The challenge, he points out, is to identify and construct possibilities for social progress from the real world as it is.

REFERENCES

Africa Policy Information Center (APIC). (1998a). *Africa at the Turning Point: Development Hinges on Success in Population, Health.* Washington, DC: APIC.
———. (1998b). *Strategic Action Issue Area: African Women's Rights.* Washington, DC: APIC.
Ashagrie, K. (1993). "Statistics on Child Labour." *Bulletin of Labour Statistics* (3), Geneva, Switzerland.
Demographic and Health Surveys. (1994). *Women's Lives and Experience: A Decade of Research Findings from the Demographic and Health Survey.* Calverton, MD: Macro International Inc.
Gwarinda, T. C. (June 1994). "The Effects of ESAP on Education."*Journal of Social Change and Development*, 35.
International Labor Organization (ILO). (1996). *Child Labor in Commercial Agriculture in Africa Report.* Dar es Salaam, Tanzania: ILO.

Inter-Parlimentary Union and United Nations Educational, Scientific, and Cultural Organization (UNESCO). (1996). *Inter-Parliamentary Conference on Education, Science, Culture and Communication on the Eve of the 21st Century Report*. Geneva: Inter-Parliamentary Union.

Karl, M. (1995). *Women and Empowerment: Participation and Decision-Making*. London: Zed Books Ltd.

Mupedziswa, R. (1997). *Empowerment or Repression? ESAP and Children in Zimbabwe*. Gweru, Zimbabwe: Mambo Press.

Neft, N. and Levine, A. D. (1997). *Where Women Stand: An International Report on the Status of Women in 140 Countries 1997–1998*. New York: Random House.

Olusi, J. (1997). "Enhancing Female Participation in African Agricultural Transformation: The Nigerian Experience." *ISSUE: Journal of Opinion*, 25(2).

Panafrican News Agency. (April 1998). "Gender Violence on the Rise in Zimbabwe."

Pronk, J. (1994). "Violence against Women as an Obstacle to Development." In *Poverty and Development, Analysis and Policy Calling for Change: International Strategies to End Violence against Women*. Leiden, The Netherlands: Development Cooperation Information Department.

Rowbotham, S. (1992). *Women in Movement: Feminism and Social Action*. New York: Routledge.

United Nations (UN). (1989). *Violence against Women in the Family*. Report No. E.89.IV.5. New York: UN.

United Nations Children's Fund (UNICEF). (1997). *The State of the World's Children 1997: Focus on Child Labour*. New York: Oxford University Press.

———. (1998). *The State of the World's Children 1998: Focus on Nutrition*. New York: Oxford University Press.

United Nations Development Program (UNDP). (1993). *Human Development Report 1993*. New York: Oxford University Press.

———. (1994). *Human Development Report 1994*. New York: Oxford University Press.

———. (1995). *Action for Equality, Development, and Peace*. Report for the Fourth World Conference on Women. Report No. E/CN.6/1995/5/Add 2.

———. (1996). *Poverty and Food Security in Sub-Saharan Africa*. Human Development Report. New York: Oxford University Press.

———. (1997). *Human Development Report 1997*. New York: Oxford University Press.

United Nations Economic Commission for Africa (UNECA) and United Nations Children's Fund (UNICEF). (1995). *Atlas of the African Child*. Nairobi, Kenya: UNICEF.

United Nations Interregional Crime and Justice Research Institute (UNICRI). (1989). *Women's Victimization in Developing Countries: Issues and Reports*. Report No. 5. Rome, Italy: UNICRI.

United Nations Program on HIV/AIDS (UNAIDS) and United Nations Children's Fund (UNICEF). (1996). *HIV/AIDS Epidemiology in Sub-Saharan Africa*. Geneva: UNAIDS/UNICEF.

World Bank. (1995). *Better Health and Nutrition for Women*. Development Brief No. 48. Washington, DC: World Bank.

World Health Organization (WHO). (1997). *Young People and Sexually Transmitted Diseases*. Fact Sheet No. 186. Geneva: WHO.
———. (1998). *Safe Motherhood: A Matter of Human Rights and Social Justice*. Geneva: WHO.

AFRICAN WOMEN
AND CHILDREN

Chapter 1

Females and Gender Status in Eastern and Southern Africa: A Comparative Critique

Anthony G. Hopkin

INTRODUCTION

This chapter offers a comparative critique of the socioeconomic, political, and educational status of women in Southern and Eastern Africa. The first section is a broad descriptive analysis of the status of women and of selected gender issues in what can be conveniently referred to as the "developed" world. Attention is then focused on women in some Islamic countries. Sub-Saharan Africa is dealt with next, and finally, Eastern and Southern Africa. Specific attention is given to the findings of the 13 gender- and education-oriented research projects reported by the Educational Research Network in Eastern and Southern Africa (ERNESA). An analysis is offered of these findings and their significance, and these are then evaluated from a regional and comparative perspective. Finally, the analysis is used to generate a discussion that highlights the disadvantaged socioeconomic, political, and educational status of women in sub-Saharan Africa in general, and in the region in particular, when considered in a comparative and world context.

Much of the data is culled from *The Economist* and its associated publications. This news journal is known both for its support of "Western" liberal capitalist economics and for the reliability of its sources with respect to data. I have found it informative and stimulating and have used it as a valuable source of comparative data relating to a diversity of issues. Nevertheless, Benjamin Disraeli's aphorism should be kept in mind: "There are three kinds of lies: lies, damned lies and statistics" (quoted in *The Oxford Dictionary of Quotations*, 1979: 187). Another important source of data is Charles Humana's *World Human Rights Guide*

(Humana, 1992). His pioneering work in this field has earned the respect of numerous world and regional organizations, and since 1991, it has served as the basis for the United Nations Development Program's Human Freedom Index of the Human Development Report, 1991. Humana frankly acknowledges that his index has the Western liberal bias reflected in the United Nations Charter whereby UN members, and all the countries referred to in this chapter as members, are called upon to uphold the principle of universal respect for individuals in relation to the observance of human rights and freedom regardless of race, sex, language, and religion (Humana, 1992). Interested readers are referred to the introduction of his book for a convincing refutation of the statistical and ideological objections made to the index. In referring to the authoritative approval given to the guide, he blandly concludes that "the accuracy of the ratings and the classification has usually been challenged only by those who are the most guilty of human rights violations" (Humana, 1992: 7).

Much of the chapter deals with controversial matters, and some readers may question the objectivity of what is written and the interpretations that are offered. Perspectives differ: we are all the prisoners of our own experience; all we can do is enlarge our cells by exposing ourselves to further experience, and learning from this. In defense, I quote what I heard that great socialist Aneurin Bevan say about his father. When debating with his opponents, his father usually concluded: "You have every right to be wrong as I have every right to be right!"

A GOLDEN CENTURY FOR WOMEN?

On the eve of the twenty-first century, *The Economist* was positive that women had made immense strides in the current century: "It has been a wonderful century for women. Whether it be reliable contraceptives and safe obstetrics or the dishwasher and the drip-dry shirt, technology has made their domestic lives easier, at any rate in the rich world" ("Breaking the Glass Ceiling," 1996: 13). The writer then extended these benefits to other areas, including work, politics, and education. Particularly females, who would presumably respond by pointing out that the century has been even kinder to males, do not universally accept such a viewpoint. The statement as a whole might be challenged. What is not open to challenge is the caveat that this applies to females in the rich world. This generalization about the century could not be made in the world-wide context.

A convincing case can be made in support of the statement vis-à-vis women in the developed world. Despite the existence of a "glass ceiling" in the United States, which forms an invisible barrier to women for entry into the director's boardrooms of American companies, women have gained entry into senior management levels. They can still be found at the basement level, doing the cleaning chores, but they also account for just under half of corporate employees at the managerial and executive level and just over a half at the professional level ("Women in American Boardrooms," 1996: 54). Salaries have improved greatly at these levels, and, while the gap is still there, it is becoming narrower. Nearly half of those studying law are females, and they make up a third of those taking advanced business degrees. Increasingly, women are running their own companies because, in the larger ones, "Corporate America is still a man's game" ("Women in American Boardrooms," 1996: 55), but the composition of the workforce at this level has changed drastically and should continue to change as females maintain their collective assault on American boardrooms.

Equal and even greater success has been gained in other parts of the developed world. Nearly a hundred years ago Marie Curie was awarded a joint Nobel Prize for Physics with her husband, Pierre, and Henri Becquerel, but only after a colleague had informed Pierre that his wife had been wrongly left out of the nomination. It appears that the nominators could not accept a mixture of womanhood and science ("The Science of Sexual Discrimination," 1996). Attitudes presumably changed—she later earned the Nobel Prize for Chemistry on her own. Women continued to suffer from discrimination in the fields of science and mathematics, but the bias has been considerably reduced and is now much less overt. In 1990, women made up less than 10 percent of university physics departments in the United States, the United Kingdom, and (the then) West Germany, while today in Hungary nearly half are women and about a third in Portugal and the former Soviet Union ("The Science of Sexual Discrimination," 1996: 98). The reasons for this apparent discrimination are subtle and can even be attributed to informal factors, such as the way males socialize and gossip which confers advantages on them. What is not generally acknowledged is that such discrimination is undesirable.

In terms of women making progress in public life, Scandinavia has shown the way to the world. Medicine in this area is almost completely feminized. Not only do females now dominate university enrollment in Sweden and Denmark, but they are increasingly making their mark in public service, such as politics and the civil service, which remain male preserves throughout the rest of the developed world. In the four main Nordic countries there is one female prime minister, two foreign ministers, and two central bank governors. Women also fill a third of cabinet posts, and of the 33 political parties a third are led by women ("Strindberg's Nightmare,"1996: 35). This has not happened by chance. The Scandinavian countries have underwritten this increased involvement of women through the provision of excellent welfare services. "They supply child-care facilities, which free women to work, and impose high taxes, which push them to do so. As a result, a higher share of working-age women are in the labour force than in any other country" ("Strindberg's Nightmare," 1996: 35). This commitment to gender equity is also reflected in the highly favorable human rights records of these countries. In the world human rights league, Norway scores 97 percent and is in third place; Sweden and Denmark are second with 98 percent; and Finland is top with 99 percent (Humana, 1992: xvii–xix). The Scandinavian countries have given meaning to the slogan that women's rights are human rights.

THE OTHER SIDE OF THE COIN

It would be quite wrong to assume from the above examples that females in the "rich" world have won equal status with respect to socio-economic and political status. Discrimination and sexist practices still prevail, many of these being both intangible and insidious. This should be viewed against the general progress that has been made in the field of human rights, especially in the last decade. Between 1986 and 1992, the publication dates of the first and third editions of his *World Human Rights Guide*, Humana observed that "[the human rights] statistics indicate an improvement over a five year period which is unparalleled in history. . . . As a percentage this represents the repudiation of one-party or one-person rule by nearly one in eight of the world's population since 1986" (Humana, 1992: xi). He tempered this claim by pointing out that, in reality, the practice of countries with respect to their constitutions and laws meant that the everyday life of the citizens of a country was not necessarily reflected in what was proclaimed in the constitution or statutes.

This was particularly the case with rating the human rights enjoyed by women in a country:

Although women enjoy political and legal equality in many countries they are always underrepresented in governments and parliaments, and frequently not represented at all. . . . For the purpose of the rating of this question, constitutional equality may not prevent the reality of an overall discrimination. (Humana, 1992: 16)

Furthermore, women's social and economic rights lag even further behind those of men. This is underlined in the case of Finland. It was not awarded 100 percent because the criterion "social and economic equality for women" was rated only as a qualified "yes." All other 39 criteria were rated as an unqualified "yes." Indeed, no country scores an unqualified "yes" on this criterion.

In general, women in the developed world do not enjoy political and constitutional representation or status that is commensurate with their number. By 1996, females had joined the ranks of football referees in France, but the percentage of deputies in the National Assembly in 1993 was 6 percent, the same as it was when women obtained the vote 50 years earlier. This figure has declined since, and the number of women in power in France today is the lowest in the European Union ("Cherchez la Femme," 1996: 37). Furthermore, in Europe and the United States, out of 16 countries, only four had a third or more women as members of parliament or senior ministers, and eight had 10 percent or less. Paradoxically, 11 had a greater proportion of women as senior ministers compared with the number of members of parliament. Women in the developed world have a long way to go to reach political equality.

In economic terms there is also much leeway to make up, but not as much as in the political arena. In the United Kingdom, during the 1980s, when a woman was the prime minister, female earnings were about 70 percent those of males for comparable posts. In France, women constitute 46 percent of the workforce, but they mostly occupy low-paid jobs and earn 80 percent of what men earn ("Cherchez la Femme," 1996: 37). For assorted reasons females still earn 19 percent less than males at senior management levels in the United States, in spite of the favorable trends identified above ("Women in American Boardrooms," 1996: 55). In socioeconomic and political terms women are still disadvantaged in the developed world, but improvement is being shown. The degree of improvement will continue to be open to dispute and will depend on many factors, including the gender of the individual assessing it.

THE IMPORTANCE OF IDEOLOGICAL FACTORS

Custom, culture, and ideology are intangibles that impinge on the status of women. In spite of the progress that has been made in the developed and the Eastern European countries toward gender equality, tradition has been one factor that appears to hamper legislation in this field. Yet current trends indicate that the basic assumptions relating to gender are being questioned in the developed world. The gender debate is becoming increasingly infused with ideological factors.

For example, monotheism (epitomized by Christianity and Judaism) prevails in the developed world, even in today's increasingly secular world, promoting the notion of God as a super-male. This notion has been reinforced by formal culture, and artists have projected the image of God as a male figure (and invariably a hirsute one). Furthermore, members of the opposition party in the debate over the ordination of women in the Anglican Church in the United Kingdom appeared to be strongly conditioned by the notion of the maleness of the divinity. In common with the Roman Catholic Church, the idea that their priests—

who represented their god—could be a female was repugnant because females could not represent a male entity. The validity of the maleness of God, however, is increasingly being subjected to scrutiny. Armstrong (1996) has drawn attention to the female attributes that many religions confer on their divinity—including Greek Orthodox Christianity—in contrast to the masculine deity worshiped by Muslims, western Christians, and Jews. Is this debate an indication that the ideological status of the female is changing in the Western world?

Conventional patriarchy is also under attack from other quarters, but the impact of this has been minimal. The experience of British males in the two world wars equipped them to become more self-sufficient in domestic matters but did not carry over later to their domestic habits as husbands (Bourke, 1996). Even the availability of paternity leave in Sweden has not led many men to actually apply for it ("The End of Patriarchy," 1996). An increasing problem in the West is the failure of males to pay for child support after divorce (Popenoe, 1996). Furthermore, the absence of a conventional male father figure in the home has detrimental effects on the family as a unit and on the way children grow up, especially males. Humes (1996) contends that the violent and pathological juvenile crime wave that is currently affecting the inner cities of the United States can be attributed primarily to the absence of resident fathers. On balance, the attack on patriarchy is an intellectual one, and it is slow in making an impact in practical terms, except among the better educated and more affluent groups. Nevertheless, the fact that such a debate is even taking place reflects the changing ideological context pertaining to gender in the developed world.

It is inconceivable that such a public debate could take place in developed countries with strong traditional values and ideologies, such as Japan or the Islamic countries. Feminism, first propagated in the 1930s by Shidzue Kato, has progressed slowly in Japan, although women have made real gains, particularly in the material sense. Increasing prosperity has lightened their domestic load, and the effects have been tangible. In 1947 a woman's life expectancy in Japan was just over 50 years. Today, at 82 years, it is the highest in the world ("Feminism Reaches Japan," 1996: 89). Prosperity has improved the lot of Japanese women in tandem with factors such as access to contraception which has enabled them to determine family size with its attendant benefits ("Feminism Reaches Japan," 1996). However, as in the rest of the developed world, the gap between males and females remains great. Women's political power is still minimal in spite of their right to vote. They earn a little over half of what males earn, and they are far more vulnerable to dismissal from employment. An Equal Opportunities Employment Bill was passed in Japan in 1985 but remained ineffective because the drafters (male) "forgot" to include a clause whereby those who broke the law would be punished ("Feminism Reaches Japan," 1996). However, the government has now acknowledged this weakness of the law.

In many respects, Japanese females may themselves be to blame for their current relatively depressed state. They have been notoriously meek, patient, seemingly inclined to accept their traditional roles, and apparently unwilling to exploit the increasing opportunities open to them to improve their lot. Yet there are signs of change. In 1995 a woman won damages for sexual harassment in a suit that did not actually involve touching. Younger Japanese females are more assertive and are prepared to say what they think in a manner hitherto considered "unfeminine." However, customary outlooks continue to hamper the fight to win recompense and justice for the "comfort women" who were forcibly recruited from Japan and other Asian countries to serve in the military brothels during the Second World War. The Japanese government itself has shown great reluctance to fully acknowledge the country's obligations arising from this sordid episode in Japanese history (Scheyvens, 1996). Japanese women have actually undermined the pressure on their government. Whereas many hundreds of abused Korean females have offered testimony in this matter, not one Japanese woman has come forward to do so. In the material sense women in Japan have made great progress, but further progress is being hampered by ideology. As Shidzue Kato has pointed out, Japanese women—who now are possibly the best educated and richest in the world—have to become much more assertive to bludgeon the minds of Japanese men if they are to achieve greater equality with them ("Feminism Reaches Japan," 1996).

That material progress is no guarantee of significant improvement in the status of females is demonstrated by the position of women in Islamic societies, particularly in the Gulf States. The principal determinant of women's status in these countries is ideological and is enshrined in the law. While the interpretation may vary from one Islamic country to another, in Muslim countries where Sharia law prevails, there is no prospect that UN treaties on women's rights can prevail

against a religion and tradition that demand total obedience and conformity. And an explanation, indisputable to those who put it forward, simply asserts that in Muslim societies women enjoy the honored status of the divine role for which they were created, that of being wife and mother. (Humana, 1992: 9)

Exacting conformity has bizarre effects. For example, in Saudi Arabia, the ability of women to undertake research into education is severely restricted (Hopkin, 1992).

But Muslim countries score badly on the human rights index in general, and not just with respect to the treatment and status of women. The elections recently held in Kuwait were perceived with foreboding by its

Arab neighbors, yet only 5 percent of the two million population voted and these, all males, had to prove their Kuwaiti ancestry. Paradoxically, when voting was first introduced in Kuwait in the first half of the 1980s, women were entitled to vote. This right was soon removed, and male suffrage was reinstalled ("Kuwait: They Voted," 1996). Since 1994, in neighboring Bahrain, women have increasingly pressured the government to move toward democratic reform and return to constitutional democracy. Protests by women have included the signing of petitions, direct disruptive tactics in the university, and public demonstrations and protests. Countermeasures have led to women losing their jobs and being imprisoned, and to action by the police and security forces against males and villages that have been associated with female protesters ("Bahraini Women," 1996).

Across the Gulf, in Iran, women ostensibly enjoy much more freedom and higher status than women in many other Muslim countries, especially the ultraconservative ones such as Saudi Arabia and the parts of Afghanistan under Taleban control. Women in Iran possess increasing access to education, are allowed to drive and to vote, and have access to the labor market. However, in matters of divorce, travel abroad (only with the husband's permission), custody of their children, and many other aspects of family life, wives do not have the same rights as husbands. This subjection is symbolized in the compulsory wearing of the chador or agneah, which is seen as public evidence of the modesty that all females over 9 years of age must observe. This inequality is reinforced by Islamic law, which asserts that a woman's testimony is worth half that of a man. Thus, the apparent "freedom" of Iranian women is misleading: the law determines that females are disadvantaged when such matters as divorce and consequent settlements arise. Above all, the absence of female judges since the revolution of 1978–1979 has ensured that, in the last analysis, any judgment made will be from an Islamic male perspective ("Behind the Chador," 1997). The status of women, especially in Iran and the Arab world, epitomizes the reality of the principle that, in the context of human rights, traditional attitudes, reinforced by ideology and compounded by a belief in the maleness of the deity, reduce the status of females as human beings.

DEVELOPMENT IN AFRICA: DECLINE OR PROGRESS?

Next to be considered is the status of women in sub-Saharan Africa, with particular reference to Eastern and Southern Africa. An initial caveat must be expressed. Africa is not, as it is often presented, a homogeneous entity. In terms of languages, ethnic groups, cultures, history, and differences between countries, it is as diverse as other continents— indeed even more diverse than some. But common elements can be identified and similarities can be found, and these will be the focus of much of the following discussion. Where applicable, significant differences will also be stressed.

It is unrealistic to reflect on the status of women without reference to the economic and developmental contexts that prevail. The preceding discussion has concentrated on the "rich" world. One significant difference between relatively wealthy and poor countries is the same as that between rich and poor individuals—the more prosperous have far more choice. In terms of lifestyle and options, the poor are restricted: Wealth opens windows of opportunity ("Economic Growth," 1996). Countries that score well in terms of human rights are, by and large, the wealthier ones. They can afford to sustain infrastructures that guarantee that the human rights of all their citizens are respected. Having limited resources, poorer countries are faced with far more demands than can be satisfied, and spending on welfare is costly. Furthermore, many poorer societies are tradition-bound, and their poverty is certainly not shared by all. The propensity of the "haves" to retain what they possess—be it material wealth or privilege—causes tensions in all societies, but these tensions are exacerbated in poorer countries where the penalty for being poor or for becoming impoverished can be calamitous. Such societies are usually male-dominated, and the males as a whole have a vested interest in maintaining their wealth and status. In so doing, a polity evolves in which the culture, ideology, distribution of wealth, and whole socioeconomic context buttress the subservient status of females. These are the features of African countries south of the Sahara and in Eastern and Southern Africa and serve as background to any debate about the status of females in sub-Saharan Africa.

Another important factor that impinges on the status of women is the economic climate. The decade of the 1980s was, with but a few exceptions, an economic disaster for sub-Saharan Africa. In relative world and absolute terms, most countries became poorer, and the standards of living declined ("A Global Poverty Trap," 1996). The reasons for this are complex and beyond the province of the present discussion, but the complexity is reflected in the words of Adebayo Adedeji, a Nigerian economist. He claims that in that miserable decade Africa faced "primarily a political crisis, albeit with devastating economic consequences" ("The Democratic Habit," 1996: 4). The adverse effects on the quality of living are reflected in the Human Development indices for the continent as a whole and for Eastern and Southern Africa in particular. Most African countries cluster toward the lower end of the United Nations Development Program scale. Of the 12 ERNESA countries, Botswana, the richest country in the region, is just in the top 40 percent in the world and the rest are all in the bottom 40 percent, six being in the bottom 20 percent ("So Little Done, So Much to Do," 1996: 4; Dallas, 1995: 22). This dismal material decline in living standards has been exacerbated by the continuing deterioration in food production, which showed a long-term decline of 12 percent from 1961 to 1995 ("Withering Indictment," 1996: 8). In such circumstances, women in Africa probably place a higher priority on family survival than on matters of equity and human rights.

DEVELOPMENT: A PRIORITY ITEM ON THE AGENDA

Even so, there are signs that economic improvement is taking place in sub-Saharan Africa ("A New Beginning," 1996), and this must lead to the issue of the status of women being included in current and future developmental agendas. Jeremy Sachs, who has pointed the way to effective economic reform in Latin America and Eastern Europe, has acknowledged the poor performances of most African countries in the last 15 years. He has argued convincingly that the malaise they suffer is not incurable, given revised policies and commitments along the lines adopted in South America and Eastern Europe (Sachs, 1996).

By 1995, per capita growth in Africa was slowly creeping up and reached 1 percent, the first time it was not negative for a decade. By the middle of the 1990s, economic growth in sub-Saharan Africa had increased to the degree that the average growth for the period 1981–1993 was positive, albeit less than 40 percent of the figure for the world as a whole. While spectacular growth was seen in a few countries, and there was none in war-torn others, on balance the growth was positive ("Sub-Saharan Africa," 1996: 46).

Another factor, which argues well for sub-Saharan Africa, is the increasing commitment to more open trading structures and more democratic regimes. Progress in these areas—some of it determined by UN structural adjustment policies—has again been uneven. Nevertheless, removing leaders by democratic means is increasingly possible. "When Benin in 1991 became the first country in mainland Africa to vote a ruling party and president out of office in free elections, it set a trend" ("The Democratic Habit," 1996: 5). More liberal approaches to trade are evident, as is reflected in the increase in stock markets on the continent. Furthermore, while some countries still rely on tariffs and place obstacles to the entry of foreign capital and expertise, there are plenty of signs that this is changing. For example, the Ashanti Goldfields Company is making its presence felt in West Africa and elsewhere ("How to Dig Yourself Out of a Hole," 1996). But the pace at which most African countries are adapting to a world economy based on open exchange is still far too slow. An *Economist* article in 1997 hypothesized that the world economy was showing signs of synchronized growth, which could bring major global benefits. It is significant that, although economic trends in the developed world and the Asian and Latin American countries were evaluated, no mention was made of the African continent or any African countries ("The Joys of Living in Sync," 1997). Any optimism about the prospects for significant economic growth in sub-Saharan Africa must be tempered by reality: In world economic terms the region is relatively insignificant.

But economic circumstances are not necessarily the principal determinants of the status of women. Tradition and ideology, either on their own or together, can be major barriers to women being accorded their rights as human beings, especially if reinforced by law. In Africa, where Christianity and animist religions prevail, tradition is the principal obstacle for women. This may take the form of acceptance of traditional roles which were essential to a group's survival, such as among the nomadic Kung San of the Kalahari. These roles rendered them less "important" than men and yet, claimed observers such as Marjorie Shostak who lived with them, such roles did not diminish their traditional authority. However, when government-generated and other related pressures affect their lifestyles the women as well as the men become increasingly marginalized ("Obituary," 1996). While outsiders may romanticize the perceptions of these groups, there is little doubt that the effect of external pressure and influence is deleterious, especially on women. For example, in recent years alcohol abuse among the Basarwa in the Kgalagadi and Ghanzi districts of Botswana has led to an increase in wife beating. Also, child beating, hitherto unknown, has been noted, and the child-rearing practices of mothers have deteriorated because of their propensity to alcohol abuse (Molamu and MacDonald, 1996).

The infringement of women's rights can be even more insidious in societies where significant change, including "modernization," has already taken place and statutory law coexists with customary law. The "new" South Africa has been lauded for its Bill of Rights, which guarantees freedom from discrimination on sexual grounds. In 1993, a newly widowed woman lost her house to her father-in-law on the grounds that she was married under traditional law and so the husband's property returned to the males in his family. On appeal, this ruling was upheld, and the Supreme Court ruled in 1996 that, in effect, African customary law prevails over women's rights ("South African Women," 1996). Current attempts to rectify such anomalies are denigrated and rejected by many male politicians.

Women are increasingly vocal and active in politics in South Africa, but the weight of customary practices remains heavy. On average, rural women spend over three hours daily carrying water and more than an hour collecting wood. As in much of Eastern and Southern Africa, *lobola* or bride price, prevails, and elite parents demand high cash prices—not the traditional cattle—for their well-educated daughters. One black woman was reported as saying, "It's degrading. It's like you're being bought from the shop" ("South African Women," 1996: 101). Educated women quite correctly see this ritual as a means whereby a husband can enforce his demands and in the way he wishes. Customary law is being subjected to increasingly critical scrutiny as democracy has begun to pervade South Africa's societies. Nonetheless, it remains a potent force for the subjection of women there.

Yet South Africa and most of the ERNESA countries are free from the worst blight that clouds the lives of women in much of Africa, that is, female genital mutilation (FGM) or circumcision. Each day, at the same time as American females are metaphorically banging their heads on the "glass ceiling," on the continent of Africa about 6,000 females are being circumcised, a practice sanctioned by tradition and their female and male relatives. Without backing from the Koran or the Bible, FGM prevails mainly in Black Muslim African societies and among some Christian groups. Over 80 percent of females are thus "butchered" in Sudan, Ethiopia, and neighboring countries, between 26 and 60 percent in Kenya, and up to 25 percent in Uganda and Tanzania ("Men's Traditional Culture," 1996: 36). Increasing opposition is being shown in the countries where it is being practiced, but the national governments of many of the countries involved do not give priority to eradicating it. Some, including Nigeria, Ghana, and the Ivory Coast, have outlawed it, but few are prosecuted for carrying out the practice. Females are increasingly active in opposing it, and the slow spread of education helps to promote public awareness of the fact that this "operation," strongly associated with the degraded status of women, is repulsive and an affront to human dignity and rights. The continued existence of FGM is a constant reminder that in some African countries women are subjected to what can only be termed the ultimate degradation. That this practice still prevails in 29 of the 46 mainland countries is damaging to the continent's image ("Men's Traditional Culture," 1996: 36).

THE EASTERN AND SOUTHERN AFRICA REGION

ERNESA is a nongovernment research organization. The countries that belong to the organization include Botswana, Ethiopia, Kenya, Lesotho, Malawi, Mozambique, Namibia, Swaziland, Tanzania, Uganda, Zambia, and Zimbabwe. The socioeconomic status of women in the region, with particular emphasis on education, will now be considered. Education is an important element in human resource development, and reference will be made to the findings derived from research into the educational status of women in the region, which was published in 1996 under the auspices of ERNESA. This publication was the result of the Educational Research Information for Practitioners project which sought to make research findings readily accessible to policy makers and practitioners in education (ERNESA, 1996). By most socioeconomic and political indices, the women of the ERNESA region, like most others on the continent, are gravely disadvantaged (see the Appendix). There are, however, differences between the countries, and Botswana, in terms of human resource development and economic and human rights indices, is atypical of the region and the continent as a whole. For example, Botswana with a score of 79 percent on the human rights indices ranked thirty-fifth out of the 105 countries on the world list. The human rights map of Africa shows that in most of the ERNESA countries many human rights are denied. In a country comparison, most rights are respected in Botswana and Namibia, while in Malawi and Lesotho most are denied (Humana, 1992: 396). Only Botswana, Namibia, and Zimbabwe score above the world mean (62%). Thus, the human rights record in most countries in the region is adverse to the status of females.

The data confirm this statement. Although most of the countries formally recognize the legal and political equality of women, three do not. In common with the rest of the world, women do not enjoy equal social and economic status in any country. In only two countries is there equality of the sexes during marriage and divorce proceedings. The payment of bride price is common, such as in Botswana and Mozambique, and cattle are still used in Zimbabwe. Traditional marriages, reinforced by customary law and attitudes that regard women as subservient, place women in an inferior status in most countries, notably Kenya, Malawi, Zambia, and Zimbabwe. Traditional male rights prevail. Therefore, in Botswana married women have to seek permission from husbands to open their own bank accounts or to have business undertakings. In Zimbabwe a large sector of the population follows customary law that allows males to treat their wives as their property: Recent legislation outlawing this custom has had no impact. In both Tanzania and Uganda there is traditional discrimination against women in relation to inheritance and divorce, which greatly disadvantages them. The regional improvement in women's political status and representation (including Zimbabwe, Mozambique, Tanzania, and Kenya) is offset by the continuing practice of female genital mutilation in parts of Kenya (outlawed but still practiced), Malawi, Tanzania, and Mozambique. Throughout the region females are exploited as cheap labor, particularly in agriculture (Humana, 1992).

Other factors place women in Eastern and Southern Africa in a more disadvantaged position than most females elsewhere in the world. The low position of the region with respect to human development indices has been noted earlier. Again Botswana is atypical and is top in sub-Saharan Africa in terms of purchasing power parity and in the top half of the countries in the world, but four of the region's countries are in the bottom 10. Women usually bear the burden of poverty and, while they generally live a little longer than men, life expectancy in the region reflects the prevailing poverty. Three countries feature the lowest age of life expectancy for females in the world: in Uganda it is 43, and in Malawi and Mozambique it is 45 years. In Botswana it is 70, the highest in sub-Saharan Africa (Dallas, 1995: 23).

Equally dismal are the figures relating to child bearing. Five countries of the region are among the 12 with the highest population growth in the world (*The Economist*, 1994: 15). In Iceland the number of deaths per 1,000 live births from 1990 to 1995 was 5, in Mozambique it was 147, in Malawi it was 142, and in Botswana it was 35, the lowest on the continent (*The Economist*, 1994: 67). Seven of the countries in the region are in the top 30 in the world in terms of fertility rates (*The Economist*, 1994: 20). In the ratio of doctors to population, education statistics, death rates, literacy rates, and other indices of standards of living, the countries of the region show up badly in world terms, apart from Botswana. The picture of the smiling African woman, which is used so often to project the image of the continent, is a misleading one: Women in Africa, including those in Eastern and Southern Africa, have little to smile about.

SCHOOLING AND GENDER EQUITY

Education is one of the strategies that could be used to raise the status of women. However, findings from the research carried out into the education of females in the region suggest that increasing their access to education does not necessarily improve their lot. If education is to be effective in getting a better all-round deal for women, then other factors have to be taken into account. Discriminatory practices, which depress the status of women, are institutionalized: Gender discrimination, like racial discrimination in "developed" countries, is a social fact. This has to be considered when dealing with such forms of discrimination, and it has to be acknowledged that whatever school strategies are developed to offset these practices, they will only be as effective as the context allows them to be. Schooling obviously does not take place in a vacuum, and the main message of the research studies under discussion is that the society at large impinges heavily on what goes on in schools and colleges.

This is graphically illustrated by the studies of the girl child in Kenya (Wamahiu, Opondo, and Nyagah, 1996) and in Botswana (Nyati-Ramahobo, 1996). Although the Botswana study acknowledged that international and national agencies have made the country as a whole increasingly aware of the needs of females and children, this awareness has had little effect on educational practice or the status of females. This is largely because socialization has a major impact on the education of the young, especially females. This is particularly well expressed in the Kenyan study where the Kenyan female is

normally born in a family and brought up in a household where patriarchal authority remains undisputed. From birth various cultural practices and symbolism persist in reminding her of the lower status she occupies in society *vis à vis* her brothers. She is socialized early into a system of norms and values, attitudes and skills that tend to emphasize gender differentiation in adult roles and aspirations. (Wamahiu, Opondo, and Nyagah, 1996: 19)

Furthermore, her status is that of a "visitor" in her parents' home, which she will leave when the appropriate commercial transaction has taken place—that is, marriage, when she enters another household. This reflects the status of most young females in the region, and it has direct effects on their schooling in such matters as the attitudes of male teachers to female pupils and the willingness or otherwise of families to send girls to school.

Attitudes strongly affect the schooling of females and in a variety of ways. In some countries, the national figures for the enrollment of females are high, but regional differences can be considerable. Juma (1996) shows that two adjacent districts in Kenya had very different participation rates for females at the primary level. The one with the high participation rates was relatively prosperous, had a record of development through association with Christian missions, and had a mainly Christian population. The other district was much less wealthy, had a poor record in terms of development, had successfully excluded Christian missions, and was predominantly Muslim. Parents in the relatively prosperous district were much more positive about the schooling of their girls. In the other, the parents were also generally positive but were strongly influenced by their religious leaders who "are not only opposed to 'Western' schooling in general, but to girls' education in particular. They advocate the confining of women to the home, and believe that sending girls to school tends to undermine what is perceived as a valuable established tradition" (Juma, 1996: 17). In this case ideology, compounded by traditional beliefs and custom, actually undermines national policy and aspirations.

Paradoxically, in matrilineal societies where females have authority, attitudes can also discriminate against the participation of girls in schooling. Zucula (1996) points out that in parts of rural Mozambique where matrilineal tradition guarantees women a positive role in decision making, the participation rates of girls are as poor as in other areas, especially with respect to dropping out. Mothers expect schools to provide good moral standards and education, and they will withdraw their daughters if this is not the case. Adult females feel secure, and they assume that their daughters will stay in the village with the family and that they will only need to be literate when they marry so only minimal schooling is necessary. Investment in schooling for a female is perceived unfavorably in terms of returns. Thus, female participation rates in schooling in such a context suffers because "the matrilineal family is not yet convinced that the school will not upset the stability which the women seem to feel within this social context" (Zucula, 1996: 28).

This "hard-nosed" attitude among females concerning schooling manifests itself in other ways. Bitamazire (1996) investigated the occupational activities of females who had successfully completed their primary schooling in a district in Uganda. The researcher established that the schooling that they had undergone had done nothing to prepare them for their lives after they left school. Furthermore, the "broad range of occupational activities in which girls engage does not reflect the level of knowledge, or the skills or the experience that they acquired at school. Girls generally engage in . . . home chores, farm activities and petty business" (Bitamazire, 1996: 39). Whether school is perceived to be useful— or otherwise—does appear to affect enrollment and retention rates. Another factor reported by a number of the researchers was the negative attitude of male teachers to female education, particularly at the secondary level (Taole, 1996; Kadzamira, 1996; Juma, 1996). The effects of this attitude are difficult to estimate, but the frequency of its being cited as a factor by the researchers does suggest that it has a negative impact on both the retention and enrollment rates of females at the primary and secondary levels.

Female achievement in science and mathematics was also investigated. Taole (1996: 10) found that the mean of the males' scores was 4.2 percent higher than that of the females in mathematics in the Junior Certificate Examination in Botswana. He claimed that his findings were in accord with comparative data, and he did not attribute these differences to intelligence. The reasons suggested for the differences were as follows: Males had been conditioned to be more confident in their dealing with mathematics; the treatment afforded to boys by teachers in class encouraged and fostered competence in mathematics; and teachers of mathematics and science at the secondary level were mainly male so that boys had plenty of role models whereas girls had very few (Taole, 1996). Nevertheless, girls were equally disposed to science-based careers as boys were, but girls were unable to fulfill their ambitions because when applying for courses in these areas, "Selection to such institutions is based on the performance of candidates in mathematics at the end of their secondary education. In this subject the girls do not perform as well as boys and are therefore less likely to be accepted" (Taole, 1996: 11).

SELF-FULFILLING PROPHECIES ARE THUS REALIZED

A somewhat different picture, though an equally disadvantageous one to females, was found in Malawi. The researcher investigated the performance of females in mathematics and science in the Malawi School Certificate examinations. As is the case with the industrialized countries, the "boys outperformed girls in mathematics, physical science, general science and biology" (Kadzamira, 1996: 24). Although girls performed best in biology, a science subject associated with females, their performance was inferior to that of the boys. Another interesting finding is that girls performed less well in single-sex schools than in coeducational schools. This finding is contrary to what the author refers to as the "dominant notion that girls in single sex schools achieve higher standards in mathematics and science subjects than those in mixed schools because they do not have to compete with boys" (Kadzamira, 1996: 24). However, while those from mixed-sex schools did do better, the difference between the two groups was not statistically significant. What was significant is that once again females performed relatively poorly in mathematics and science. Wamahiu, Opondo, and Nyagah (1996) also noted the unsatisfactory performance of females in science in the Kenya Certificate of Education. Their alarming conclusions were that the disproportionately few females who managed to reach the tertiary level of education would be clustered in the arts and education. Furthermore, they predicted that in Kenya there was "a strong possibility that the gender disparity in participation of girls and boys in university education may become wider" (Wamahiu, Opondo, and Nyagah, 1996: 21).

Females who enroll at the tertiary level will continue to experience gender discrimination. This is suggested by the findings arising from Mannathoko's depressing insight into gender factors in teacher education in Botswana. She traced the gender inequities in teacher education to the "traditional domination of men and sexual politics of pre-colonial Botswana states" (Mannathoko, 1996: 2). Although the colonial and postcolonial periods increased opportunities for females in terms of occupations outside the home, the males gained the greatest access to tertiary education and decision-making positions. Females had much less opportunity to enter upper secondary and higher education. Mannathoko further noted that teacher trainers, in line with other lecturers at the tertiary level, were gender blind and used authoritarian methods that ignored gender issues. Moreover, the texts and materials used sustained the dominant male culture, which was further reinforced by their teaching. Students in teacher training institutions were not exposed to materials and methodologies that facilitated the discussion of gender issues and the status of males and females in society at large (Mannathoko,

1996). Her view was that unless strategies were developed to offset the all-pervading male culture prevailing in teacher education in Botswana, the schools would continue to reinforce current practice, ideology, and custom vis-à-vis gender in Botswana. This can be assumed to be the case for the region as a whole.

Gender is a factor in teacher training in Botswana, and it manifests itself in assorted ways. For example, the students in the two colleges that train junior secondary teachers have representation on the University Board of Affiliation, which governs them with respect to academic matters. No females have been representatives on this body or on the Advisory Board, which deals with the colleges on behalf of the Ministry of Education. In the seven teacher training institutions (including the University Faculty of Education), there are very few females at the senior management levels, but they predominate at the middle and lower levels (Hopkin, 1994). Although examination results—including mathematics, science, and teaching practice—indicate that the females perform much better than the males, this is not statistically significant (Hopkin, 1997). However, to establish the validity of these results in relation to achievement in terms of gender, it would be necessary to include (as a variable) the prior qualifications of those being assessed prior to their enrolling in these courses. It may be hypothesized that the females who enroll in teacher training courses are better qualified than the males who enroll, primarily because females have much more limited access to other tertiary education institutions than males do in Botswana. This disadvantage in status is probably true for females in the region as a whole.

SOME SOCIOECONOMIC FACTORS IN THE ERNESA REGION

One disadvantage faced by women, particularly in rural areas, is that, while they are often responsible for growing food and maintaining the household, they are rarely involved at a decision-making level if a development project is initiated for which funds are provided. Development involving funding is the domain of the males. Kimweri and Swai (1996), through their research into a nonformal environmental education project in Tanzania, established that females have the potential to play a significant role in afforestation, that is, tree planting programs.

Traditional mores prevailed during the project, and its effectiveness was undermined because females were not involved in the decision-making processes and related executive matters. Their involvement was found to be crucial in that they were best able to determine how their environment could be effectively used. The officials and members of the public concerned with the project recognized that, without the support and participation of women in its operation, it would not have fulfilled its goals. In short, the findings showed that by extending ownership and decision making to females, environmental projects were much more likely to succeed.

Furthermore, women's potential is not being realized in the modern sector of the economy, where they continue to suffer because of traditional male attitudes. Women have had very limited access to skills-upgrading programs in engineering in Dar Es Salaam, Tanzania. Mongella's research showed that of the 232 workers (15% female) in a company, less than a quarter of the females had been enrolled in the three upgrading programs over five years, compared with 70 percent of the males (Mongella, 1996: 35). Indeed, more than half of the females were in jobs that did not provide for further training, and requests to enroll in programs not related to direct training needs, such as in computer programs, were turned down. This was attributed to the gender bias displayed by the male heads of departments when nominating people for such training. Furthermore, women participated more in programs conducted after working hours than they did on those conducted during working hours. In all, the upgrading program did little to promote or equalize opportunities for women to be upgraded.

Women in middle management are equally, if not more, disadvantaged. Females have increasingly been participating in the labor market in Uganda, and yet it is still assumed that their domestic obligations hamper the performance of their job duties. Musiimire's study of women middle-level managers in the civil service in Uganda was designed to assess the extent of the conflict between their domestic and employment responsibilities (Musiimire, 1996). The patriarchal nature of Uganda's society meant that these middle-level managers enjoyed few or no concessions, and the married ones had sole responsibility for child-care and domestic duties.

Family obligations—particularly if young children were involved—led married women to face problems with time management, unlike their unmarried counterparts. It was thought that their marital status, which generated obligations to their husbands and children, affected their work performance. This was particularly so when there was lack of family support; in these cases, the female manager was more likely to be inefficient and to be subject to considerable strain. An important result of women coping with unsympathetic working and domestic environments was that they were unable to exploit training opportunities. "Women middle-level managers tended to miss out on training opportunities thereby limiting their chances of career development" (Musiimire, 1996: 43). These are examples of the professional women's disadvantages in the region.

The picture of disabled women in Ethiopia offered by Gebretensay (1996) shows that traditional practices with respect to women must not be universally denigrated. Without the support of neighbors—many of them very poor—the 440 individuals who were the subject of the study would be in an even worse state than they were. The positive attitudes shown by families and neighbors, much of them based on religious conviction, partly made up for the government's inability to provide sufficient rehabilitation centers and services for the disabled. However, as is the case with the rest of the region, these women, of whom less than a quarter were employed, constitute an issue that is least known about and acknowledged by both governments and society at large (Gebretensay, 1996). In terms of status and degradation, the disabled women remain among the lowest strata of society.

In most of the ERNESA, countrywomen enjoy political and legal equality. However, as this discussion suggests, this equality is notional rather than real. This is exemplified by the status of women in Zimbabwe in relation to the Convention on the Elimination of all Forms of Discrimination Against Women, which was adopted by the United Nations in 1979 and ratified by the Zimbabwean government in 1991. Gaidzanwa and Maramba (1996) have investigated the status of women in Zimbabwe in relation to this convention. Their findings are salutary and vividly depict the difference between rhetoric and reality when gender issues are involved.

The constitution of Zimbabwe does not guarantee nondiscrimination on the grounds of sex. This has led to assorted anomalies whereby married women are unable to raise loans without the consent of their husbands. Also, women do not have an independent right to citizenship to confer on their children, nor has any attempt been made to monitor initiatives made to enforce women's rights in Zimbabwe or to publicize them, such as by translating the Convention into the main local languages. Registered customary marriages are recognized and are common in rural areas, but women in these unions are at a marked disadvantage in terms of security of property and inheritance compared with those who have undergone civil marriages (Gaidzanwa and Maramba, 1996). Soliciting for purposes of prostitution is an offense, and punitive measures are taken against women who do so. But little or no action is taken against men for buying sexual services, which is also against the law. Some gains have been made in primary education, but males still dominate secondary and tertiary education and very few women hold high level posts in the government, the civil service, or the private sector. In the matter of the promotion of female rights, the Ministry of Community and Women's Affairs has been assigned responsibility for action, but "the UN convention has not been put into action" (Gaidzanwa and Maramba, 1996: 47). This sorry litany is probably replicated—in most cases, to a greater degree—in all the countries of the region, each of which is a member of the United Nations.

CONCLUSION

By all standards, women in the ERNESA region are grossly disadvantaged in terms of their socioeconomic and political status and their rights as human beings. From a male perspective, it could be argued that such a judgment is invalid because the cultural perspective of the individual making the judgment has to be taken into account. In any case, it has been acknowledged that women are disadvantaged all over the world and that the disadvantages they suffer in Africa in general, and in Eastern and Southern Africa in particular, are only matters of degree.

These differences in degree warrant scrutiny, however. Disadvantaged females in the developed world do not experience the poverty or the miserable living conditions that are faced by women in the ERNESA region, and, when delivering children, their expectations of a safe delivery are up to 30 times as great. In terms of employment, females in the United States may face difficulty in getting to the very top in corporate America and may bump their heads on the "glass ceiling." Women in Africa do not experience such a ceiling: In struggling up the steep slopes of their professional avenues, they face a series of barred and buttressed gateways, and for each a male holds the key. In the university physics departments of the developed world, females are underrepresented on the staff, particularly at the senior levels. In the ERNESA countries, females are grossly underrepresented in science, let alone physics, as students at the upper secondary and tertiary levels.

To many in the developed world, Sharia law is an affront to the status and dignity of women, as is much of the ideology that reinforces the law and the status of women associated with it. But at least the rights it confers provide far greater security for widows and wives than does the customary law which legally prevails in much of Africa. Present practice in customary law ensures that numerous material benefits and advantages accrue to males. However, the security for females, which was guaranteed in traditional societies and which legitimated such advantages, has been eroded, and even eliminated, with modernization and the adoption of monetized economies. Furthermore, legal sanctions and UN conventions still fail to guarantee women social and economic equality in developed societies. In operational terms, the disadvantages they suffer are minor ones when measured against the harassment, economic persecution, and subjection that females suffer in societies in which culture, tradition, and customary law are allowed to prevail to retain the entrenched interests of dominant males. This is in direct contravention of the United Nations' conventions on female rights to which the governments of these countries have committed themselves.

As noted earlier, just over half a century ago the Japanese government grossly abused the rights and bodies of many Japanese and Asian women by forcefully recruiting them for military brothels. This stain remains, and current efforts to remove it have been comparatively feeble. But was the degradation experienced by these women any worse than that currently experienced by thousands of African girls who undergo female circumcision? Perhaps it was, but the only ones who can really tell are those who experienced such degradation. Similarly, the educated females who are subjected to circumcision increasingly see the practice of "buying" wives, resulting in their being owned by their husband, so prevalent on the African continent, as particularly barbarous. The indignities women in developed countries face in relation to employment, rates of pay, and professional opportunities must appear insignificant in comparison. Again, only those subjected to these affronts can determine the relative significance of these practices.

In a survey of sub-Saharan Africa entitled *Africa for the Africans* published in *The Economist* (1996), the title is presented as a caption on the first page superimposed on a crowd scene. Most of the group are males: it is difficult to see whether any females are present. The last page features a crowd of celebrating women, which is intended to illustrate the idea that the continent is still smiling. Perhaps this exemplifies the plight of women in Africa: They remain smiling, while the men determine who is to control the continent. If women are to gain the status and power to which they are entitled on the continent in general, and in Eastern and Southern Africa in particular, they will have to undergo a long and grueling struggle. It is a battle that they themselves will have to fight, but there will be help from some male quarters. There will always be men to assist and advise. Indeed, this tradition goes back to Aristophanes (1973), who had particularly helpful suggestions for women with respect to strategies and tactics.

In gaining the rights of women throughout the world, it will be women who will be the principal actors in the movement. To look forward to the eve of the twenty-second century and to predict that women in Africa will be enjoying the same rights and privileges as women do in much of the rich world today would be both patronizing and even neo-colonialist. Such a mistaken perception of the linear nature of development is akin to that shown by development specialists like Curle (1963) and Rostow (1960) three decades ago. Countries on the continent of Africa will be as varied in a hundred years time as they are now, for they will each follow their own developmental paths. In common with the rest of the continent, however, it can be predicted with confidence that women in Eastern and Southern Africa will have contributed greatly to this development and will have won for themselves the status to which they, as human beings, are entitled.

REFERENCES

Aristophanes. (1973). *Lysistrata*. A. H. Sommerstein, trans. Harmondsworth: Penguin.

Armstrong, K. (1996). "Divinity and Gender: A God for Both Sexes." *The Economist*, December 21–27, pp. 35–40.

"Bahraini Women: Screaming for Democracy." (1996). *The Economist*, April 6–12, p. 52.

"Behind the Chador." (1997). *The Economist: A Survey of Iran*, January 18–24, pp. 9–10.

Bitamazire, G. N. (1996). "A Study of the Occupational Activities of Female Primary School Leavers in Five Selected Villages in Mpigi District." In Educational Research Network in Eastern and Southern Africa (ERNESA), *Educational Research Information for Practitioners* (pp. 38–40). Gaborone: ERNESA.

Bourke, J. (1996). *Dismembering the Male*. Chicago: University of Chicago Press.

"Breaking the Glass Ceiling." (1996). *The Economist*, August 10–16, p. 13.

"Cherchez la Femme." (1996). *The Economist*, December 7–13, p. 37.

Curle, A. (1963). *Educational Strategies for Developing Countries: A Study of Educational and Social Factors in Relation to Economic Growth*. London: Tavistock Publications.

Dallas, R. (1995). *The Economist: Pocket Africa: Profiles, Facts and Figures about Africa Today*. London: Penguin Books.

"The Democratic Habit." (1996). *The Economist: A Survey of Sub-Saharan Africa: Africa for the Africans*, September 7–13, pp. 4–6.

Disraeli, B. (1981). Quoted in *The Oxford Dictionary of Quotations* (3rd ed.) (pp. 185–187). London: Book Club Associates and Oxford University Press.

"Economic Growth: The Poor and the Rich." (1996). *The Economist*, May 25–31, pp. 23–29.

The Economist. (1994). *The Economist: Pocket World in Figures* (1995 ed.). London: Penguin Books.

———. (1996). *A Survey of Sub-Saharan Africa: Africa for the Africans*, September 7–13.

Educational Research Network in Eastern and Southern Africa (ERNESA). (1996). *Educational Research Information for Practitioners*. Gaborone: ERNESA.

"The End of Patriarchy." (1996). *The Economist: The Economist Review*, May 18–24, p. 5.

"Feminism Reaches Japan." (1996). *The Economist*, June 1–7, pp. 89–90.

Gaidzanwa, R., and Maramba, P. (1996). "United Nations Convention on the Elimination of All Forms of Discrimination Against Women: A Zimbabwean Report." In Educational Research Network in Eastern and Southern Africa (ERNESA), *Educational Research Information for Practitioners* (pp. 45–48). Gaborone: ERNESA.

Gebretensay, M. (1996). "The Status of Disabled Women in Selected Kebeles in Addis Ababa." In Educational Research Network in Eastern and Southern Africa (ERNESA), *Educational Research Information for Practitioners* (pp. 12–14). Gaborone: ERNESA.

"A Global Poverty Trap." (1996). *The Economist*, July 20–26, p. 36.

Hopkin, A. G. (1992). "Qualitative Research Methodologies: A Cross-Cultural Perspective." *Compare*, 22(2), 133–141.

———. (1994). "Self-Study in the Primary Teacher Training College: A College Staff Perspective in Botswana." *Journal of Practice in Education for Development*, 1(1), 25–26.

———. (1997). *Diploma in Secondary Education External Moderation Exercise 1996/7: Report of the Co-ordinator, Affiliated Institutions*. Unpublished manuscript.

"How to Dig Yourself Out of a Hole." (1996). *The Economist: A Survey of Sub-Saharan Africa: Africa for the Africans*, September 7–13, pp. 12–13.

Humana, C. (1986). *World Human Rights Guide*. London: Pan Books.

———. (1992). *World Human Rights Guide* (3rd ed.). Oxford: Oxford University Press.

Humes, E. (1996). *No Matter How Loud I Shout*. New York: Simon & Schuster.

"The Joys of Living in Sync." (1997). *The Economist*, January 4–10, pp. 71–72.

Juma, M. N. (1996). "Determinants of Female Participation in Primary Education: A Case Study of Kwale and Taita Taveta Districts." In Educational Research Network in Eastern and Southern Africa (ERNESA), *Educational Research Information for Practitioners* (pp. 15–18). Gaborone: ERNESA.

Kadzamira, E. C. (1996). "Sex Differences in Performance of Candidates in MSCE Mathematics and Science Subjects 1982–1986." In Educational Research Network in Eastern and Southern Africa (ERNESA), *Educational Research Information for Practitioners* (pp. 23–25). Gaborone: ERNESA.

Kimweri, P. H., and Swai, N.M.P. (1996). "The Involvement of Women in Non-formal Environmental Education Programs: The Case of Hai District Afforestation Project in Kilimanjaro Region Tanzania Mainland." In Educational Research Network in Eastern and Southern Africa (ERNESA), *Educational Research Information for Practitioners* (pp. 30–33). Gaborone: ERNESA.

"Kuwait: They Voted." (1996). *The Economist*, October 12–18, p. 58.

Mannathoko, C. (1996). "Politics of Gender in Teacher Education Curriculum and Pedagogy." In Educational Research Network in Eastern and Southern Africa (ERNESA), *Educational Research Information for Practitioners* (pp. 1–4). Gaborone: ERNESA.

"Men's Traditional Culture." (1996). *The Economist*, August 10–16, p. 36.

Molamu, L., and MacDonald, D. (1996). "Alcohol Abuse among the Basarwa of the Kgalagadi and Ghanzi Districts in Botswana." *Drugs: Education, Prevention and Policy*, 3(2), 145–152.

Mongella, C.M.R. (1996). "Factors Influencing Women's Participation in Skill Upgrading Programs in Business Oriented Enterprises in Tanzania: The Case of Pamba Engineering." In Educational Research Network in Eastern and Southern Africa (ERNESA), *Educational Research Information for Practitioners* (pp. 34–37). Gaborone: ERNESA.

Musiimire, C. C. (1996). "Inter-role Conflict: A Study of Middle-Level Women Managers in the Uganda Civil Service." In Educational Research Network in Eastern and Southern Africa (ERNESA), *Educational Research Information for Practitioners* (pp. 41–44). Gaborone: ERNESA.

"A New Beginning." (1996). *The Economist: A Survey of Sub-Saharan Africa: Africa for the Africans*, September 7–13, pp. 17–18.

Nyati-Ramahobo, L. (1996). "The Girl-Child in Botswana: Educational Constraints and Prospects." In Educational Research Network in Eastern and Southern Africa (ERNESA), *Educational Research Information for Practitioners* (pp. 5–8). Gaborone: ERNESA.

"Obituary: Marjorie Shostak." (1996). *The Economist*, October 19–25, p. 109.

Popenoe, D. (1996). *Life without Father*. New York: Free Press.

Rostow, W. W. (1960). *The Stages of Economic Growth: A Non-Communist Manifesto*. Cambridge: Cambridge University Press.

Sachs, J. (1996). "Growth in Africa: It Can Be Done." *The Economist*, June 29–July 5, pp. 23–25.

Scheyvens, H. (1996). *The External Politics of ODA: A Case Study of Japan*. Palmerston North, New Zealand: Institute of Development Studies.

"The Science of Sexual Discrimination." (1996). *The Economist*, June 22–28, pp. 97–98.

"So Little Done, So Much to Do." (1996). *The Economist*, September 7–13, pp. 2–4.

"South African Women." (1996). *The Economist*, October 12–18, pp. 101–102.

"Strindberg's Nightmare." (1996). *The Economist*, June 8–14, p. 35.

"Sub-Saharan Africa: Inching Ahead." (1996). *The Economist*, May 11–17, pp. 46–48.

Taole, J. K. (1996). "A Comparison of Performance in Mathematics Between Boys and Girls in the 1990 Junior Certificate Examination in Botswana." In Educational Research Network in Eastern and Southern Africa (ERNESA), *Educational Research Information for Practitioners* (pp. 9–11). Gaborone: ERNESA.

Wamahiu, S., Opondo, F. A., and Nyagah, G. (1996). "Educational Situation of the Kenyan Girl-Child." In Educational Research Network in Eastern and Southern Africa (ERNESA), *Educational Research Information for Practitioners* (pp. 19–22). Gaborone: ERNESA.

"Withering Indictment." (1996). *The Economist: A Survey of Sub-Saharan Africa: Africa for the Africans*, September 7–13, pp. 8–12.

"Women in American Boardrooms: Through a Glass, Darkly." (1996). *The Economist*, August 10–16, pp. 54–55.

Zucula, C. (1996). "Socio-cultural Aspects of the School Attendance of Girls at Primary Level in Mozambique." In Educational Research Network in Eastern and Southern Africa (ERNESA), *Educational Research Information for Practitioners* (pp. 26–29). Gaborone: ERNESA.

Chapter 2

The Impact of Parental Separation and Divorce on Children: A Southern African Perspective

Tapologo Maundeni

INTRODUCTION

This chapter examines the dynamics as well as the impact of parental separation and divorce on children, with special reference to Southern Africa. It focuses on conflict and violence between parents, decline in family standards of living following divorce, lack of communication about divorce and separation, and loss of supportive networks. The above-mentioned experiences cause a considerable amount of stress to children. Therefore, measures need to be taken to reduce the level of stress on children emanating from parental separation and divorce. In discussing issues on which little written evidence exists, the literature from developed countries is cited and related to countries in Southern Africa, taking into account differences in political, cultural, and economic backgrounds. The implications for research, policy, and practice are outlined.

Because of increasing divorce rates in both developed and developing countries, the issue of how divorce and marital separation affects children has been the subject of increasing academic interest. Most research on the situation of these children, however, has been conducted in developed countries. This is largely because it is assumed that there are lower divorce rates in developing countries. It is assumed that women in Africa, for example, have limited opportunities outside the home and so are more likely to stay in abusive marriages. Yet cumulative evidence from Africa indicates that divorce rates are increasing and that the marriage institution is now less stable than it used to be (Klingshirn, 1971;

Iro, 1976; Ahmed and Letamo, 1989; Solivetti, 1994; Bhebhe and Mosha, 1996).

In most Southern African countries, the figures on divorce may be an underestimation because many marital partners separate permanently without going through the official legal channels to seek a divorce. This is partly because of the stigma associated with divorced people, especially women in rural areas. It is widely believed that women have to persevere and try their best to keep their marriages together, so that when marriages fail, women, rather than men, are likely to be blamed. In urban areas, some people separate permanently without utilizing official channels because they fear the high fees involved in the legal process of divorce. Although some agencies provide legal services to low-income people, for example, the legal clinic of the University of Botswana and the legal clinics in Zambia and Lesotho, such services are usually available only in urban areas, and many people do not have access to them.

DYNAMICS AND CONSEQUENCES OF DIVORCE

Domestic Violence and Conflicts

One of the issues facing children of divorced parents in Southern Africa as well as in developed countries is domestic violence. Parental separation and divorce frequently happen after a long period of heightened conflict between parents. A perusal of divorce cases brought by women at one high court in Botswana shows that wife battering is a common problem, and many women have experienced assaults over many years (Molokomme, 1990). This problem has been found to be on the increase in all countries in the Southern Africa region. Holm (1995) and Women and the Law in Southern Africa (the latter being a nongovernmental organization which, among other things, researches on women and law and empowers women through legal literacy campaigns) note that violence against women in Botswana, Lesotho, Mozambique, Swaziland, Zambia, and Zimbabwe is increasing at an alarming rate and that most women stay in abusive relationships for a long time. It is difficult to ascertain the exact incidence of women battering because of lack of accurate statistics.

Various factors compel women to stay in abusive relationships. First, women are generally reluctant to report violence in the family to the extended family members, the police, or other legal authorities. This is partly because there is lack of recognition or services for battered women. Thus, women are aware that even if they report abuse, they are unlikely to get help. In addition, the cultural attitude that encourages subordination of women and what seems to be a custom permitting men to chastise their wives results in women being reluctant to report domestic violence (Molokomme, 1990). According to Taylor and Stewart (1991), there is still widespread acceptance of violence against wives in Zimbabwe as reflected in the court reports. These authors contend that husbands are likely to be excused or pardoned for having assaulted their wives, while if the assault had been done on another family member, the court would likely treat the case as completely inexcusable.

Second, some women are reluctant to move out of the violent relationships because they feel that their families will not help due to fears that the man's family might reclaim the bride price (Holm, 1995). Other factors that hinder women from seeking assistance include self-blame and criticism; fear that the men will kill them if they realize they have told other people about the violence; threats from their husbands that they will take their children away; women's fear that their husbands may be put in prison and that consequently no one will financially support them and their children; and fear that once the husbands are released from prison, they will be more violent (Taylor and Stewart, 1991).

Although there is considerable documentation about women and domestic violence in the Southern Africa region, little research has been done on children's exposure to domestic violence and its effects on them. Research from Western countries shows that children of on-going divorce disputes and violence tend to be highly distressed as a result of witnessing parental fights (Johnston et al., 1987), aggressive (Jacobson, 1978), depressed, and prone to antisocial behavior (Peterson and Zill, 1986). These effects tend to be more severe for children who continue to be exposed to parental conflicts and violence after divorce, for it has been found that legal separation and divorce do not necessarily end conflicts between parents (Emery and Forehand, 1994). In some cases, conflicts and violence continue in the form of custody disputes long after the legal divorce is finalized. Such conflicts may focus largely on the children because children are one of the few ties that give angry former spouses an excuse for fighting (Emery, 1992). The fact that women in the Southern Africa region experience severe violence for prolonged periods of time implies that the consequences of such violence for their children can be more traumatic than for their counterparts in western countries whose parents are unlikely to stay very long in violent relationships since they can readily get assistance.

Domestic violence has been linked to child abuse and incest (Jaffe et al., 1990). This has serious implications for children who experience parental violence. Yet, welfare services for abused children in the Southern Africa region are few. Where such services exist, they are found in urban areas. Therefore, a large proportion of children do not have access to them. This implies that rural children who are abused rarely get help from formal agencies. Therefore, they continue to live under conditions of abuse for prolonged periods of time, if not for the rest of their childhood years.

Not only are child victims of domestic violence likely to be abused, they also tend to be socially isolated. Research conducted in Western countries shows that perpetrators of domestic violence routinely isolate their victims from social contact with friends, family members, and supportive community institutions (Gelles and Straus, 1988). Such isolation makes both the children and their mothers helpless. Battered women and their abused children who are denied contact with friends and extended family members have great difficulty in getting help. The social isolation imposed on children and their mothers by the perpetrators may be particularly severe for children and women in some Southern African countries where men are viewed as unquestionable heads of households. This view of men as unquestionable is associated with the payment of bride price by the man's family to the woman's family. Some men in Southern Africa feel that they have the right to maltreat their wives simply because they have paid the bride price (Holm, 1995). Not all cultural groups in Southern Africa require men to pay a bride price. However, domestic violence exists even among such groups. This shows that domestic violence is embedded in society and is not attributable to bride price alone.

When discussing domestic violence and children in Southern Africa, it should be recognized that it may have a different impact on children who live in rural areas than on those who live in urban areas. For example, it could be difficult for perpetrators of violence to isolate women and child victims in rural areas because rural people are likely to know their neighbors, to have good relationships, and to visit each other more frequently—to the degree that incidents of domestic violence that happen in one family may not be easily hidden from neighbors and relatives who can sometimes provide assistance. Because divorce and marital separation are more common in urban areas of Africa (Wilson, 1968), where neighbors are less likely to know and help each other, a large number of child victims are likely to be socially isolated.

The effects of domestic violence on children do not necessarily end during childhood; sometimes they spill over into adulthood. Thus, childhood experience of family violence has been linked to domestic violence in adult relationships. Although some parents who were abused during their childhood become loving and supportive, others, partly because of their unmet emotional needs, abuse their children as they themselves were abused (Jaffe et al., 1990). Despite the fact that parental violence associated with divorce has adverse effects on children, not all children of divorced parents experience parental violence.

LOW FAMILY INCOME

Decline in children's standard of living in mother-custody families following parental separation and/or divorce is another problem that affects children. The decline in children's standard of living following divorce is not a phenomenon peculiar solely to children of divorced parents in Southern Africa; indeed, it affects a large number of children of divorced parents in developed countries as well. According to the Select Committee on Children, Youth, and Families (SCCYF) of the United States House of Representatives (1989), after divorce, 90 percent of children resided primarily with their mothers, and in the first year following a divorce the average family income of such mothers declined from 26,000 U.S. dollars to 15,000 U.S. dollars.

In Southern Africa, as in Western countries, most women get custody of children after divorce, especially when young children are involved or when former husbands were violent. Such women and their children are likely to experience a decline in their standard of living for several reasons. First, the earning capacity of men in most Southern African countries is higher than that of women. This partly stems from the differences in educational attainments between men and women. In Malawi, Tanzania, Botswana, and other countries in the region, the discrepancy in average levels of educational achievement between the genders, and the proportions of enrollment of males compared to females at all educational levels are high (Croll, 1981; Segal and Berheide, 1994; Hope, 1996). In Botswana, for example, in 1991 there were 15,037 male cash earners in the economically active population who had completed secondary school compared to only 8,171 females with this educational level. Similarly, there were 11,122 male cash earners who had attained a tertiary education compared to 5,485 females (Hope, 1996). The small number of girls who attain higher education has been attributed to differences in the socialization practices of girls and boys in some Southern African countries and to the girls' high pregnancy rates. In her study of women in Botswana, Enge (1985) found that girls are socialized to value marriage and child bearing more than education.

Cooper (1979) attributes the high earning capacity of men relative to that of women in some towns in Southern Africa to the fact that men in general have more opportunities open to them. This is particularly so because of the heavy construction nature of some of the jobs, for example, digging toilets and roofing huts, and the fact that men quite often use skills from formal employment to generate more income for themselves. For example, many men work as part-time builders, carpenters, and mechanics, whereas women engage in activities such as sewing and beer brewing, which do not enable them to get as much money as the men.

Second, child support payments in most Southern African countries are inadequate to meet the needs of children. The writer's personal discussions with several divorce lawyers in one Southern African country in 1996 and 1997 revealed that the system is generally lenient to men in terms of child support payments. One reason for this leniency is that most men rather than women hold influential positions (policy makers, judges, lawyers, etc.); therefore, they are likely to make decisions and policies that favor husbands. In Botswana, for example, it was as late as January 1998 that a woman judge was first appointed. This step is a right move toward empowering women, and it is hoped that in the long run (as more and more women enter positions that can allow them to influence policies), policies and decisions that are fair to women and children will be made. In addition, women are usually too poor to afford lawyers' fees, and therefore representation is quite often on behalf of male respondents only (Women and Law in Southern Africa, 1991a). In Leribe, a village in Lesotho, WLSA found that 71 percent of the female litigants who were involved in civil proceedings in 1991 were not represented legally.

Third, monitoring and enforcement of child support payments in Southern Africa countries is inadequate (Women and Law in Southern Africa, 1991a). Discussions during a regional seminar on maintenance law which was conducted by WLSA, in which six countries of Southern Africa were represented (Botswana, Lesotho, Zambia, Swaziland, Mozambique, and Zimbabwe), revealed that child support systems in these countries have serious problems in enforcing child maintenance orders, especially where the men concerned were either unemployed or self-employed.

The problems of enforcing and monitoring child maintenance orders are prevalent not only in the developing countries of Southern Africa, but also in South Africa (a semideveloped country). According to Sinclair (1983), the legal machinery is unable to cope with the volume of cases of maintenance defaulters. Furthermore, the fact that judicial determination of entitlement to maintenance for children is rare in South Africa disadvantages divorced women and their children economically. Private ordering of child support payments without proper legal assistance available to women makes them powerless in the decision-making process and leads to severe decline in their living standards.

Poor monitoring and enforcement of maintenance orders discourage women from making maintenance claims. Other factors that discourage them include fear of violence from former husbands, women's limited knowledge of the laws, lack of information about aid agencies, and fear of witchcraft. In Swaziland, men often threaten women that if they take maintenance matters to the courts, they will bewitch the children. Some children have died following such threats (WLSA, 1991a).

Fourth, children in mother-custody families experience a decline in their standard of living because most men tend to associate maintenance with custody. In Swaziland, for example, it is common for fathers to refuse, even on pain of imprisonment, to pay periodic sums to the mother, insisting that they want their children to live with them (Nhlapo, 1990). The fact that men insist that they can maintain children only if they live with them may lead some women to drop maintenance charges. This can be particularly so because divorced men may have remarried and many women do not want their children to live with stepmothers. Similarly, some divorced women may have already remarried, and this makes divorced fathers reluctant to support children living in the home of another man (Armstrong, 1992). According to Armstrong, it is perceived that the new husband is getting the benefit of being with both the woman and the children and therefore should have the responsibility of maintaining them.

Fifth, children in mother-custody families are likely to live in poverty because men in Southern Africa find themselves torn between their traditional obligations to support their extended family members and their duty to maintain their nuclear family. Research conducted by Holm (1995) and WLSA (1991a) found that in some cases men considered it more important to maintain their extended families than their own children, particularly in cases where they were living apart from their children. Also, customary laws in countries such as Zambia and Botswana which entitle women to maintenance by their husbands only during the marriage, but not after divorce, lead children to live in poverty (Maundeni, 1997). Lastly, the absence of welfare programs that cater for poor children in Southern African countries also contributes to poverty among children of divorce.

Not all children of divorced parents in Southern Africa experience decline in the family's standard of living following divorce. For those women whose husbands were using the family resources irresponsibly, the end of the marriage can mean the wife's greater control over the resources she produces and more efficient use of funds to meet the children's needs. Research from Tanzania shows that single women who are heads of households are more assured of receiving just returns for their labor than married women. They are also able to organize their labor as they wish and to control the products they get from plowing, whereas husbands of married women continue to control the resources and market products of women's labor at both the household and village levels (Croll, 1981).

The effects of poverty on children whose parents are divorced is well documented. Lack of finance restricts family access to food, shelter, and clothes, and deprives children of opportunities for play, leisure, and education. Poverty can also impact on families by increasing levels of stress, tension, sense of stigma, and ill health (Kilmurray, 1995). These experiences can affect family functioning and the quality of parenting that parents provide for their children. For example, poor parents are usually more concerned about meeting basic food and clothing needs than recreational, social, and emotional needs. They are also likely to work very long hours and to spend little quality time with their children. Coming home exhausted, poor parents may not have the time to listen to their children's experiences of the day and to provide them with social and emotional support.

Low income also impacts on children's educational performance. Whelan (1994) has found a relationship between low family income and poor educational performance. In his study of poverty, social class, education and intergenerational mobility in Ireland, Whelan found that households exposed to the highest risks of unemployment and poverty were also the source of those school leavers who entered the labor market each year lacking qualifications.

Research on poverty in Southern Africa shows that overcrowding is a feature of severe poverty, especially for very poor female households that lack assets and employment. Female-headed households have also been found to have higher household sizes or dependency ratios (BIDPA, 1997). The BIDPA found that poor people rely more on wood/charcoal for cooking and on paraffin and gas for lighting. This has serious implications for the health of household members and for their ability to study and work during weekends because they live in such unhygienic environments. These factors explain the high incidence of acute respiratory infections and avoidable communicable diseases among children in rural areas and contribute to the problem of poor children failing to devote sufficient time to school homework (BIDPA, 1997).

LACK OF COMMUNICATION BETWEEN DIVORCEES AND CHILDREN

Little has been documented on parent-child communication about divorce in Southern Africa. Available literature from Western countries shows that most divorcing parents are reluctant to communicate with their children about their divorce (Wallerstein and Kelly, 1980). According to Wallerstein and Kelly (1980), the difficulty usually arises from the fact that parents are apprehensive that their children may be unhappy, frightened, or angered by their decision. Parents are also worried about the present and future psychological, social, and economic effects of their decision on their children. However, it seems that the reluctance of parents to communicate with their children about divorce does more harm than good to the children. Children tend to feel confused, angry, and unhappy. If a child's views on issues of custody and access are not sought, the child may be placed into the custody of an abusive parent, just because the other parent is mentally unwell. If a child's views have been sought, however, he or she might have revealed the abuse and options such as placement with relatives considered.

Apart from the reasons highlighted in the preceding paragraph, children of divorced or separated parents are likely to lack information because of the cultural belief that exists in some Southern African countries such as "children should be seen but not heard." Banda's (1994) study on children whose parents have been separated or divorced in Zimbabwe found that children are rarely provided with any information about their parents' divorce, nor are they given the opportunity to express their views and opinions on issues of custody and access to noncustodial fathers. These findings should not be generalized to all Southern African countries because countries have different cultures, manifesting different degrees of complexity. In addition, factors such as parents' individual characteristics, their educational backgrounds, and their socioeconomic status can influence parent-child communication about divorce. Therefore, making general statements that are not substantiated by research evidence can be misleading.

Advocates of children's rights stress the need for children to have information and to participate in decisions that affect their lives. Such participation rights are included in the United Nations Convention on the Rights of the Child that almost all the Southern African countries have signed. The importance of parents' communication with children about divorce has been stressed by Jewett (1994: 35), who asserts that "if parents have separated, questions from their children are as important and as inevitable as they are when there is a loss through death." However, Jewett cautions that parents should avoid burdening children with constant discussions.

LOSS OF SUPPORTIVE NETWORKS

Parental separation brings changes in the nature of children's social networks. Although little is known about how divorce affects the nature of these networks in Southern Africa, lessons can be drawn from the research findings emanating elsewhere. Research from Western countries, for example, shows that children of divorce and their families are more likely to have fewer supportive people in their networks than do their counterparts from nondivorced families (Sprenkle and Cyrus, 1983).

Several reasons explain why children of divorced parents lack supportive networks. First, children of divorced parents are likely to change schools, neighborhoods, peers, and other familiar environments, partly because of decreased family income. Both economic and residential changes sharply alter children's lives, and such changes adversely affect them. Second, divorce brings changes in relationships between parents and children. Children are likely to have less contact with their noncustodial parents following divorce. Several American researchers (Seltzer and Bianchi, 1988) have found that most children whose parents have divorced experience loss of contact with nonresidential parents. Not only does this contact decrease following divorce, but also the quality of their relationships changes, and this affects the support that children get from their fathers. Father-child relationships have been found to be less close and more indulgent in divorced than in married families (Emery and Forehand, 1994).

Divorce also affects the quality of support children receive from their custodial parents. Research shows that most custodial parents go through a process of adjustment following divorce. This process involves adapting to being a single parent, starting employment outside the home, especially for those who did not engage in such work before, depression, and mourning the loss of a relationship. These experiences may affect the custodial parent's ability to be supportive to the children. For example, divorced mothers in the United States have been found to be less affectionate and more inconsistent in relation to their children, and boys have been found to receive less positive feedback and more negative sanctions from their mothers than daughters (Hetherington et al., 1982). Divorce has also been found to increase the risk of psychological stress for parents (Bloom et al., 1978), and parents with psychological problems are less likely to offer adequate support to their children. Bloom and colleagues have found high admission rates to psychiatric institutions, high suicide rates, and a greater prevalence of alcoholism among the divorced than the married, with obvious negative effects on the children.

Little is known about how divorce affects the support that parents give to their children in Southern Africa. Findings from Western countries which show that divorce increases the risk of psychological problems for parents and that such parents are less likely to offer adequate support to their children may be less applicable to parents who stay for prolonged periods of time without their spouses. This can be so because women, for instance, may be accustomed to living alone and getting less emotional, recreational, moral, and other types of support from their husbands. It is common in some Southern African countries for husbands to leave their wives and children to work either in urban areas of their own countries as migrant labor or in other countries. The extent of both internal and external migration, however, varies among countries. In Lesotho, for example, 40 to 60 percent of married women are left behind by their husbands who work in South Africa, particularly in the mines (Gordon, 1981). According to Gordon, men leave their families behind primarily because the labor laws prohibit women and children from living with migrant workers.

Although women who do not live with their spouses for a prolonged period of time may be less psychologically affected by divorce and therefore their ability to provide support to children is unaffected, it is also possible that the rate of juvenile delinquency, crime, and deviance among children can be high due to the absence of fathers. This is because fathers in most Southern African countries are traditionally the disciplinarians. Fathers can also act as role models, especially for boys. In her study of parental availability and academic achievement among rural primary school children in Swaziland, Booth (1996) found that grade repetition rates were significantly higher for boys in father-absent homes. Booth attributes the high repetition rate to the fact that boys experienced a lack of educational motivation in the absence of the male role models. The experience of failure and repetition by the boys may lead some of them to have low self-esteem or to leave school and engage in deviant activities.

The finding that noncustodial fathers provide less support to their children following divorce is relevant to children of divorced parents in Southern Africa. This is particularly so because, as mentioned previously, most noncustodial fathers in Southern Africa do not pay adequate and frequent amounts of child support. Some do not pay child support at all, despite the fact that they are usually ordered to by the courts. Fathers who do not support their children financially are also less likely to provide emotional, social, religious/moral, and recreational support to their offspring.

Yet children's lack of emotional, recreational, and other types of support from their noncustodial fathers may not be felt by children who stayed apart from their fathers for prolonged periods of time; those who did not have frequent contact with their fathers; and those who did not have close relationships with their fathers prior to the divorce. Not all Southern African children whose parents are married live with both parents. Some, because of their own education demands, imprisonment, labor laws, and parents' work demands, live with one parent. There are also children of married parents who do not live with either parent for a long time as a result of wars that have been rampant in countries such as Mozambique and Angola. Although some of these children are able bodied, others are disabled, and still others suffer from malnutrition. They are therefore likely to be more concerned about meeting basic needs of food, shelter, and clothing, and reunification with their parents and relatives, than about whether their parents are still married or divorced. The number of children who do not stay with both parents is difficult to quantify, and it also varies among countries. Although work demands force some fathers not to stay with their children on a full-time basis, in countries such as Lesotho, some of them remain in close contact with their families by seeking location for work in South Africa whose proximity to Lesotho allows them close contact, with frequent weekend visits home (Gordon, 1981). However, for those unable to do this, divorce may have minimal effect on their children's relationships with them, as well as on the support they receive.

Children in countries such as Tanzania, where agriculture is the backbone of the economy, are also less likely to be affected by the lack of support (emotional, recreational, and social) from their fathers following a divorce. This is particularly so because they spend more time with their mothers and other women working in the fields, are able to produce some food for themselves, and have less contact with their fathers. Less contact with fathers largely emanates from some fathers' migration to urban areas to work and from their involvement in activities such as carpentry and brick-making which do exist in some rural areas (Croll, 1981). Women in Tanzania are responsible for almost all domestic work and spend more hours on the farms than men. Such labor burdens compel them to rely on their children as the most easily accessible source of help (Madulu, 1995). In cases where hired labor is used, it is largely the men's infrequent and heavier labor that is replaced, not the women's. Child labor, which is common among poor agricultural societies, is not a feature of middle- and upper-class families in urban areas of Southern African countries because affluent parents provide all the basic (and non-basic) needs of their children, and consequently the children are heavily dependent on their parents. Such children are more likely to be adversely affected by divorce than their counterparts in agricultural societies who are accustomed to taking care of themselves and to participating with adults in the process of social reproduction.

Parents are not the only members of children's networks; other members include extended family members, friends, and professionals. Children of divorce and parental separation are also likely to get less support from extended family members than their counterparts in nondivorced families. This is particularly so because the modern way of living (money economy, competition over scarce resources, etc.) places serious restrictions not only on the extent to which relatives can help each other, but also on the extent to which governments can provide services to the people. In traditional African societies (prior to industrialization and urbanization), societies were dependent on a subsistence economy characterized by self-sufficiency and joint family organization. Several family members who were related to one another by blood, marriage, or adoption lived together in the same compound or part of the village, and their needs (e.g., material, emotional) were provided for by the extended family as a unit (Himonga, 1985). When situations such as divorce occurred, divorced women and their children were absorbed into their kinship group or self-sufficient family organization and were taken care of by their relatives in the same way as before marriage. Therefore, children's life experiences were not so adversely affected by divorce, for the social structure was such that marital disruption resulted in minimal disruption of the family's material resources and social supports (Bilge and Kaufman, 1983; Himonga, 1985).

The support and protection for women and children that existed in traditional societies is now reduced under modern living conditions. Such a system has been transformed by changes such as the money economy, industrialization, migration, urbanization, decrease in agricultural produce, and changes in religious beliefs, which have brought with them different patterns of life and values. People need money to buy food, and since the income levels of most families in some Southern African countries are low (because of low wages and unemployment), it is difficult for some people to maintain extended family members. People are increasingly spending the money they earn on their nuclear family members; therefore, the extended family ties are weakened (WLSA, 1991a).

Research evidence indicates that divorced women and their children in Southern Africa lack support from members of their networks. In her study of support for women with dependent children in Botswana, Griffiths (1987) found that a majority of women in her sample did not use the customary courts to file for maintenance charges from the fathers of their children because they lacked the necessary cooperation from their elderly relatives. In order for the mothers to effectively utilize customary courts, their elderly relatives, especially males, have to play an active role in reporting the cases, following them up and ensuring that the decisions reached by the customary courts about the cases are fair and enforceable.

This discussion does not mean that all people in Southern Africa do not help their extended family members. Some still maintain adequate links and provide a certain level of support to relatives. According to WLSA (1991b), Lesotho still has some households in which extended family members stay together. In such circumstances, working members of the family help with maintenance of the other members. Nevertheless, WLSA found that the extended family ties seem to be getting looser in the urban areas of Lesotho than in the rural ones.

Although many extended family members in contemporary societies live and work outside their own villages or even outside their countries and are beyond the reach of senior family members who may want to enforce obligations of support, their ability to provide support to their relatives is adversely affected (Molokomme, 1987). Yet it should be recognized that the provision of support in contemporary societies, unlike in traditional societies, is a voluntary exercise. One need not be forced to provide support for his or her relatives. It should also be recognized that support can be provided from a distance. That is, a person does not have to be living in the same place with a relative in order to provide support to that person. Improved communication systems (telephones, e-mail, transport, and so on) are features of modern living that enable people to contact each other frequently despite the distance between them. It should also be emphasized that children of divorced parents and their mothers do not necessarily have to be supported in financial terms; this support can also be informational, emotional, spiritual, or recreational. The elderly members of a family in particular provide this kind of support to children.

African researchers and scholars have not reached consensus on the role of the extended family and whether it is strong or weak. They have not developed instruments or ways to measure its strength or weakness. It can therefore be contended that although some divorced women and their children in Southern Africa get help or support from extended family members, the extent and value of such support is difficult to determine.

IMPLICATIONS FOR RESEARCH, POLICY, AND PRACTICE

Before examining the implications of the impact of divorce on children in Southern Africa, some features of the region relevant to the subject under discussion should be pointed out. First, the Southern Africa region comprises 12 countries, with different cultural, economic, social, historical, and political backgrounds. These features influence children's experiences in relation to divorce as well as its impact. For example, women in Zimbabwe and South Africa have, for many years, been subjected to discrimination on the basis of both race and gender. In contrast, women in other Southern African countries have largely been subjected to discrimination on the basis of gender only. Black South African women's experiences of race and gender discrimination may explain why a large proportion of them work as domestic workers and are poor. Children of black women in Zimbabwe, South Africa, and other Southern African countries experience more severe economic hardships than children of white women because of the enduring effects of discrimination on the basis of gender, race, or color.

Second, the human rights profile differs in the various countries of Southern Africa. Whereas poor countries such as Tanzania are faced with the problem of meeting their people's basic needs, countries such as South Africa have made considerable progress. This does not mean that poverty has been eradicated in South Africa. Rather, it means that in relative terms, most people's minimum basic needs are met. Third, economic factors causing the internal and external migration of fathers who then leave their families behind also greatly influence children's experiences of divorce and its impact on them. For example, children who stayed with their fathers and those who had frequent contact with them prior to the marital rupture are likely to be more adversely affected by divorce than their counterparts who did not stay with their fathers and those who did not have frequent contact with them.

This chapter has implications for research, policy, and practice. Given the increase in divorce and parental separations in Southern Africa, more research must be conducted on the sources, characteristics, and effects of divorce on children. Such research should be guided by theories such as the social construction perspective which emphasizes the perceptions of people who experienced certain situations. Information should therefore be collected not only from parents, but more importantly from children themselves. In addition, the research should focus on the conditions of children from various backgrounds: cultural, ethnic, age groups, and socioeconomic.

Policy makers, researchers, and practitioners must also propose or find ways of reducing the stress associated with divorce on children. Measures should be taken to prevent domestic violence, which often precedes and accompanies divorces. These measures can be in the form of public education programs to sensitize people about the effects of violence on children and women. In addition, battered women's shelters could be developed to cater for women who have experienced severe violence but feel that they have nowhere to go. This service should be provided on a temporary or permanent basis, depending on individual circumstances. The shelters that already exist in urban areas of some Southern African countries need to be improved and expanded so that they can be made accessible to a wider population. Furthermore, there is need to educate women about their rights. The Women and Law in Southern Africa Project has already started such programs, which should be expanded and improved.

Given research findings that link domestic violence to child abuse and incest, it is imperative that services for abused children be developed, improved, and expanded. Child abuse is a complex issue, especially if the perpetrator is a family member. The absence of child welfare services such as foster care and safety institutions for children in some Southern African countries may result in some victims of child abuse continuing to live with the perpetrators. This has serious implications for the children's welfare.

Child support systems in the various Southern African countries are grossly inadequate. Greater attention should be paid to the systems in general. Issues of enforcement and monitoring are critical. Action should be taken against defaulters of child support payments. Holiday imprisonment (that is, imprisoning defaulters during their holidays rather than imprisoning them during the time when they could be working) should be imposed on defaulters. If defaulters are put in prison during the time that they could be working, they might earn low wages and their ability to pay adequate child support amounts could be affected. The practice of putting defaulters in prison during the holidays has been attempted in Swaziland on defaulters who subsequently paid their child support money (WLSA, 1991a).

Given the findings that many parents do not communicate with children about divorce and separation, parents should be made aware of the benefits of open communication with children about divorce. This task can be facilitated by human service professionals such as social workers, lawyers, psychologists, and medical workers. These professionals cannot perform the task unless they have been appropriately prepared and trained. Child welfare specialists need to conduct seminars for the professionals so as to disseminate information about divorce and its consequences and to sharpen the professionals' skills on working with divorced families. Communication is a process that involves information giving, understanding, expressing feelings, and responding. Children should be provided with information about what is happening or has happened in the family, and this information should be presented in a way that will enable the children to understand. Also, children should be allowed to express their feelings and to respond. Smith (1995) contends that if children are given adequate information about the divorce, they will be less likely to blame themselves for their parents' separation or divorce. She also observes that if the separation and divorce are not discussed, children can be anxious about the possibility of parents not loving them and about what will happen in the future.

Mediation, pre-divorce counseling, post-divorce counseling, and social support groups should be established for both mothers and children to share experiences and to get support in countries where they are nonexistent. A primary goal of mediation is to foster the cooperation and involvement of divorcing adults in the decision-making process required for the organization of the family's future, with special attention to issues affecting children. Mediation therefore contrasts with the adversary process, which invites abdication by one of the parties and places them in competitive opposition (Sinclair, 1983). It must be recognized, however, that mediation will not be suitable for all clients. For example, those who exhibit destructive behavior cannot participate profitably in mediation. But spouses who have achieved a certain level of emotional independence and are ready to bargain can be assisted by the mediator in the clarification of goals, objectives, and issues affecting their children, including custody and visitation. Although counseling and support groups existed in traditional societies, the people involved usually knew each other for some time, whereas nowadays the practices are coordinated and led by professionals, and the participants are more likely to be meeting each other for the first time. This can make some participants reluctant to share their experiences and provide support to each other. Trained counselors are therefore needed to help victims of domestic violence to participate more comfortably in these programs. Places such as churches and community halls can be used as meeting places for such groups.

The problem of domestic violence is multifaceted, and its resolution requires a multidisciplinary approach. Research on domestic violence in the Southern Africa region shows that medical workers are usually the first to get in contact with victims of domestic violence. It is therefore imperative that medical workers link victims with other professionals who can help them, including social workers, lawyers, and psychologists. The referrals should only be made with the consent of the victims. Although most domestic violence victims contact medical workers first, some of them do not verbally reveal the violence to them because of feelings of shame and guilt associated with the traumatic experiences. In such cases, medical workers may have to initiate the discussion. By beginning the dialogue, they will be communicating to the women that the problem is not all that shameful or irrelevant to talk about, that they understand the woman's discomfort and other reactions to victimization, and that the situation is not so hopeless that it cannot be changed.

The police are also likely to get in contact with victims of domestic violence. It is therefore vital that they be trained to be sensitive to the issues involved. During several workshops attended by the writer in Africa and abroad (e.g., a workshop on probation work with juvenile delinquents in Botswana, 1995; a workshop on violence against women in Scotland, 1997), it was reported that the police are generally not sensitive to victims of domestic violence partly because they lack training. Lastly, confidential toll-free phone arrangements should be put in place so that victims (both women and children) can call and seek assistance whenever there is a need. Because this service may not be easily accessible to women without telephones, such women should be encouraged to use public telephones. For the sake of effectiveness and efficiency, pilot projects of the programs being suggested coupled with research should be embarked upon to provide information for the development of future appropriate strategies.

The implementation of some of these suggestions will require money, and most parts of Southern Africa have limited resources. Because governments in Southern African countries play a vital role in economic development and policy making, they are expected to play a leading part in the field of welfare. Unfortunately, this may not be the case because welfare services do not bring any income to the governments, but they may be seen as liabilities, and governments do not want to perform poorly economically. One way of overcoming the problem of limited resources is to invite or encourage nongovernmental organizations

(NGOs) such as Women and the Law in Southern Africa and Childline to develop the services. Such action can be initiated by governments, policy makers, practitioners, clients, and advocates for women and children (through subsidy from governments and practitioners giving their services to clients free). In addition, the NGOs can equip women volunteers with skills and knowledge so that they can provide services to women and children who are in need of help. The use of volunteers in NGOs is not a new phenomenon in Southern Africa. NGOs such as Red Cross Societies have a long history of relying on volunteers, and it is a good way to reduce costs. Women should also be encouraged to engage in fund-raising activities to finance the programs.

Issues of domestic violence and low income of divorced custodial mothers are closely associated with male dominance over women in Southern Africa. This dominance has social, economic, and health implications for both women and children. One of the social implications of this dominance is that children who grow up under such conditions are likely to learn that female oppression or exploitation is normal. The process of male dominance can therefore be transmitted from one generation to another. Another social implication is that children of violent fathers are likely to fear their fathers so much that a positive relationship may not exist between them, resulting in such children lacking male role models. Economically, male dominance implies that women will continue to depend on men for economic survival, so that when divorce takes place, their children are likely to experience decline in their standards of living. Male dominance also affects women's health. Because women in some rural areas of Southern Africa spend most of their time working on farms, they are likely to have health problems. Intensive efforts to raise the educational level of women through literacy campaigns and formal educational reforms and to equip them for a larger role in economic and political development programs should be embarked upon. Lastly, long-range policies aimed at changing gender relations are needed.

CONCLUSION

This chapter has examined the dynamics of divorce and separation and their impact on children. Some of the problems discussed begin before divorce, and although they may be resolved as time passes, divorce undeniably poses many problems for children. The issues of low family income, family violence, poor parent-child communication about divorce, and loss of supportive networks are sources of stress and need to be attended to if children are to live as healthy and productive human beings. Not all children of divorced couples in the Southern Africa region are negatively affected by divorce and its consequences. Some children emerge as competent, mature, and productive individuals, especially when divorce is a positive solution to destructive family functioning. It therefore seems reasonable to conclude that if children are not exposed to parental conflicts and violence, if they do not experience drastic deterioration in their standard of living, and if their social network members are supportive, the impact of divorce on them may not be so traumatic.

REFERENCES

Ahmed, G. and Letamo, G. (1989). *Causes and Consequences of Current Marriage and Family Transformation: What Batswana Think about These Changes.* Unpublished monograph, University of Botswana.

Armstrong, A. K. (1992). *Struggling over Scarce Resources: Women and Maintenance in Southern Africa Regional Report: Phase One. Women and the Law in Southern Africa.* Harare: University of Zimbabwe Publications.

Banda, F. (1994). "Custody and the Best Interest of the Child." *International Journal of Law and the Family,* 8(2), 191–201.

Bhebhe, B. and Mosha, A. C. (1996). *The Concept of Women Remaining Single and Its Economic Consequences.* Unpublished paper.

Bilge, B. and Kaufman, G. (1983). "Children of Divorce and One Parent Families: Cross Cultural Perspectives." *Family Relations,* 32, 59–71.

Bloom, B. L. et al. (1978). "Marital Disruption as a Stressor: A Review and Analysis." *Psychological Bulletin,* 85(4), 867–894.

Booth, M. Z. (1996). "Parental Availability and Academic Achievement among Swaziland Rural Primary School Children." *Comparative Education Review,* 40(3), 250–263.

Botswana Institute for Development Policy Analysis (BIDPA). (1997). *Study of Poverty and Poverty Alleviation in Botswana, Phase One, Vol. 2.* Gaborone: Ministry of Finance and Development Planning.

Cooper, D. (1979) *Rural-Urban Migration and Female Headed Households in Botswana: Town Case Studies of Unskilled Women Workers and Female Self Employment in a Site and Service Area in Selibi-Phikwe.* Gaborone: Central Statistics Office.

Croll, E. J. (1981). "Women in Rural Production and Reproduction in the Soviet Union, China, Cuba and Tanzania: Socialist Development Experiences." *Signs,* 7(2), 361–399.

Emery, R. E. (1992). "Family Conflict and Its Developmental Implications: A Conceptual Analysis of Deep Meanings and Systemic Processes." In C. U. Shantz and W. W. Hartup (eds.), *Conflict in Child and Adolescent Development* (pp. 270–298). Cambridge: Cambridge University Press.

Emery, R. E. and Forehand, R. (1994). "Parental Divorce and Children's Well-Being: A Focus on Resilience." In R. J. Haggerty et al. (eds.), *Stress, Risk and Resilience in Children and Adolescents: Process, Mechanisms and Interventions* (pp. 64–99). Cambridge: Cambridge University Press.

Enge, M. (1985). *Women in Botswana: Dependant Yet Independent.* Stockholm: Swedish International Agency.

Gelles, R. J. and Straus, M. A. (1988). *Intimate Violence: The Causes and Consequences of Abuse in the American Family*. New York: Simon & Schuster.

Gordon, E. (1981). "An Analysis of the Impact of Labor Migration on the Lives of Women in Lesotho." *Journal of Development Studies*, 17(3), 59–76.

Griffiths, A. (1987). "Support for Women with Dependent Children: Customary, Common and Statutory Law in Botswana." In A. Armstrong and W. Ncube (eds.), *Women and Law in Southern Africa* (pp. 164–178). Harare: Zimbabwe Publishing House.

Hetherington, E. M. et al. (1982). "Effects of Divorce on Parents and Children." In M. Lamb (ed.), *Non Traditional Families: Parenting and Child Development* (pp. 233–289). Hillsdale, NJ: Lawrence Erlbaum Associates.

Himonga, C. N. (1985). *Family Property Disputes: The Predicament of Women and Children in a Zambian Urban Community*. Unpublished Ph.D thesis.

Holm, G. (1995). *Women and Law in Southern Africa*. Copenhagen: Danish International Development Assistance (Danida), Ministry of Foreign Affairs.

Hope, K. R. (1996). "Growth, Unemployment and Poverty in Botswana." *Journal of Contemporary African Studies*, 14(1), 53–67.

Iro, M. I. (1976). "The Pattern of Elite Divorce in Lagos: 1961–1973." *Journal of Marriage and the Family*, 38, 177–182.

Jacobson, D. S. (1978). "The Impact of Marital Separation/Divorce on Children: Inter-parent Hostility and Child Adjustment." *Journal of Divorce*, 2(1), 3–19.

Jaffe, P. G. et al. (1990). *Children of Battered Women*. Newbury Park, CA: Sage Publications.

Jewett, C. L. (1994). *Helping Children Cope with Separation and Loss*. Child Care Policy and Practice, 2nd ed. London: Batsford Ltd. in Association with British Agencies for Adoption and Fostering.

Johnston, R. et al. (1987). "Ongoing Post-Divorce Conflict and Child Disturbance." *Journal of Abnormal Child Psychology*, 15(4), 493–509.

Kilmurray, A. (1995). "Children and Poverty in Ireland." *Children and Society*, 9(2), 5–18.

Klingshirn, A. (1971). *The Changing Position of Women in Ghana: A Study Based on Empirical Research in Larteh, A Small Town in Southern Ghana*. Marburg: Lahn.

Madulu, N. F. (1995). "Population Growth, Agrarian Peasant Economy and Environmental Degradation in Tanzania." *International Sociology*, 10(1), 35–50.

Maundeni, T. (1997). *Children's Experiences of Divorce and the Role of Social Networks in their Adjustment: A Review of the Literature and Implications for Developing Countries of Africa*. Unpublished paper.

Molokomme, A. (1987). "The Mosaic of Botswana Maintenance Law." *Botswana Notes and Records*, 19, 129–135.

———. (1990). "Women's Law in Botswana, Laws and Research Needs." In J. Stewart and A. Armstrong (eds.), *The Legal Situation of Women in Southern Africa* (pp. 7–46). Harare: University of Zimbabwe Publications.

Nhlapo, R. T. (1990). *The Legal Situation of Women in Swaziland and Some Thoughts on Research*. Mbabane: Webster's.

Peterson, J. L. and Zill, N. (1986). "Marital Disruption, Parent-Child Relationships and Behavior Problems in Children." *Journal of Marriage and the Family*, 48, 295–307.

Segal, M. T. and Berheide, C. W. (1994). "Access Is a Beginning: Education and the Advancement of Women in Malawi." New Albany: Indiana University.

Select Committee on Children, Youth and Families (SCCYF) of the United States House of Representatives. (1989). *US Children and Their Families: Current Conditions and Recent Trends.* Washington, DC: U.S. Government Printing Office.

Seltzer, J. and Bianchi, S. M. (1988). "Children's Contact with Absent Parents." *Journal of Marriage and the Family*, 50, 663–677.

Sinclair, J. (1983). "The Financial Consequences of Divorce in South Africa: Judicial Determination or Private Ordering?" *The International and Comparative Law Quarterly*, 32(4), 785–811.

Smith, H. (1995). *Unhappy Children: Reasons and Remedies.* London: Free Association Books.

Solivetti, L. M. (1994). "Family, Marriage and Divorce in a Hausa Community: A Sociological Model." *Africa*, 64(2), 252–271.

Sprenkle, D. H. and Cyrus, C. L. (1983). "Abandonment: The Stress of Sudden Divorce." In D. McCubbin and C. R. Figley (eds.), *Stress and the Family, Vol. II: Coping with Catastrophe* (pp. 53–75). New York: Mazel Publishers.

Taylor, J. and Stewart, S. (1991). *Sexual and Domestic Violence: Help, Recovery and Action in Zimbabwe.* Harare: Glehn and Taylor in Collaboration with Women and the Law in Southern Africa.

Wallerstein, J. S. and Kelly, J. B. (1980). *Surviving the Breakup: How Children and Parents Cope with Divorce.* New York: Basic Books.

Whelan, C. C. (1994). "Poverty, Social Class and Education and Intergenerational Mobility." In T. Callan and B. Nolan (eds.), *Poverty and Policy in Ireland.* Dublin: Gill & Macmillan.

Wilson, G. (1968). "An Essay on the Economics of Detribalisation in Northern Rhodesia." The *Rhodes-Livingstone Papers*, No. 6. Manchester: Manchester University Press.

Women and Law in Southern Africa (WLSA). (1991a). *Findings of Maintenance Law Regional Seminar.* Protea, Piggs Peak, Swaziland.

———. (1991b). *Maintenance in Lesotho.* Johannesburg: Women and Law in Southern Africa Research Project.

Chapter 3

Child Abuse: A Sociological Perspective

Norma Romm and Apollo Rwomire

INTRODUCTION

This chapter explores various arguments that have arisen in sociology to explain child abuse, an issue that needs to be kept on the social agenda of public concern. The different implications for action attendant on these explanations are discussed. The following discussion shows how sociological reflections can make input into this agenda. Before offering sociological arguments, the complexities involved in defining "child abuse" are presented.

DEFINING CHILD ABUSE

As a starting point to delimit the area of consideration, child abuse is defined following Nagi's discussion in the *Encyclopedia of Crime and Justice* to mean "maltreatment of children" (Nagi, 1983: 1624). This maltreatment, as Nagi states, "can take many forms, including physical violence such as battering and other expressions of rage and excessive punishment." He adds that "maltreatment that is equally damaging, if not physically evident, includes mental cruelty" (1983: 1624). The child abuse that is the focus of this chapter thus includes both physical and emotional battering. The issue of sexual abuse is not included in the discussion because this matter deserves separate attention.

The definition of maltreatment invoked in Nagi's discussion is not clear-cut. Nagi points out that in order to determine whether maltreatment has occurred or is occurring, two components may be referred to: namely, intent and severity. With regard to these components, the aim is to establish whether a perpetrated physical or mental (emotional) abuse had intent to harm and whether forms of maltreatment are to be regarded as "disciplinary, excessive or abusive" (Nagi, 1983: 1625). Although some people would perhaps prefer the category of abuse to be more clearly defined, others argue that its vagueness is its strength. This is because it "permits flexibility" in decision making in the context of particular cases, allowing for case-by-case assessment of whether "abuse" can be said to have occurred or be occurring (Nagi, 1983: 1625).

A complicating factor in discussions of child abuse is how one goes about defining the "normative," or what may be regarded as justifiable or appropriate behavior in a particular society or social context. In some situations, it might be argued that certain forms of "abuse" are appropriate as long as the aim is to have a disciplining/reformative influence on the children's behavior. Neither members of society nor the international literature on the subject may have reached agreement on the cutoff point where disciplining action becomes abusive behavior. There seems to be a consensus, however, that action leading to hospitalization or death of the victim is unacceptable. However, there may be vast differences of opinion about cases that thus far may have been argued not to lead to lasting physical or emotional harm. As Magagula (1991) points out, there may be disagreement, too, about how to interpret or decide when lasting harm has been inflicted. Magagula suggests, for instance, that corporal punishment could be said to endanger children's health and cause permanent physical damage, as well as foster long-lasting feelings such as "doubt, inferiority complex and helplessness" (1991: 11).

Related to the difficulty of defining abuse is the question of its magnitude in society (assuming people could come to a minimal definition of how it can be identified). One reason it is difficult to assess its magnitude is that it is often not reported. As an article written by the Public Policing Unit in the Ugandan paper *The New Vision* indicates (1994: 10), "unfortunately, accurate data on child abuse are impossible to obtain because of the refusal of many children to report the crime and the unwillingness of parents to report to the authorities." This concern echoes the claims of a reporter in the *Swazi News* (Angelica, 1992: 5) that well-off parents are more likely than those less well off to "be able to conceal the true cause of their child's injuries." This reporter (Angelica) indicates that perceived occurrences of child abuse depend on how "injuries" are labeled and on when they occurred. Nagi (1983) suggests that other family members may fail to report abusive acts to the authorities because they fear violence to themselves or the breaking up of the family. And of course many victims find it difficult, if not impossible, to make their plight known (Nagi, 1983: 1625–1626). Physicians, social workers, teachers, and other professionals may also decide not to report cases.

But fully accurate figures are not needed to argue that it is important to draw attention to this important issue. Otherwise, a cycle of muting the voices/concerns of victims and potential victims is perpetuated. One may agree with Marzouki (1997: 119) that it is important to "raise awareness among us [all concerned] and among the public about this specific violation of a basic child's right: The right to the enjoyment of the highest attainable standard of physical and psychological security." A full accounting of the phenomena of child abuse and neglect in society in order to find ways of increasing the chances that children can be prevented from falling prey to these violations is required. Children's claims to rights, whether made by themselves or by committed adults, need to be accounted for in our social fabric. (In this respect see also Roche, 1996: 37.)

This chapter seeks to offer certain sociological explanations of what can be called the "deviance" of child abuse. The discussion focuses on the action implications of these explanations. Hopefully, this focus may help those concerned to reconsider ways to address the issue. The (sociological) input into the discussion may help to ensure that at least the discussion will indeed be kept alive.

The literature on deviance and abuse has not advanced just sociological theories; other kinds of theory include theological, biological, and psychological ones. By and large, these theories concentrate on exploring the characteristics of deviance by considering their demonic features, their genetic inheritance, or their psychological makeup. However, from a sociological point of view, this discussion concentrates more on social and environmental factors and processes that might be relevant to the debate on child abuse rather than on so-called individual wickedness or individual deficiencies.

SOCIOLOGICAL THEORIES OF DEVIANCE

Sociological theories of deviance can be divided broadly into two types: those that concentrate on "social structure" as contributing to and accounting for certain forms of deviance, and those that concentrate on "social processes" through which individuals might become deviant.

The *structural approach* (e.g., strain theory) examines such factors as the economic system, social inequality, family destabilization, and social disorganization as crucial determinants of deviant behavior (Goode, 1994: 74–82). The *processual approach* instead concentrates on the avenues whereby people become deviant, particularly through learning processes. According to one version of such an approach (e.g., control theory), "deviants" in society have failed to internalize (accept) the norms of the society in which they live, that is, the generally shared view in that society about what is justifiable behavior. Other versions of process theory argue that deviant behavior itself is learned—that is, it is passed from generation to generation or from one person to another through interaction processes in society. Arguments to this effect suggest that there is not necessarily just one set of "normative prescriptions" present in society at any point in time. Hence, it is possible to learn certain forms of behavior in a setting that deems such behavior acceptable—even though the behavior is regarded as unacceptable from other points of view in society. The processes by which contradictory discourses are dealt with are also explored by (certain) process theories of deviance.

Strain Theory: A "Structural" Approach

Strain theory derives from Durkheim's sociological viewpoint, especially his concept of "anomie" or lack of social regulation (Durkheim, 1964). According to this theory, social disorganization, largely as a result of rapid changes in the social structure, produces a state of confusion and uncertainty characterized by a feeling of rootlessness or social disorientation. A person suffering from anomie lacks a sense of belonging and continuity: She or he is like a ship without a rudder. As Dressler (1969: 251) puts it allegorically, "the anomic individual has lost his [or her] past, foresees no future, and lives only in his [or her] immediate present, that is virtually nowhere." Merton (1957) elaborated and refined the concept of anomie and developed an influential theory of deviant behavior, drawing a distinction between culturally prescribed goals and institutional means of achieving the goals. He argues that should a society place too much emphasis on obtaining certain goals without providing appropriate means of achieving those goals, a state of anomie will prevail, resulting in all sorts of social problems.

Referring to the United States as an (extreme) exemplar, Merton points out that cultural goals tend to extol material success. For instance, advertisements are a recognized way of urging people to buy material goods, whether a car, new clothes, or an electric toothbrush. (See also Scarpitti's discussion, 1977: 475.) However, even though many people might want these goods, not everyone can afford them. Because the social structure limits the available means to material success, people might feel frustrated. (This kind of scenario is of course possible not only in the United States, but wherever people feel that opportunities for participating in socially recognized goal-achievements are denied them. In less developed countries, such conditions are exacerbated by similar maldistributions of opportunities as may be present in so-called developed ones.) One mode of response of individuals that is specifically relevant to this investigation of child abuse is what Merton calls "retreatism."

The retreatist, in response to what he or she perceives to be a lack of opportunity for attaining desired goals, rejects both societal goals and institutionalized means and, as it were, drops out of the struggle, thus becoming increasingly isolated from significant social contact. The frustrating existential circumstances, such as lack of (or minimal) education, a broken or unsatisfactory marriage, or difficult family conditions, unemployment, disruption of occupational ambitions, and so on might lead them into a depressive state unconducive to caring for children.

A number of studies have tried to explore a range of antecedents to child abuse, including societal, cultural, and situational factors, as well as personality attributes specific to the adults and children involved (see Rodriguez and Green's discussion, 1997: 367). Self-reported parental characteristics that have been correlated with abuse potential include unhappiness and intrapersonal and interpersonal difficulties, which in turn may lead to unrealistic expectations regarding children's behavior (Milner, 1986). Adult stress and anger built up through a sense of frustration with life in general may issue in unrealistic demands for "obedience" and for comfort from children. This unrealism has been argued to be a good predictor of child abuse potential (Rodriguez and Green, 1997: 366). Strain theory would explain this abuse potential with reference to factors in the social structure that contribute to generating a sense of rootlessness among members.

The action implication of this argument is that one cannot address issues of child abuse without providing the relevant social support networks that can militate against people's feelings of rootlessness and uninvolvement in society. In this vein, Bennett argues that "all levels of society have their particular responsibility [in finding ways for addressing the issue]" (1996: 45). He argues that the micro- and meso-systems of families (the home environment) and of settings immediately outside it (such as the school) may be influenced by patterns of economic and social production generated on other levels of society (what he calls exo- and macro-systems). He refers to the exo-system as those social structures that can be seen to impinge on the home and the school. Components of the exo-system are social services, mass media, economic circumstances, workplace conditions, and law and order. Furthermore, other structural features in the macro-system also cannot be ignored in considering ways of supporting family responsibilities toward children. Such structural features include the type of economy, culture, ideologies, and customs (1996: 53). Here it could be argued that economies that provide maximum opportunities for people to participate in becoming more self-reliant and more in control of their employment potential would make a difference to people's conceptions of themselves, and thus of their relations with others (including the children in their care). Or again, culture, ideology, and customs that allow people more scope for participating in, for example, civics education, permit people to experience the possibility of participating in society rather than feeling excluded from its mainstream. Bennett also refers to school–family partnerships as another way of creating social support.

In this way Bennett, along with other structurally oriented theorists, suggests that we cannot place full responsibility on families to deal somehow with parenting tasks in an appropriate fashion, without at the same time examining other "systems" in which the family can be seen to be embedded. Social circumstances that may be argued to generate (or at least exacerbate) feelings of frustration also must be taken into account in any discussion of parenting/caretaking.

Apart from variations of structural theories such as those described above, there are what can be called process theories which place the emphasis on processes of social interaction that might explain the deviance of child abuse. A number of these theories are explored immediately below.

Control Theory: Processes of Socialization or Unsuccessful Socialization

Control theory seeks to explain why some people more than others become (more or less successfully) socialized to conform to widely upheld norms in society. The theory revolves around the concept of social control. This refers to the planned or unplanned, formal or informal, processes whereby people become socialized or feel compelled to conform to norms and laws. The effective achievement of social control involves the use of sanctions, which may be positive (e.g., praise, prize, smile, certificate) or negative (e.g., ridicule, ostracism, fine, imprisonment). According to control theory, many people conform to norms because of the operation of internal and external constraints. Reckless (1961: 44), for example, distinguishes between "inner containment" and "outer containment." Inner containment consists mainly of self-control, whereas outer containment refers to the individual's social environment which keeps him or her within bounds. The family setting is an important agent for engendering restraint. Law enforcement agencies, educational institutions, and other agencies of social control also play a role in restraining people from deviating.

Control theory suggests that deviance is a result of inadequate socialization, or the weakening of social bonds (feelings of attachment) in society, so that people do not feel bound by the demands of those equipped to "socialize" them into acceptable channels of behavior (see also Conklin, 1984: 106). In regard to the deviance of child abuse, control theory concentrates on the way absence or weakening of social attachment leads to a weakening of the control mechanisms whereby people (in this case parents/caretakers) regard seriously the opinions of others in connection with their own behavior.

The suggestion (from the standpoint of this theory) is that although in theory the family (and other agents of socialization) should be equipped to "pass on" a desired morality to the next generation—for example, the necessity not to be abusive of children and other "victims"—it is not always performing this function. This may be partly because the bonds of intimacy and social attachment through which people might come to identify with such a morality are not strong enough to evince an acceptance thereof. Hence, people remain inadequately socialized, and, with regard to child abuse, they do not internalize the necessity to refrain from adopting abusive behavior when they become parents/caregivers. Furthermore, the adults involved in family settings may be unable to exert pressure on one another to refrain from abusive behavior toward the children.

Control theory suggests that it is crucial to try to engender in society processes whereby people learn to take seriously the concerns of others in regard to their own behavior. In this sense, control theory is a kind of learning theory that hopes to encourage people to appreciate the importance of relating to others rather than disregarding their influence. Control theory suggests the importance of exploring ways of creating "socializing" experiences wherein people are encouraged to take seriously others' concerns and suggestions. One avenue for doing so would be to investigate possibilities for all concerned to play an active part in defining the "norms" that they develop in their interactions with others, so that they do not feel that these norms are somehow alien to them. Other avenues (not necessarily mutually exclusive with the first) would be for law enforcement agencies or other agencies in the social environment (e.g., social workers) to try to ensure that adverse consequences do indeed arise for adults who consistently fail to appreciate the minimal normative requirement to protect the children in their care.

Cultural Transmission Theory: Learning "Deviant" Behavior

Cultural transmission theory focuses on the processes by which "deviant" behavior is learned. The best known transmission theory is the theory of differential association developed by Sutherland (1939). To a great extent, this theory is a sophisticated version of the "bad companion" explanation of deviance. It is premised on the assumption that deviant behavior is learned through interaction with a group that offers rewards to the learners. Sutherland argues that deviance is a consequence of being socialized in the context of such interaction.

Sutherland argues that when a person associates with other people in society, some encourage conformity to accepted norms while others encourage violation of them. This is what "differential association" means.

According to Sutherland, a person is likely to become deviant if he or she receives an excess of definitions favorable to violation of norms over definitions unfavorable thereto. Such exposure takes place in the context of social interaction. Moreover, definitions or statements approving "deviance" will vary in their power to influence behavior, depending on the status of the person who utters them and the age of the listener. According to Sutherland, variations depend on the following factors.

- Frequency: number of times the definition occurs.
- Duration: over what period.
- Priority: at what stage in one's life (it is assumed that childhood socialization is more important than that which takes place in later life).
- Intensity: the prestige of the person making the definition.

Sutherland's theory may be relevant in considering child abuse if one wishes to argue that sometimes those with whom the parents/caretakers associate (as well as the frequency, duration, priority, and intensity of the interactions) may have definitions conducive to accepting a level of child abuse. Or, one could argue that such associations may lead parents/caretakers to appreciate the "advantage" of some level of child abuse—such as being able to control the household, elicit fear in people, vent their own frustrations, and so on.

Although this perhaps seems a forced argument, it may be relevant to consider cases in which people accorded high status in society incline to the belief that "punishment" even if excessive is a worthwhile aim to promote "order" within the family or the school. Insofar as parents/caretakers/teachers frequently interact with people espousing these types of arguments/lifestyles, and insofar as they themselves gain (or believe that they gain) the "reward" of retaining order in enforcing "strict discipline," they may indeed be inclined to approve of this behavior. Their obsession with discipline becomes a kind of self-righteous overdiscipline (Jones et al., 1987: 94). This may be the case even when they know that others in society regard them with disdain. They may not accord such others the same prestige (in their eyes) as those from whom they learn (potentially) abusive behavior.

This theory would also explain cases in which people live by the sense of "reward" of severe treatment of those under their care, while not intending to cause lasting physical and mental harm. However "accidentally," their actions may at times lead to such results, so that their behavior then falls somewhat unintentionally into the category of severe maltreatment leading to damage (hospitalization or death). Although this aspect of their behavior may not have been "transmitted" through their association with those advocating "severe discipline," it can be said that their "identifications" with such people lead them to the actions that (albeit partly unintentionally) become classified as indeed criminal (in terms of the laws of the society).

How might cultural transmission theory offer recommendations for turning these behaviors around? From the standpoint of cultural transmission theory, people must be exposed to a wide range of cultural patterns so that they learn and experience the rewards of building different relationships. Cultural climates where rules of conduct can become negotiated, so that "order" is not seen as necessarily contingent on following of preset rigid rules, can be developed (see, for instance, McKay and Romm's discussion, 1995). If these cultural climates are experienced in school settings, people might later (as adults) be better equipped to carry them over into their own relationships with others (including children in their care). In addition, cultural transmission theory would propose the immediate relevance of parental education in that parents are exposed to parental forms that are not premised on enforcing harsh discipline as a way of generating "order" in their family settings.

Thus, cultural transmission theory would endorse the more frequent "display" in society of forms of interaction in that people do not feel that they have to use force to generate ordered relationships. New definitions of order in human relationships need to become more widely transmitted in society, so that people can become exposed to these and may also experience the rewards of such relationships.

Neutralization Theory: Neutralizing Demands for Conformity

This theory argues that people's actions are guided by their thoughts (Hagan, 1987: 156) and that "good" people come to violate norms because they themselves do not interpret these norms as morally compelling. Important theorists in this regard include Sutherland (1939) and Sykes and Matza (1957). Sutherland's theory of differential association is complementary with neutralization theory. The suggestion of this theory is that "deviants" and "nondeviants" are not qualitatively different kinds of people. The argument is based on the observation that deviants usually show guilt or shame when they violate what they see as "normative" prescriptions, and they frequently approve of certain forms of conforming behavior. Sykes and Matza see the "deviant" as a person who drifts into a deviant pattern through a process of justification, that is, "neutralization." They identify five techniques of neutralization:

• Denial of Responsibility: Here deviants see themselves as helpless to control the situation.

- Denial of Injury: Here deviants argue that their behavior does not really cause great harm.
- Denial of the Victim: Here the "victims" of the deviance are transformed into wrongdoers.
- Condemnation of the Condemners: Here deviants allege that those who accuse them of deviance are themselves hypocrites or deviants in disguise.
- Appeal to Higher Loyalties: Here deviants view themselves as caught between the demands of society at large and the needs/commitments to others more significant to them.

Sykes and Matza suggest that deviants tend to cherish subterranean values (hidden values) which exist side by side with more "conformist" feelings. This means that people need to neutralize their feelings of conformity to what they believe is socially demanded, so as to develop a justification for the line of "nonconformist" behavior that they take.

Applied to the case of child abusers, all of these techniques of neutralization can be invoked by abusers. They can believe that they themselves cannot control their own abusive behavior which they attribute to having been provoked or being unable to cope with the situation; they may deny that they are really causing harm, or, in any case that they intend to cause harm; and they may deny that it is they who are the aggressors and instead shift the blame onto the child whose so-called misbehavior prompted the abuse. They may condemn those who try to sanction their abuse, arguing that they too, if placed in such difficult circumstances, would react in the same way; and they can appeal to the demand to, for example, retain "discipline" in the home as a higher loyalty that transcends the requirements of (the rest of) society not to be too "severe" in the treatment of children.

The theory of neutralization that focuses on these justificatory techniques can be seen as linked to differential association in the sense that individuals are seen as able to resist the demands to conformity through associating with others who do not disapprove of their conduct. This lends credence to their own wish to see their actions as justifiable.

One way of further exploring the justification techniques parents (or other caretakers) use to account for their own behavior is through discourse analysis in which their speech is questioned. Gough and Reavey propose that interviewing can take place with the intention of locating and making visible the contradictions in people's accounts of "physical punishment." By conducting their own interviews with parents, they uncover the tension between conformity (to some accepted codes) and nonconformity (flouting of the "accepted" codes). For instance, they point out that although parents might invoke a discourse of duty (the accepted duty to discipline children), at the same time they recognize that such norms can come into conflict with "personal interpretations of when and how to punish, that are usually more erratic (than what is deemed acceptable)" (1997: 419). Gough and Reavey sum up the position as follows: "Despite the culturally pervasive discourse of duty, any particular instance of physical punishment of children may well be occasioned by more subjective criteria, informed by one's personal biography and emotional state" (1997: 419).

Other contradictions pointed out by Gough and Reavey are between parental beliefs on the one hand that, as children, they were themselves justifiably punished by their parents. On the other hand, their sense (drawn out by interviewers by posing questions from a different angle) is that often the severity of the punishment was not justifiable. Gough and Reavey found that "mothers frequently made excuses for their own mother's harshness (when they saw this as fulfillment of 'duty') . . . but sometimes recollection of punishment that seems unjustified still rankled" (1997: 420). Thus, there were contradictory repertoires that could be unraveled as people tried to justify their own practices in regard to physical punishment of children (PPC) by referring to "excuses" which in some way they recognized to be capable of contradiction.

Gough and Reavey conclude that researchers should draw out the conflicting rationales that people use to justify their punishment practices. The researcher's role as "interrogator" helps to highlight contradictions for the people involved (and for other audiences), so that it is then less easy to "make excuses" that do not stand up to a more considered argument. This is not to say that the complex and conflicting discourses about the need for forms of punishment can ever be fully reconciled in society—but at least by unfolding these manifold discourses, they can become more open to reconsideration. Concerned parents (who are indeed often very concerned about their children when "injury" is recognized to have occurred), as well as others in society, can revisit the discourses that allow people to "make excuses" that do not stand up to further accounting. Gough and Reavey also suggest that added to the cultural arena should be a "discourse of child's rights wherein young people are accorded a voice, a position that allows for discussion of and resistance to the methods of punishment favored by parents" (1997: 428). Following Gough and Reavey one could argue, that because this discourse is by and large "missing" in our communications about child care in society, people can more easily "neutralize" (normative) requirements that children be protected both physically and psychologically. A stronger discourse on children's rights might make it less easy for parents and other caretakers to turn to the neutralization techniques currently utilized to neutralize the claims of children to protection.

Social Learning Theory: Learning to Evaluate Behaviors in Social Contexts

Social learning theory is another theory closely allied to the theory of differential association. Within this theory the concept of "differential reinforcement" is used to explore the processes by which deviant behavior becomes dominant over conforming behavior in certain situations (Akers, 1977). Akers argues that an individual learns to evaluate behavior as either good or bad and that these definitions can be reinforced (in social interactions) and thereby become reinforcers (of continuing behavior). As he puts it: "A person will participate in deviant activity to the extent that it has been differentially reinforced over conforming behavior and defined as more desirable, or at least as justified as conforming alternatives" (1977: 58).

Social learning theory has been employed to account for the widely recognized observation that abusive parents themselves tend to have been the victims of child abuse (cf. Helfer and Kempe, 1976; Nagi, 1983: 1626; Spencer, 1985: 429; Sears et al., 1991). Sears et al. (p. 341) cite the argument of the social learning theory as follows: "Parents are the primary models for a child during the early years. Since parents are both the major source of reinforcement and the chief object of imitation, a child's future aggressive behavior depends greatly on how parents treat the child and on how they themselves behave."

The social learning theory draws on the following maxim to explain the continuance of child abuse from one generation to another: "Children will do what their parents do" (Sears et al., 1991: 343). Watching the aggression of parents teaches people that aggression is acceptable if one can get away with it (Sears et al., 1991: 343). Thus, people learn that it is appropriate behavior to aggress against those weaker than one. Because learning theory emphasizes the notion that abuse is a learned response, it also highlights the requirement for cultural programs aimed at disseminating alternative norms as a means of remedying the mode of abusive/violent behavior as practiced by people in a society. Straus and Gelles (1986) cite the effectiveness of publicity programs in the United States between 1975 and 1985, where attention was given to changing the norms concerning allowing physical punishment. As these norms changed, they claim, so did the frequency of parents' severe violence against children.

In short, social learning theory focuses on the idea that people might learn to regard abusive behavior as appropriate. Their behavioral patterns may, however, be altered through attempts to disseminate alternative norms aimed at instilling new "learning" processes (through, for example, publicity campaigns).

Symbolic Interactionism: Another Kind of "Learning Theory"

Symbolic interactionist theory draws attention to the way people develop symbols in communication with others to make sense of their world. The argument is that the way people construct a meaningful world depends on the interactions they have with others, and it also depends on the way they interpret the behavior and meanings of others in social situations. According to this theory, people's actions are grounded in definitions that they have of "the situation"—as their definitions of situations change, so do their actions. Furthermore, every situation "has the capacity to establish, educate, and redefine the self," that is, people's view of who they are and how they expect themselves to react (Downes and Rock, 1988: 171). Social life involves people rehearsing their own ideas as to how to respond to others' meanings and actions, while also considering others' responses to oneself. So life is patterned by the way people "continuously interpret themselves, their settings, and their partners" (1988: 172). Symbolic interactionists accept the suggestion of Sykes and Matza (1957) that the experience of oneself as free to deviate (from seemingly required patterns of conduct) depends in part on one's ability to find the appropriate symbol (word) to justify one's intended or actual conduct. As Downes and Rock put it: "When acts and states can be reassessed as . . . innocuous, when they can be presented [to oneself and to others whom one regards as relevant] as not 'really' deviant, it is a little easier to accept them" (1988: 173).

With regard to child abuse, symbolic interactionists would argue that deviance depends on the way both the perpetrators and the "audience" define the situation. As far as the perpetrator (abuser) is concerned, the cycle of abuse might arise in response to his or her definition of the situation in one of the ways described under neutralization theory above. As far as the audience is concerned, symbolic interactionists note that deviance will often be normalized and be built into the fabric of accepted life. A crisis develops when others will not or cannot cope with deviant behavior (Downes and Rock, 1988: 177). Thus, abuse assumes the proportion of "criminality" when the audience (which may include the victim or others equipped to "report" the abuse and indeed name it as abuse) takes action against the "criminal." Otherwise, what may have been seen as "deviant" may nevertheless not become officially defined as such and not be reported to relevant policing agencies in society. Therefore, it may go unnoticed officially, although of course those who do not wish to endorse the behavior as "acceptable" notice it.

Symbolic interactionist theory draws attention to the malleability of people's meaning constructions in society and to the idea that meaning is not fixed. Hence, if potential abusers feel that others will not cope with their intended (abusive) action, and if they are unable to convince themselves of its justifiability (perhaps because there are insufficient numbers of people who support the "reasons" that they might advance to attempt to justify/neutralize their actions), this can have a decisive influence on the potential perpetrator. In this sense, symbolic interactionism is a learning theory. However, symbolic interactionism does not state that one can count the number of associations/positive reinforcements/learning experiences and then come up with a statement of how a person is likely to behave. For the likelihood of one response over another depends on the sense-making abilities of the person in question and on how he or she attributes meaning to the various social influences.

What are the action implications of symbolic interactionist theory? Symbolic interactionists agree with other learning theorists that one's ways of moral reasoning can be influenced through the kinds of meaning with which one comes in contact, especially if the meanings are presented in a way that appears to the self/subject to make sense and if, furthermore, the person involved has a part to play in contributing to the matrix of events.

Symbolic interactionists would therefore find the kind of publicity programs cited by Straus and Gelles (1986) to be appropriate—in that people are made aware of the inappropriateness of emotional and physical violence toward children (where violence is in turn defined as in some way violating the self-image and self-actualization of others). Such kinds of publicity can render potential and actual abusers more aware of the possible harmful consequences of their behavior and can draw attention to alternative modes of treating the issue of "discipline."

In this regard, attention should be given to Magagula's suggestion that the ultimate goal of discipline may be seen as "self-discipline, self-esteem, trust, respect for others, self respect, and self-direction." To achieve this goal, corporal punishment can be said to be largely ineffective, for it may be seen to foster feelings of "shame, guilt, hostility, fear, resentment, doubt, inferiority complex, and helplessness" (1991: 11). Downey and Kelly support this suggestion, adding that punishment (not necessarily of the corporal kind) may be justified when rules appear (to both the punisher and offender) as having moral import, and when children understand the point of the rule (1986: 146). But they caution (as does Magagula) "to keep in mind the evidence of the possible psychological effect of punishment on children." Instead of looking for a justification for punishment, people should be working toward "devising methods of control that will as far as possible obviate the need for it" (1986: 146). One way they suggest this can be achieved is by drawing attention to the need to negotiate the rules of interaction and to remember that indeed "the fewer the rules we have and the less explicit we are about them the more flexibility and room for maneuver we will have in our interpretation of them" (1986: 146). This idea of negotiation of potential and actual disagreements is also echoed in the advice given by Stark (1985: 302) who points out the need for parents (and other caretakers of children) to "negotiate disagreements so that they get settled rather than escalate." (See also McKay and Romm's discussion of this matter specifically in schooling contexts, 1995.)

Jeffery (1976: 212) points to a number of practical ways in which such advice may be implemented. Caretakers, she observes, can learn to respond positively to those in their care. Learning such responding means learning to give "positive" attention to children in the sense of focusing on "listening to, and responding to" the child's communications. Positive responding is the adverse of (negative) responding to children only when their behavior seems to be found "unacceptable," or responding primarily in terms of issuing "commands" (Jeffery, 1976: 212). Parents (and other caretakers) who are in the habit of "negative responding" are prone to believe that the child is "bad" because, as Jeffery points out, the (apparent) "bad" behavior "is all that they notice" (1976: 212). In such contexts, abusive patterns of response to such "unfavorable" behavior may set in. Learning the skill of positive response/communication may thus help to prevent abuse.

Jeffery suggests organizing relationships (between parents/caretakers and children) around implicit or explicit contracts arrived at through negotiated settlements. As she points out, "Contracts or agreements can be drawn up to avoid particular [acrimonious] conflicts and situations that lead to negative interactions" (1976: 216). The experience of learning the mutuality of negotiated interactions may, Jeffery notes, be facilitated by interventions on the part of social workers and other personnel, where this is deemed necessary/supportive.

Initiatives in organizing facilities for learning parental skills (parental education) also are relevant in this respect. Campbell-Forrester and Lee (1991) cite an example of a successful intervention aimed at parent education in Jamaica, in which parents themselves (the vast majority) evaluated the program as having increased their awareness. Ninety percent stated that they had learned to be active listeners, and 50 percent reported that they had a better understanding of themselves (Campbell-Forrester and Lee, 1991: 5).

Giddens (1989) also draws attention to the possibility that people will look back critically on their behavior in the light of additional challenging input such as ideas gleaned from conversations with others and from exposure to alternative experiences (and alternative interpretations thereof). People's ideas about the meaning of their (potentially abusive) behavior may change, and this itself may feed back into their mode of behavior. Giddens believes that sociologists themselves can perform important tasks in allowing people to become more reflective about their behavior. This can help generate awareness of possibilities that transcend current patterns of behavior (cf. 1989: 21).

The main argument in this chapter is that people can learn through interaction with others; that also means that they can learn to set up relationships that are less abusive (than they otherwise might be). The insights offered by learning theories can be accepted as long as they do not set themselves up as predicting behavior based on counting people's "learning experiences." In this respect, there is some truth in the argument of symbolic interactionism that it is people's sense-making activities that are paramount in defining how they will respond to various experiences and how they might learn from them.

Undeniably, frustrating life conditions as elucidated with reference to strain theory might have some influence in affecting people's meaning-making (and conduct). But only if people, individually and in groups, decide to address "life conditions" in ways that will permit some form of active response, will moves toward better conditions in society ensue.

Therefore, how people (including potential and actual abusers) decide to attribute meaning to their life circumstances is a precursor to finding ways to live "better" lives. This does not imply that a better way of life can easily be defined or practiced. It suggests that the principle of non-violation of others should penetrate social life on all levels of society and should allow people to recognize forms of abusive conduct and set up debates about how these can be mitigated in society. The abuse of children is a special case of abusive conduct that may generally become perpetuated as a form of social relationship, unless efforts are made to counteract this possibility.

CONCLUSION

Abuse is sometimes associated only with severe physical harm. However, as indicated earlier, it is associated with all circumstances in which force is turned to in order to generate obedience/compliance without consideration for the reasonableness and fairness of the rule in the first place and without consideration of the perspective of the person supposedly required to obey the rule. Abuse also embraces mental and emotional battering, which tends to foster the low self-esteem of the victim who is given the feeling that he or she is worthless as a person. The opposite of abuse is communication/understanding/consideration, which implies the possibility of some form of negotiation between parties who develop rules for the benefit of their mutual interaction (see Romm, 1994, 1996, for more detailed accounts of what might be involved in such "negotiation"). To the extent that children learn these values, they are afforded the cultural resources (principles and experiences) to draw on in their later interactions (in adult life) and to input into the next generation. Of course, the principle of nonviolation of "the other" itself includes the possibility of further debates on the subject, so that all concerned parties should have the chance to contribute.

This chapter has focused primarily on processual theories of deviance, with particular attention to accounts of socialization, cultural transmission, neutralization, and (other) learning processes. Symbolic interactionism also was discussed in terms of its links with learning theories. The action implications of these various theories were explored as a way of increasing awareness of possible ways in which the issue of child abuse might be addressed.

The so-called structural factors mentioned in relation to strain theory are indeed relevant to discussion on deviance. Nevertheless, it is absolutely important to include a consideration of the way people might learn to respond differently to "circumstances" in the socioeconomic world (and to find fresh ways of addressing social and economic questions). This requires a learning process that focuses on the possibility of participants learning certain skills for a rapidly changing world in which past recipes for action cannot be relied upon to provide social solutions. The learning of these skills requires both family and other educational contexts in which people develop (in practice) patterns of interaction based on managing and tolerating (working with) "strains" that arise in the process of social change. Without the development of these skills, the frustrations of people might be exacerbated, with consequent implications for child abuse potential.

REFERENCES

Akers, R. (1977). *Deviant Behavior: A Social Learning Approach*. Belmont, CA: Wadsworth.

Angelica, D. (1992). "The Abuse of Children." *The Swazi News*, July 11.

Bennett, J. (1996). "Supporting Family Responsibility for the Rights of the Child: An Educational Viewpoint." *The International Journal of Children's Rights*, 4, 45–56.

Campbell-Forrester, S. and Lee, P. D. (1991). "Parent and Provider Education in Jamaica." *The International Association for Adolescent Health*, 5(5).

Conklin, J. E. (1984). *Sociology*. New York: Macmillan.

Downes, D. and Rock, P. (1988). *Understanding Deviance*. Oxford: Clarendon Press.

Downey, M. and Kelly, A. V. (1987). *Theory and Practice of Education*. London: Paul Chapman.

Dressler, D. (1969). *Sociology: The Study of Human Interaction*. New York: Alfred A. Knopf.

Durkheim, E. (1964). *The Division of Labour in Society*. George Simpson, trans. New York: The Free Press.

Giddens, A. (1989). *Sociology*. Cambridge: Polity Press.

Goode, E. (1994). *Deviant Behavior*. Englewood Cliffs, NJ: Prentice-Hall.

Gough, B. and Reavey, P. (1997). "Parental Accounts Regarding the Physical Punishment of Children: Discourses of Disempowerment." *Child Abuse and Neglect*, 21(5), 417–430.

Hagan, J. (1987). *Modern Criminology*. New York: McGraw-Hill Book Co.

Helfer, R. E. and Kempe, C. H. (eds.). (1976). *Child Abuse and Neglect*. Cambridge, MA: Ballinger.

Jeffery, M. (1976). "Practical Ways to Change Parent-child Interaction." In R. E. Helfer and C. H. Kempe (eds.), *Child Abuse and Neglect*. Cambridge, MA: Ballinger.

Jones, D. N., Pickett, J., Oates, M. R., and Barbor, P. (1987). *Understanding Child Abuse*. London: Macmillan.

Magagula, C. (1991). *To Flog or Not to Flog, That Is the Question*. Occasional paper, University of Swaziland.

Marzouki, M. (1997). "Thoughts from the Human Rights Perspective." *Child Abuse and Neglect*, 21(2), 117–123.

McKay, V. I. and Romm, N.R.A. (1995). "The Practice of Discipline in Education." In C. Allais and V. I. McKay (eds.), *A Sociology of Educating*. Johannesburg: Heinemann.

Merton, R. (1957). *Social Theory and Social Structure*. New York: The Free Press.

Milner, J. S. (1986). *The Child Abuse Potential Inventory*. Webster, NC: Psyctec.

Nagi, S. Z. (1983). "Child Abuse." In S. H. Kadish (ed.), *Encyclopedia of Crime and Justice*. New York: The Free Press.

Public Policing Unit. (1994). "Child Abuse Major Public Heath Problem." *The New Vision*, December 15.

Reckless, W.C. (1961). "A New Theory of Delinquency and Crime." *Federal Probation*, 25, 42–46.

Roche, J. (1996). "The Politics of Children's Rights." In J. Brannen and M. O'Brien (eds.), *Children in Families*. London: Falmer Press.

Rodriguez, C. M. and Green, A. J. (1997). "Parenting Stress and Anger Expression as Predictors of Child Abuse Potential." *Child Abuse and Neglect*, 21(4), 367–377.

Romm, N.R.A. (1994). "Symbolic Theory." In N.R.A. Romm and M. Sarakinsky (eds.), *Social Theory*. Johannesburg: Heinemann.

———. (1996). "A Dialogical Intervention Strategy for Development." In J. K. Coetzee and J. Graaff (eds.), *Development, Reconstruction and People*. Johannesburg: International Thomson Publications.

Scarpitti, F. R. (1977). *Social Problems*. Hinsdale, IL: Dryden Press.

Sears, D. O., Peplau, L. A., and Taylor, S. E. (1991). *Social Psychology*. Englewood Cliffs, NJ: Prentice-Hall.

Spencer, M. (1985). *Foundations of Modern Sociology*. Englewood Cliffs, NJ: Prentice-Hall.

Stark, R. (1985). *Sociology*. Belmont, CA: Wadsworth.

Straus, M. A. and Gelles, R. J. (1986). "Societal Change in Family Violence from 1975 to 1985 as Revealed by Two National Surveys." *Journal of Marriage and the Family*, 48, 465–479.

Sutherland, E. H. (1939). *Principles of Criminology*. Philadelphia: Lippincott.

Sykes, G. and Matza, D. (1957). "Techniques of Neutralization: A Theory of Delinquency." *American Sociological Review*, 22, 664–670.

Chapter 4

Traditional Institutions and the Violation of Women's Human Rights in Africa: The Nigerian Case

Abdul-Mumin Sa'ad

INTRODUCTION

It is common knowledge that women all over the world are considered and treated as inferior to men. There appears to be a consensus, too, that this oppression is even more endemic in traditional societies such as the African societies. A cursory look at the literature on the various institutions (economic, political, legal, religious, familial, etc.) of precolonial societies in Nigeria alone is enough to reveal the endemic nature of woman's oppression in traditional societies.

In Nigeria, even the government recognizes the oppression of women, and attempts have been made to improve their situation, leading to the emergence of organizations like Better Life for Rural Women, the Women Commission, and now the Family Support Program and Federal Ministry of Women Affairs and Social Services. All of these efforts notwithstanding, the condition of women in Nigeria leaves much to be desired. It appears that the reason for this is the deep-rooted traditional attitudes and practices of the Nigerian people, especially the most rural and traditional of them. The tenacity of these traditional attitudes and practices in matters concerning women in rural areas should not be surprising. Women constitute the most important rural labor force, and a traditionalist form of control may be the most cost-effective social control device. Accordingly, any genuine search for effective solutions to inequalities between the sexes must focus on the cultural impediments to women's rights. Undoubtedly, the scope of this chapter is a very wide one, so what is intended here, is limited to discussing only the major issues, with a view to suggesting broad solutions.

Most issues pertaining to rights conferment and enjoyment, or the absence of them, in traditional African societies revolve around five major cultural institutions: familial, economic, political, educational, and religious. The following discussion is therefore organized around these institutions in Nigeria as an African example. The extent and nature of sex discrimination embedded in each of these institutions will be discussed as much as possible. Government policies and programs designed to realize de facto equality of sexes will also be examined. An attempt is made to provide explanations for the violations of women's human rights and to propose some broad policy recommendations. First, the issues of what human rights are and whether women's rights are human rights are examined.

WHAT ARE HUMAN RIGHTS?

A short answer to this question is that human rights are "universal moral rights." They are universal in that they are the rights that people possess by virtue of being human beings, regardless of race, sex, nationality, occupation, income, religion, and other social and cultural characteristics (Milne, 1979: 23). They are also moral in that people possess these rights whether or not they form part of their familiar way of life and whether or not they have been enacted into the operative laws of their societies (Milne, 1979: 23). In short, human rights transcend customary, social, and positive legal rights. As the above definition makes clear, a proper understanding of human rights requires an understanding of at least two important concepts: morality and right.

Morality

To understand what morality means, we should compare it with law. "Both," according to Milne, "have to do with conduct, especially in relation to other people" (1979: 23). The two, however, are different in the sense that morality is more inclusive than law. In other words, morality can exist without law but not vice versa. Telling the truth, keeping a promise, or taking care of parents in their old age, for example, are moral rules. Breaking them might bring about only disapproval and probably hostility from the general public. They become legal in addition only when breaking them also entails being tried, sentenced, and punished by a body with the authority to do so.

Again, as Milne rightly notes, an essential concept in morality is "obligation" (1979: 25). When one is under a moral obligation to do something, one ought to do it whether or not doing it is in one's self-interest. For human social life to exist, such an obligation is very necessary because, according to Milne, an essential element in human social life is "trust" for which moral obligation is the basis (p. 25).

Right

Simply put, a right means an "entitlement" (Milne, 1979: 26). To have a right to vote, to your own opinion, to legal representation, and so on, means to be entitled to all these provisions. This simple definition entails three important implications. First, every substantial right also places a correlative obligation on other people. For example, to be entitled to legal aid means that some person or agency has the correlative obligation to provide it.

Second, for one to exercise a right, one's claim to have the right must first of all be justified. Milne identified three ways one's claim to a right can be justified, depending on the nature of the right: legal, customary, or moral (1979: 28). In the case of a legal right, you can refer to the particular law in your community/society that confers the right on you and imposes correlative obligation. In the case of a customary right, you can refer to the particular custom in the community in which you live that confers the right on you and imposes correlative obligation. In the case of a moral right, you can refer to an appropriate moral rule or principle assuming that you share the same moral code with whomever you think is under the correlative obligation. Human rights appear to fall within this last category of rights.

Finally, and corollary to the second point above, it can be argued that a right, whether legal, customary, or moral, is essentially social in character. That is, one can have these rights only as a member of a given community or society with its own legal system, body of customs, and moral code, and therefore they cannot be universal. Although it may be true that both legal and customary rights are essentially social, it cannot be true in absolute terms that all moral rights are social (unless, of course, there is nothing that can be called human rights). This is because, as noted earlier, human rights, properly so-called, are universal moral rights. They are supposed to be correlative to universal moral obligations owed by every human being to other human beings.

The issue now is whether any such universal moral obligations exist. We agree with Milne that they do. The fundamental reason for such a position, as Milne puts it, is the fact that all human beings, whatever their cultural differences, are fellow human beings. They are moral and social beings "capable of social living, of co-operation, and of the moral commitments that" go with it (1979: 24). What then are these universal moral obligations and their correlative rights? Do they apply to both men and women equally? In other words, are women's rights also human rights?

ARE WOMEN'S RIGHTS HUMAN RIGHTS?

Once women are recognized as full human beings, their rights, as those of men, are seen as human rights. The first International Bill of Rights, the United Nations Universal Declaration of Human Rights (UDHR), adopted on December 10, 1948 (acceded to by Nigeria in 1960 upon becoming a member of the United Nations), was unequivocal on the subject of the universality of human rights, including the equal rights of men and women. Article 1 of UDHR proclaims that "All human beings are born free and equal in dignity and rights." This statement is reinforced by Article 2:

Everyone is entitled to all the rights and freedoms set forth in this declaration, without distinction of any kind, such as race, color, *sex*, language, religion, political or other opinion, national or social origin, property, birth or other status (emphasis added). Furthermore, no distinction shall be made on the basis of the political jurisdiction or international status of the country or territory to which a person belongs whether it be independent, trust, non-self-governing or under any other limitation of sovereignty.

No doubt, in their broadest terms, the principles that various articles of UDHR address are truly universal. They include the right to life (Art. 3), the right to respect for one's dignity as a person (Arts. 4–6), the right to justice (Arts. 7–11), the right to freedom (Arts. 12, 13, 18–20, and 27), the right to work (Art. 23), and the right to have one's distress relieved (Arts. 22 and 25). All these rights, as broadly stated, can be said to have derived from the moral status of the human being regardless of sex, for example. Therefore, as fellow human beings, we have the correlative moral commitment or obligation to observe these rights without discrimination, whether on the basis of sex or otherwise.

Two other international bills of rights followed on December 16, 1966, eighteen years after UDHR was born. They are the International Covenant on Civil and Political Rights (ICCPR) and the International Covenant on Economic, Social and Cultural Rights (ICESCR). Both covenants were meant to apply to men and women equally, and Nigeria ratified both in 1993. Generally, the ICCPR recognizes the rights to life, integrity, liberty, and security of persons, and the rights pertaining to administration of justice. Other rights include the rights to freedom of assembly, association, and political participation. It also recognizes freedom of religion, belief, opinion and expression. ICESCR for its part recognizes the rights to work, to food, clothing, and shelter, to education, and to health care, and the right to partake in the cultural life of one's society. All three international bills of rights are reflected in the 1979 Nigerian constitution. The groups of rights under UDHR and ICCPR are guaranteed by Chapter IV of the 1979 constitution, whereas the group of rights under ICESCR is included in Chapter II of the constitution.

In addition to the three international bills of rights applicable to individuals universally, regardless of sex, race, religion, and so on, the United Nations also adopted certain rights that have found their way into the Nigerian constitution and many international bills of rights specific to women. They include the Convention on the Political Rights of Women, the Convention on the Nationality of Women, and the Convention on the Consent of Marriage, Minimum Age of Marriage, and the Registration of Marriage. The idea that cuts across all of these bills of rights is gender equality. The most comprehensive of all the conventions on women, however, is the Convention on the Elimination of all Forms of Discrimination Against Women (CEDAW), adopted on December 19, 1979 and ratified by Nigeria on June 13, 1985. This Convention brings together in one single international instrument a number of prior conventions concerning women's human rights. Many UN resolutions pertaining to women are also brought into force and even expanded upon by CEDAW. It is made up of 30 Articles that state the meaning of equality between sexes (Art. 1), provide an international bills of rights for women to enable them to achieve equal rights with men (Arts. 12–16), and establish an agenda for action by every country to enable the enjoyment of those rights by women (Arts. 17–30). In short, CEDAW condemns and seeks to remove all forms of discrimination against women that it defines as "any distinction, exclusion or restriction made on the basis of sex that has the effect or purpose of impairing or nullifying the recognition, enjoyment or exercise by women, irrespective of their marital status, on a basis of equality of men and women of human rights and fundamental freedoms in the political, economic, social, cultural, civil or any other field" (CEDAW: Art. 1).

The African Charter on Human and People's Rights, adopted on January 19, 1981 by the Organization of African Unity is another human rights document relevant to women's equality with men, and it applies to Nigeria in particular and Africa in general. The African Charter on Human and People's Rights (henceforth referred to as the African Charter) is a regional treaty binding individual African countries that have ratified it. Out of the 52 member states of the OAU, 49, including Nigeria, have ratified the Charter. The provisions of the Charter are similar to those of the UDHR except that the UDHR does not attach people or collective rights to its economic, social, and cultural rights. All the provisions of the African Charter are meant to be enjoyed by both men and women without any discrimination. This is clearly stated in one of the charter's preambles that touches on its objectives, which, among others, is "to dismantle . . . all forms of discrimination, particularly those based on race, ethnic group, color, sex, language, religion or political opinion."

As should be clear by now, all those rights that are inherent in our nature as human beings are human rights, and Nigerian women are entitled to all the human rights provisions in the international and national bills of rights and the constitution of Nigeria. Above all, the right to be treated equally with men is itself a woman's human right. Unfortunately, however, it appears that in many rural communities in Nigeria the human rights of women are neither recognized nor respected. Sex discrimination of various dimensions is the order of the day. The next section identifies and discusses critically the extent and nature of sex discrimination that is embedded in each of the five major social institutions known to every rural community, namely, familial, economic, political, educational, and religious/normative institutions.

TRADITIONAL INSTITUTIONS AND SEX DISCRIMINATIONS IN NIGERIA

Family Institutions

Most activities within small-scale traditional societies revolve around the family; hence it is a big arena for contests over rights. The inequalities of rights between sexes within the family institution manifest themselves in such areas as marriage, divorce, and inheritance.

Marriage

Most important in a discussion of marriage is the age at which the sexes get married, the choice of a spouse, consumption of the bride price, sexuality, and child bearing. In regard to age, in most rural communities in Nigeria, child marriage is still practiced. Recent studies in rural Bura, Gwoza, Bachama, Fulani, and Kilba communities indicated that most women are married before the age of 15. Most men, on the other hand, marry at the minimum age of 25 (Haruna, 1992; Sa'ad, 1994b, 1995; Sa'ad, Shettima, and Babagana, 1994; Ghide, 1994; Rufa'i, 1994; Murrey, 1994). Women, as rightly noted by Nwabara, are regarded as "past it" if they are still unmarried by the time they are 23 or so, if not even by the time they are 18. It is thought that something must be wrong with the girl if she has not found a husband by then (1989: 10).

In these societies, too, most first marriages are either arranged by parents without seeking the consent of the girl in particular or are teleguided by the parents to happen, as though the girl had consented to the marriage. In short, the selection of a marriage partner is the prerogative of the family rather than a matter of romantic love. Thus the bride's kin fix the bride price. As rightly noted by Okonjo, among the Igbo people, during the process of the fixing of the bride price, "those resources that the bride is endowed with by nature, such as beauty, native intelligence and industry are sometimes made most of by her kin." That "makes her look like a commodity on sale to the highest bidder" (Okonjo, 1991: 189). The bride is, of course, a commodity as far as her kin are concerned. Otherwise, one cannot explain why the bride price paid is generally consumed by the head of the family, who is usually the father and/or other male relations, for example, the uncle of the bride, not by the bride herself (Thomas-Emeagwali et al., 1985: 132; Sa'ad, 1988; Haruna, 1992; Ghide, 1994; Sa'ad et al., 1994; Murrey, 1994; Rufa'i, 1994; Sa'ad, 1995).

Once married, the woman becomes the personal property of her husband. She has no right to refuse making love to her husband even if she is not in the mood, and this is not considered to be rape. Modern law in Nigeria does not recognize marital rape:

The law in Nigeria, as it stands, would not punish a husband who forcibly had sexual intercourse with his wife without her consent. . . . Similarly, a man who violates a woman where there is separation or divorce proceedings subsisting will not be responsible for rape against her. (LRRDC, 1995b: 55)

What is more, it is considered "unwomanly" for a woman to demand sexual intercourse from her husband even if she needs it (Sa'ad et al., 1994; Ghide, 1994). In a recent nationwide study comparing urban, semi-urban, and rural women's opinions on who should initiate sex in a relationship, it was found that only a very few women, including those from the urban areas, felt a woman should initiate sex: 22.29 percent (urban); 14.89 percent (semi-urban), and 18.49 percent (rural). The study therefore concluded as follows: "This therefore emphasizes the role of culture in determining the extent that women are prepared to accept or to perceive themselves as persons with the right to self-determination and control over their bodies" (LRRDC, 1995b: 62). It is not surprising therefore that a man with many wives can decide to abstain from sexual intercourse with other wives and stick to just one of his many wives for even a year or more, and those who have been abandoned have no right to complain (Sa'ad, 1995). In fact, nursing mothers may welcome such sexual abstinence in the traditional belief that sexual intercourse will contaminate the mother's milk, which "may weaken or even kill the child" (Pittin, 1989: 93).

Just as the woman does not have control over her sexuality, so she does not have the right to limit the number of children she should have in her reproductive life. Her major goal, as set for her by her society, is to marry early and have many children, most especially male children, without minding the attendant health risks. Consequently, being appropriately fertile is one of the woman's major challenges that her male counterpart is free from. For example, a national survey found that only

38.82 percent of respondents believed that a woman who had no children could still be regarded as an accomplished woman. Furthermore, only 42.08 percent felt that a woman with only female children could still be regarded as an accomplished woman (LRRDC, 1995b: 40). In light of the societal pressure on the woman to be appropriately fertile, she may naturally feel that she needs frequent sexual intercourse with her husband. Ironically, however, it is unacceptable for a woman either to initiate sex in a relationship or to have sexual intercourse while breastfeeding.

Divorce

Divorce among many traditional rural communities in Nigeria is unpopular. Once married, women are deemed to be property of their husbands forever. Thus, most men never divorce their wives on their own accord. Rather, a disgruntled wife can only escape from her husband, thereby forcing a divorce. For example, among traditional Gwoza, Kilba, Mumuye, and Jukun rural communities in Nigeria, a wife seeking divorce usually escapes from her husband's residence and takes refuge in the residence of her lover, or she elopes with the lover and resurfaces after some days or weeks. She becomes the wife of her lover upon repayment of her bride price to her husband either by her lover or her relations (Mahmud and Mahmud, 1985: 83). The bride price has to be refunded even if the wife has spent the best part of her life in the service of her husband. The sex discrimination here is very obvious. What is more, she must forfeit to her divorced husband the custody of all the children she might have borne him (Amadi, 1972: 75; Mahmud and Mahmud, 1985: 84; Ghide, 1994; Sa'ad et al., 1994; Sa'ad, 1995).

Inheritance

As properties of men rather than their equals, women are themselves inheritable items in many traditional rural communities in Nigeria. A man's wife can be inherited by his male relations on his death. However, if the wife of the deceased "chooses" to marry somebody else, her bride price is paid to the relation of her deceased husband who would have inherited her as his wife (Thomas-Emeagwali et al., 1985: 134; Sa'ad, 1988, 1994, 1995; Haruna, 1992; Sa'ad et al., 1994; Ghide, 1994; Murrey, 1994; Rufa'i, 1994).

Being inheritable items, women inherit neither their fathers' nor their husbands' properties or positions. The male children of her deceased husband inherit almost everything, especially land. Even where there are no male heirs, a daughter cannot inherit the land of her father. She can only claim the land on behalf of her husband or sons (Thomas-Emeagwali et al., 1985: 129; Imam, Ngur-Adi, Laniran and Makeri, 1985:

24, 25). However, a widow "has the legal right to be in possession, and make use of the matrimonial home" as well as her deceased husband's farmland before "she remarries or otherwise leaves the family" (Mahmud and Mahmud, 1985: 88).

Among the Fulbe nomads, cattle are the most important item of inheritance. They are inherited by the younger brother of the deceased or by the eldest son in the absence of a younger brother. The wives of the deceased may remain in their matrimonial home as helpers, but with no cattle, until they remarry elsewhere in the absence of a younger brother of the deceased to inherit them all as his wives (Thomas-Emeagwali et al., 1985: 136).

Economic Institutions

Many labor activities take place both within and outside the home among the traditional rural communities in Africa. Within the home, important labor activities include hewing firewood, fetching (or even finding) water, thrashing and grinding grains, cooking, tendering domestic animals, washing (especially domestic utensils), cleaning the surroundings, and looking after children. All of these tasks are done mostly by women (Stevens and Date-Bah, 1984: 17–18; Sa'ad, 1988, 1994, 1995; Sa'ad et al., 1994; Haruna, 1992; Ghide, 1994; Murrey, 1994; Rufa'i, 1994). Men only construct and mend the family compounds, which are occasional activities rather than recurrent. In fact, among the nomadic Fulani, even the constructing and mending of compounds are women's work (Hopen, 1958). Thus, the only recurrent activity of men at home appears to be the maintenance of discipline within the home (Sa'ad, 1988, 1994, 1995; Sa'ad et al., 1994; Haruna, 1992; Ghide, 1994; Murrey, 1994; Rufa'i, 1994).

The major economic activity outside the home in most rural societies in Africa is farming, and, again most farming activities are carried out by women (Boserup, 1970: 16; UNECA, 1974; Dhamija, 1984: 75; Stevens and Date-Bah, 1984: 17; Tadesse, 1984: 65). In addition to farming, women in Africa are said to be responsible for 70 percent of marketing (Imam et al., 1985: 1). The African situation in general is true of most rural communities in Nigeria, whereby "about 80% of the labor force is supplied by rural women" (Imam et al., 1985: 8).

Clearly, therefore, women in rural areas do a lot more work than men do, which also means that they generally work longer hours per day than do men. In fact, it has been estimated that women spend between 10 and 16 hours working per day as compared to the less than 10 hours a day men put in. Yet women own neither farmlands nor the bulk of farm products being marketed. They also receive far less remuneration than do men. For example, one study among the Yoruba has estimated that although women spend 41.9 percent of their time on farm operations as compared to 48.9 percent for men, the women receive only "a token annual cash gift in return for services rendered throughout the year" (Imam et al., 1985: 8).

What else does one expect for a sex that is regarded as a property of another (i.e., the male sex) who owns both the farmland and farm products? Thus, among the rural communities with which the writer has had contacts through research, particularly the Kilba, Mumuye, Jukun, Bura, or Babur and the Gwoza hill dwellers, economic wealth is a status exclusively for men. According to the elders of these rural communities, people can only talk of a man being wealthy or poor. It is meaningless to talk of a woman being wealthy because the number of women a man has as wives is itself one of the indices of his wealth (Sa'ad, 1988, 1994, 1995; Sa'ad et al., 1994).

Political Institutions

According to Marxists, the class that has the economic power also controls the political affairs of the society (Marx, 1971). This is apparently the case among the rural communities of Nigeria, though along gender lines rather than class. Just as wealth is the exclusive right of men, political leadership and decision/policy making, thus political power, are exclusively for men. The leadership positions women occupy are those within the private sphere such as those of motherhood over their children, of senior wives over the junior wives, and leaders of women associations. And even in these positions the degree of power and influence a woman exerts is still determined by the "head" of the household, who has always been a man (Sa'ad, 1994, 1995; Sa'ad et al., 1994).

Gender discrimination in political leadership has existed since precolonial days, with only a few exceptions. Among the Yoruba of Ibadan, for example, the Iyalode's office was said to be "equal to all other chieftaincy offices. . . . The Iyalode . . . was the voice of women and she represented their constituency upon regular consultations with them. . . . Often times, the power of the women's constituency was determined by the political dynamism of the Iyalode-in-Council" (LRRDC, 1995b: 13; see also Awe, 1992: 57–71).

Among the Igbo of Anambra and Imo, Okonjo observed that since precolonial times "rural women have had their own councils where they deliberated on current issues affecting their interest and the interests of their community. Their decisions are as binding and as recognized as those of the men folk and are equally respected" (Okonjo, 1985: 192).

Finally, among the Hausa people of Zaria, historical accounts have shown that apart from women's equal access with men to political offices within the government of Zazzau, they also had equal access to the exalted office of the king. Hence, the emergence of the famous Queen Amina of Zazzau in A.D. 1576 (Sa'ad, 1992: 11–25). What these few exceptions have shown is that even though women have always had less political power and influence than men, women have had more political clout in the traditional precolonial times than they have had since the inception of colonialism.

Educational Institutions

Literacy is undoubtedly very low in Africa, but almost all adults in rural Africa, even before the advent of alphabets, were educated in the sense that education does not simply mean the ability to read and write. Education is a process whereby norms, values, beliefs, attitudes, and skills are inculcated into the learner to enable him or her to deal as efficiently and as effectively as possible with the physical/natural and social environment. Education therefore goes beyond the three "Rs": Reading, Writing, and Arithmetic. It is true, moreover, that women in rural Africa are educated differently from men and for different purposes, that education appears discriminatory, or to even aid discrimination, against women.

Since time immemorial, women in rural Africa, including Nigeria, have been trained to be good wives and mothers, to run affairs at home effectively, to be morally upright, to help men in farming, and to process and distribute food. Men, on the other hand, have been trained to farm, head the family units, and run the affairs of the community, including wars. The training started very early in life, as the case of nomadic Fulani indigenous education demonstrates. Education of the nomadic Fulani is not the formal school type, and true to the nomadic Fulani profession, its emphasis is on good herdsmanship. In other words, male children learn herding, which is the main occupation of nomadic Fulani, from members of their families rather than from school or from other nomads as apprentices, and they begin very early in age. The learning method involves observation and practice.

This is all in an effort to inculcate in the nomadic Fulani child good herdsmanship (*ngainaka*)—one of the elements of nomadic Fulani ideology (the *pulaaku*). Herdsmanship is a value attached to men rather than to women. Hence, only boys are involved in herding unless, of course, the family does not have a male child. Boys are taught early in life "to identify their herds by their color, size, types of horns or their individual specific names" (Lar, 1989: 25). They also "learn a lot about wild fruits, flowers and grass varieties. They know the edible and poisonous grasses" (Lar, 1989: 25). Courage (*ngorgaku*) is also an element of nomadic Fulani ideology that is attached to males. Boys are therefore taught this virtue through various means, one of which involves a special dance festival referred to as Sharo. As described by Lar, Sharo

involves beating the dancer, sometimes to a state of unconsciousness, yet the dancer has to brave it with great courage. He is not expected to indicate or show any sign of hard feelings. Sometimes, this game exhausts the youth to death. The game is a kind of festival of initiating youths into manhood. And a man is exposed to all sorts of dangers from wild beasts and hostile people that they are supposed to face and conquer. (Lar, 1989: 25)

With regard to girls' education, the virtues of *dewal* (service, particularly to her husband) are taught to them early in life through examples and practice. Girls are therefore involved in such activities as cooking and looking after the young calves and their younger sisters and brothers. They also receive training in milking, milk processing, and sales through observation and practice. *Semteende* (shyness, reserve), which is emphasized in women, is also part of *ndewaku*, (that is, behavior depicting submission or inferiority complex) and this is taught to girls through examples. A girl watches as her mother prostrates herself and bows down her head while she is either talking to the girl's father or giving something to, or taking something from, him. She also observes as the mother runs away in absolute embarrassment when she accidentally meets a man eating. The mother herself avoids eating in public. Clearly, therefore, training children differently to perform their traditional roles can only result in the subordination of females in their adult life by men.

Religious and Normative Institutions

Religious and normative institutions have always served effective social control functions to enable the smooth working of the society. The latter depends largely on the "cooperation" of the most productive section of the society that usually constitutes the majority. The most productive section of the society in rural agrarian societies is that of the women, which is also the largest. Hence, most religious and normative injunctions are directed more toward women than men.

Generally, African Traditional Religions (ATR) regard women as naturally inferior to men. Consequently, they are precluded from performing equal roles with men in religious services, notwithstanding the fact that there are many goddesses and priestesses in most ATR. Apparently, there are two cultural "smokescreens" that becloud and justify discrimination against women in ATR. The first has to do with the fact that a significant portion of the rites and rituals of the ATR are shrouded in secrecy, taken together with the belief that women cannot keep secrets. The second reason is the traditional belief that a woman is unclean for a significant part of her life because of her monthly menstrual period and the bleeding that follows for a maximum of 40 days after childbirth. Thus, only women who "are either in their pre-menarche or post-menopause stages of their life" are sometimes allowed "to participate in carrying out religious rites with male religious leaders" (LRRDC, 1995b: 65).

In keeping with their lower status in ATR, more religious and cultural taboos and practices in Nigerian rural communities are designed to control the behavior of women than of men at every stage of their lives. From birth through puberty to first marriage (which takes place within the first 15 years of a woman's development), a myriad of cultural taboos and practices permeate her life. From marriage and beyond, she is introduced to further religious taboos and practices to ensure that she never grows out of her subordinate status. Some of the more serious religious and cultural practices to be considered here include female circumcision, sex taboos, and widowhood rites.

Female circumcision is still being practiced in rural communities in Nigeria, especially in the south. The practice ranges from removal of the clitoris to extensive mutilation of the labia minora or the major part of the female genitalia. This practice has been found to cause the following problems to victims:

1. Extensive damage to body tissue of the victim's genitalia.
2. The risk of complications such as surgical shock, bleeding, and infections during the operation, which may be fatal.
3. Prolonged and obstructed labor and delivery complications.
4. Social ostracism of the victim as a result of rectal or urinary incontinence.
5. Psychological trauma of sexual frustrations where, for example, the clitoris has been mutilated (LRRDC, 1995b: 52).

Despite all the possibly serious effects of female circumcision, the practice persists in the attempt to ensure that the woman arrives at her husband's house a virgin and remains faithful during marriage. Similarly, "the powers of deities are often conjured to keep the fidelity of the wife to the husband and not the other way round" (Elumoye, 1985: 144). Among the Yoruba, for example, the husband has the right to put *magun* on his wife, but not vice versa. Magun is a native/traditional medicine used by husbands to check on their wives' fidelity. It has the power to kill a man who has had sexual intercourse with another man's wife on whom the medicine had been applied. Another way of imposing a check on the woman's fidelity in many rural Nigerian communities is through "confessions" in the process of childbirth. The expectant mother is required to call out (before the assembly of midwives) the names of all those she had gone to bed with during pregnancy in the belief that she may have serious problems in giving birth if she fails to tell the full story (Kukah, 1989: 70). In complete contradistinction, the man has the divine right to marry as many wives as he wishes or can afford. Consequently, sex taboos/offenses such as adultery and fornication are concepts entirely woven around the women in ATR. In most Nigerian rural communities, fines are the most popular punishment for adultery, whereby only the husband of the adulterous wife has the right to compensation from his offender. The wife or wives of the adulterous husband is/are not entitled to even an explanation from their husband, much less any compensation. This, undoubtedly, underscores the belief that the wives are properties of their husbands.

Finally, widowhood rites discriminate against women. Women who lose their husbands are made to observe a mourning period, usually for a whole year, and suffer much during this period, whereas men are not subjected to the same treatment. In fact, a widower can "marry another wife within a matter of weeks after his wife's death" (Amadi, 1982: 75). Despite the discriminatory nature of widowhood rites, a recent survey found that the practice is still rampant in many areas in Nigeria. The survey found many types of widowhood rites being practiced. They range from rites designed to express grave and adequate sorrow for the loss suffered to rites designed to cleanse/purge the woman from her bad luck to rites that require her to vouch for her noninvolvement in her husband's death (LRRDC, 1995b: 53). The survey revealed how these different types of widowhood rites are variously practiced:

She [i.e., the widow] may be required to shave her hair, mourn by wearing black for as long as the customary prescribed period that sometimes extends to a year. Sometimes, a widow is required to mourn her deceased husband by sitting and sleeping on the bare ground for a prescribed period of mourning period and is not allowed to bathe herself or change her clothing. . . . Some of these practices could be hazardous to a woman's life and safety. . . . [She may, for example, be required] to swallow concoctions or other dangerous substances to prove her non-involvement. She is sometimes required to [perform] some sacrificial rituals that may involve her exposure to physical harm as where she has to take long treks on lonely paths or routes alone at night time. (LRRDC, 1995b: 53)

The survey then concluded by noting that failure to carry out the prescribed widowhood rites is frowned upon seriously and usually "give(s) rise to suspicion about the involvement of the widow in her husband's death, or the depth or genuiness of her love for the deceased" (LRRDC, 1995b: 53).

GOVERNMENT POLICY AND PROGRAMS TO REDRESS GENDER INEQUALITY

Even though it is now recognized worldwide that women's rights, like men's, are human rights, as indicated by the existence of many international bills of rights, rural women in Nigeria still suffer serious discrimination. It would seem that the Nigerian government has not taken any step or action to protect or enforce women's human rights, particularly in the rural areas. On the contrary, however, within the last decade the Nigerian government has adopted several programs geared to redress inequalities between the sexes. The following section discusses the various policies and programs the Nigerian government has adopted with a view to highlighting their lack of positive impact on women's human rights.

The Directorate of Food, Roads, and Rural Infrastructure

This agency, popularly known as DFRRI, was established under Decree 4 of February 6, 1986, to identify and promote programs that would effectively lead to the achievement of the following objectives (Koinyan, 1987–1988: 440–448):

1. The improvement of the quality of life and standard of living of the majority of the rural people by substantially improving the quality, value, and nutritional balance of their food intake;
2. Raising the quality of rural housing, living and working environment;
3. Improving the health conditions of the rural people; and
4. Creating opportunities for greater human development and employment, by encouraging self-employment and enhancing income levels.

Despite its commendable objectives, DFRRI has not had any positive impact on the condition of life of the rural people in general and women in particular. Rural areas remain largely in poverty, poor health, and without electricity, portable water, and good access roads.

Better Life for Rural Women Program

This program, which has now been replaced by another called Family Support Program (FSP), was initiated in 1987 specifically to enable the rural women to improve their lives. It includes education, gainful employment (especially in the arts, crafts, and agriculture), healthy living conditions, political participation, and so on. The program (henceforth referred to as BLPRW) was a private initiative of the wife of the former military president, Mrs. Maryam Babangida. Even though BLPRW did not have budgetary allocations from the government, it was largely funded by donations from the government purse.

The BLPRW undertook many activities to achieve its objectives. In the field of vocational education, for example, it worked closely with the National Directorate of Employment to help impart to women income-generating skills. Women were also exposed to labor-saving technologies to improve their productivity. Some women were also helped to organize themselves into groups or cooperatives in order to enable them to have access to loans to finance their farming activities and/or small businesses. BLPRW also encouraged the women's groups to open day care centers to help relieve women of the burden of child care so as to enhance their productivity within and outside the home.

Undoubtedly, the BLPRW had commendable objectives and did pursue some relevant activities toward the realization of the objectives. Nevertheless, the rural women's poor conditions of life remain unchanged. The program's only achievement appeared to be that of putting women's issues on the national agenda, which brought about some awareness of such issues by both women and men. Several factors appear to be responsible for the BLPRW's lack of impact on rural women. To begin with, it pursued too few activities in rural areas, and it had too little sense of commitment. Second, the technologies it acquired and introduced to women in agriculture were largely not "women-friendly," and they also were too expensive. Third, most women felt BLPRW was simply meant to provide some ego-boosting and money-making extracurricular activities for the initiator of the program, Mrs. Babangida, and the wives of governors and local government chairmen, who were the chairpersons of the program at the national, state, and local government levels, respectively.

Following the United Nations' declaration of 1994 as the International Year of the Family, FSP was inaugurated in September 1994 to replace the BLPRW. The Family Support Program (FSP) is a private initiative of the wife of the late head of state, Mrs. Maryam Abacha, headed at the national, state, and local government levels by Mrs. Abacha and the wives of the state governors and local government chairmen, respectively. Like BLPRW, FSP also has no budgetary allocations from the government but depends largely on government donations. Unlike BLPRW, however, FSP's focus is on family needs/interests rather than on "women in development" per se. There is therefore the fear that women's concerns may be overshadowed by "the perceived and more compelling interest of children and family as a whole" (LRRDC, 1995b: 33). This fear has yet to be either confirmed or allayed since the program (i.e., FSP) is still not fully off the ground.

The Peoples' Bank

The government established the Peoples' Bank of Nigeria on October 2, 1989 in order to "open up an-easier-to-obtain financial vista" (Okeje, 1990: 14) to the poor, most of whom are women. In this way they can have access to credit with which to open up or finance their petty businesses to enhance their incomes. Unfortunately, this program, like DFRRI, had little real impact on improving the condition of the poor and women. Its problems appear to be mainly twofold: inadequacy or absence of accurate information about its activities; and "general skepticism about the genuineness of any governmental programs designed to alleviate the conditions" of the masses (LRRDC, 1995b: 38). As a result, the local savings networks such as ajo, adashi, susu, and esusu, still serve as the only sources of finance for most women in Nigeria.

The National Commission for Women

The National Commission for Women (NCW) was established in 1989 in compliance with the requirement by CEDAW that each state party to CEDAW should establish a national machinery with a strong power base and an independent budget to monitor effectively the implementation of the provisions of CEDAW in their respective state parties. Apart from the national headquarters headed by a woman as the executive chairperson, the NCW has branches in all the states of the federation headed by executive secretaries who are also women. Section 2(a) of the decree (1989 No. 30) establishing NCW vested in the agency has the following key objectives:

1. To promote the welfare of women in general.
2. To promote the full utilization of women in the development of human resources.
3. To bring about the acceptance of women as full participants in every sphere of national development, with equal rights and corresponding duties.
4. To eliminate totally social and cultural practices tending to discriminate against and dehumanize womanhood.

The NCW is also expected to carry out the aims and objectives of the BLPRW, support the work of NGOs, and mediate "between government and Nigerian women organizations" (LRRDC, 1995b: 30).

It is very hard to separate the successes and failures of the NCW from those of the BLPRW in that the NCW is also expected to, and in fact, has attempted to carry out some of the aims and objectives of the BLPRW. It is clear, however, that the NCW did make its mark on the military regime of General I. B. Babangida. The regime, for example, had "openly identified with the political aspirations of Nigerian women and even encouraged them to run for political offices. Among the civilian deputy governors it appointed in 1990, two were women" (Ifowodo, 1993: 170).

The establishment of a ministry specifically for women in January 1995, namely, the Federal Ministry of Women Affairs and Social Services, to work hand-in-hand with the NCW, may be counted as one of the positive impacts of the NCW's activities in General Sani Abacha's military regime. It is envisaged that machinery at such a high level of government will be able to ensure adequate resources and authority to pursue and implement, hand-in-hand with NCW, many government policies meant for the development of women in the country.

The National Commission for Mass Literacy, Adult, and Nonformal Education

To be sure, the significant role education plays in personality development and empowerment of individuals cannot be overemphasized. It follows, therefore, that discriminatory educational principles and practices against women (as we have seen in the section on educational institutions in traditional rural communities) usually translate into women's exploitation and underdevelopment. In order to address this problem, among others, through increased participation of women in education, the National Commission for Mass Literacy, Adult and Nonformal Education (henceforth referred to as NCMLA and NFE) was initiated in July 1991.

The NCMLA and NFE is saddled with responsibility for developing and carrying out literacy programs, with special attention to disadvantaged groups such as women, nomads, and the handicapped. The summary of the activities of the NCMLA and NFE over three years indicates that it has made great efforts to bridge the gap between male and female enrollment into its various educational programs. Consequently, by 1993 the NCMLA and NFE had enrolled a total of 1,529,522 females in its various programs, as against 1,771,099 males, a difference of 241,577 (LRRDC, 1995b: 35).

The problem, however, is that the total number of women enrolled is too small to have any impact on millions of rural women in a Nigeria of 120 million people, about half of whom are women. Second, females enrolled in NCMLA and NFE programs tend to go for courses which, to quote Ijere, "reflect the society's idea of the role assigned to women, namely cookery, sewing, laundry for house keeping, and home management for rearing children" (1991: 15), rather than for courses that will enable them to compete on an equal footing with males or secure wage employment.

The National Policy on Population

The sexual and reproductive rights of women that are being abused in rural communities should be central issues in any population policy in Nigeria. The government in its population policy targets for the year 2000 indirectly addressed this issue. These included, among others, the reduction of the proportion of women who get married before the age of 18 by 80 percent; of pregnancy to mothers below 18 years and above 35 years of age by 90 percent; and of women bearing more than four children by 80 percent (Federal Republic of Nigeria, 1988: 13).

Government efforts, have been directed more toward reducing infant and child mortality as evidenced in the Expanded Program on Immunization. Issues pertaining to female genital mutilation, VVF and RVF, early marriages, number and spacing of children, nutritional value of the food pregnant women eat, cancer of the cervix, AIDS, and so on, have never been pursued seriously. Most of these issues are left almost entirely to the initiatives of nongovernmental organizations. Even with regard to the area of family planning where there is a government policy and program, it was found "that not more than 6% of Nigerian women of reproductive age are currently on contraceptives" (LRRDC, 1995b: 41). Therefore, the government has made no concerted effort to improve the reproductive health of Nigerian women, especially rural women.

CONCLUSIONS

The facts marshaled under each of the five institutions known to human societies in history have clearly demonstrated that women in Nigeria, a predominantly rural African country, are far from being liberated, much less equal to their male counterparts. This is the case notwithstanding the existence of many commendable international bills of rights for the promotion of women's rights globally that Nigeria has acceded to or adopted, and of the policies and programs embarked upon to realize those rights in Nigeria. The major reason for this is the overwhelming nature of the cultural ideas and attitudes embedded in the five traditional institutions and the practices arising therefrom.

The traditional ideas, attitudes, and practices that deny a woman her rights as a human being vis-à-vis men in rural Nigeria are bound also to affect the status of even a modern woman in an urban area. This is because most people in urban areas, whether educated or otherwise, have their roots in rural areas. Thus, attention needs to shift to the plight of the rural woman in Nigeria if the women folk as a whole are to be

successfully liberated. First and foremost, therefore, the rural peoples
must be removed from the stranglehold of their traditional cultures that
justify and encourage the oppression and exploitation of the rural
women. It appears that the first thing that needs to be attacked is the
marriage contract, which appears to be the primary source of livelihood
and oppression for women in both traditional (rural) and modern (urban) settings. As rightly noted by Quick (1972: 3), marriage for women
"is a contract that is theoretically entered into freely by a man and a
woman," whereas in reality "there is little choice involved" for the
woman. Quick then draws an analogy between the marriage contract for
women and the wage contract for the working class: "members of the
working class may choose their employers, but they will not remain unemployed if they can help it, and they cannot be independent since they
own no capital" (1972: 3).

This analysis has demonstrated that among rural communities of Nigeria mate selection is the prerogative of the family rather than of the
couple, especially the female spouse. Similarly, it has been shown that
once she is married, a woman cannot remain without a husband. She
can change husbands only through abduction or eloping. Thus, she remains married forever, rendering both sexual and labor services in return
for the bride price paid on her once in her lifetime, even though the
bride price was consumed by her kinsmen rather than by herself. In other
words, the bride price, which is a form of exchange between the husband
and the male relations of the wife, becomes the justification for men's
overwhelming rights over women, just as the wage contract becomes
justification for the overwhelming rights of the capitalist over the worker.

Unlike exchange in the capitalist mode, however, the bride price is not
a commodity exchange as such; it is more or less a gift exchange. According to Fitzpatrick, whereas "commodity exchange is an exchange of
alienable things between transactors who are in state of reciprocal independence," gift exchange is "an exchange of inalienable things between transactors who are in the state of reciprocal dependence" (1982:
231). Thus, like the gift exchange, bride price is inalienable from the
husband, and it creates a reciprocal dependence between the couple as
husband and wife. Hence, this discussion has revealed that a woman
who prefers to remain with her abductor/eloper can do so only if her
newfound man can refund her former husband his bride price. Similarly,
when a husband dies, his brothers or children can inherit his widows,
or marry them out to other people and use the bride price to acquire
other wives. Thus, once exchanged for a bride price, women are rendered
dependent on men (they must always have husbands), for men are dependent on their labor and other services.

One of the best ways to begin to remove the marriage contract as the
basis of oppression and exploitation of women is to open up the family

that hitherto has been considered a private domain. There is also a need for direct governmental and nongovernmental scrutiny and implementation of policy recommendations aimed at liberating the woman within the family structure in Nigeria. Apparently, all the programs embarked upon by the government have failed to do this.

Second, there is a dire need to educate members of the rural communities (both women and men) as to the importance of respecting women's rights. As we have seen, the fundamental rights provisions in the Nigerian constitution, and in other human rights documents such as the CEDAW, would guarantee equality of rights among the sexes very adequately if they were implemented. What is needed is to take these documents down to the rural areas and enlighten the rural folk, both men and women. The NCW, in conjunction with the FSP, has the primary responsibility of doing this. To be more effective, however, the NCW should liaise very closely with NGOs concerned about rights in general and women's rights in particular. These include the National Council of Women Societies (NCWS), Women in Nigeria (WIN), Legal Research and Resource Development Center (LRRDC), Civil Liberties Organizations (CLO), Committee for the Defense of Human Rights (CDHR), Nigerian Bar Association (NBA), and the trade unions. The NCW also needs to forge close ties with universities and research institutes throughout the country to carry out on its behalf policy-oriented in-depth research projects on various issues of women's rights in order to guide the commission's crusade against the abuses of women's rights in rural Nigeria.

Third, NGOs concerned with human rights should intensify their efforts, both in terms of their range of activities and of the geographical spread of these activities. Most of these organizations are presently located in the southern states of the country, and they also tend to give priority to the rights of the urban poor in almost total neglect of the rural populace. There is therefore an urgent need for them to establish many more branches in the northern states and to redirect a lot of their human rights activities to ameliorate the plight of rural people, particularly rural women.

Finally, women's nongovernmental national associations, such as the NCWS and WIN, should mobilize local women's associations scattered throughout the country to put constant pressure on the government at the state and federal levels, through the NCW and the newly established federal ministry of women affairs, in order to provide rural areas with more infrastructures (health, portable water, energy, light, etc.), "women-friendly" labor-saving devices, easier-to-obtain credit facilities for women, and mass literacy and legal centers that give priority to the enlightenment of women and men on gender issues, including women's legal and human rights in contemporary Nigerian society.

REFERENCES

African Charter on Human and People's Rights. (1981). January 19.
Ajomo, M. A. (1993). "The Development of Individual Rights in Nigeria's Constitutional History." In M. A. Ajomo and B. Owasonoye (eds.), *Individual Rights under the 1989 Constitution*. Lagos: NIALS.
Amadi, E. (1972). *Ethics in Nigerian Culture*. Ibadan: Heinemann Educational Books Ltd.
Awe, B. (1992). "Iyalode Efunsetan Aniwura (Owner of Gold)." In B. Awe (ed.), *Nigerian Women in Historical Perspectives*. Lagos: Sankore/Bookcraft Ltd.
Boserup, E. (1970). *Women's Role in Economic Development*. London: George Allen & Unwin.
Constitution of the Federal Republic of Nigeria. (1979).
Convention on the Elimination of All Forms of Discrimination Against Women. (1979). December 19.
Dhamija, J. (1984). *Income-Generating Activities for Rural Women in Africa: Some Successes Dwellers in Borno State*. Unpublished B.Sc. dissertation.
Elumoye, R. (1985). "Women and Religion." In Women in Nigeria (WIN), *Conditions of Women in Nigeria and Policy Recommendations to 2000 A.D.* Zaria: WIN.
Ezeomah, C. (1988). *Education of Nomadic Families*. Jos: University of Jos, Nomadic Education Unit.
Federal Government of Nigeria (FGN). (1988). *Fifth National Development Plan*. Lagos: Government Printer.
Federal Republic of Nigeria. (1988). *National Policy on Population and Development, Unity, Progress and Self-Reliance*. Lagos: Department of Population Activities, Federal Ministry of Health.
Fitzpatrick, P. (1982). "The Political Economy of Dispute Settlements." In C. Sumner (ed.), *Crime, Justice and Underdevelopment*. London: Cambridge University Press.
Ghide, I. A. (1994). *Traditional Rights and Duties of Women: A Case Study of Gwoza Hills*. Unpublished.
Haruna, L. D. (1992). *Legal and Human Rights of Women in a Traditional Society: The Case of Kilba Community*. Unpublished B.Sc. dissertation.
Hopen, C. E. (1958). *The Pastoral Fulbe Family of Gwandu*. Oxford: Oxford University Press.
Ifowodo, O. (ed.). (1993). *Human Rights in Retreat*. Lagos: CLO Publication.
Ijere, M. O. (1991). "Mobilising Women Power for Nigeria's Economic Development." In M. O. Ijere (ed.), *Women in Nigerian Economy*. Enugu: Acena Publishers.
Imam, A. M., Ngur-Adi, N. D., Laniran, Y., and Makeri, G. (1985). *Conditions of Women in Nigeria and Policy Recommendation to 2000 A.D.* Zaria: Women in Nigeria (WIN).
Koinyan, L. (October 1987–September 1988). "Everything You'd Always Wanted to Know about the DFRRI: Social Mobilisation Strategies for Development." *Giant Strides*, 1.
Kukah, M. H. (1989). "Women, the Family and Christianity: Old Testament, New Testament and Contemporary Concepts." In A. Imam, R. Pittin, and A. Omole (eds.), *Women and the Family in Nigeria*. Senegal: CODESRIA.

Lar, M. (1989). *Aspects of Nomadic Education in Nigeria.* Lagos: Fab Educational Books.

Legal Research and Resource Development Centre (LRRDC). (1995a). *Human Rights Made Easy.* Ibadan: Bookcraft Ltd.

Legal Research and Resource Development Centre (LRRDC). (1995b). *Women Rights as Human Rights: The Nigerian Experience.* Ibadan: Bookcraft Ltd.

Mahmud, P. and Mahmud, M. (1985). *Women and the Law: Conditions of Women in Nigeria and Policy Recommendations to 2000 A.D.* Zaria: Women in Nigeria (WIN).

Marx, K. (1971). *A Contribution to the Critique of Political Economy.* Moscow: Progress Publishers.

Milne, A.J.M. (1979). "The Idea of Human Rights: A Critical Inquiry." In F. E. Dowrick (ed.), *Civil Rights: Addresses, Essays, Lectures.* London: Teackfield Ltd.

Murrey, P. A. (1994). *Traditional Rights and Duties of Women in Bachama Community of Adamawa State.* Unpublished B.Sc. dissertation.

Nwabara, Z. I. (1989). "Women in Nigeria the Way I See It." In A. Imam, R. Pittin, and A. Omole (eds.), *Women and the Family in Nigeria.* Senegal: CODESRIA.

Okeje, R. N. (1990). *The Integration of Women: An Essential Factor in Economic Development.* Paper presented at the National Workshop on Strategies for the Integration of Women in National Development, Owerri, December 11–14.

Okonjo, K. (1991). "Rural Development in Nigeria: How Do Women Count?" In M. O. Ijere (ed.), *Women in Nigerian Economy.* Enugu: Acena Publishers.

Pittin, R. (1984a). "Gender and Class in Nigeria." *Review of African Political Economy,* 31.

———. (1984b). "The Documentation and Analysis of the Invisible Work of Invisible Women." *ILO Review.*

———. (1989). "The Control of Reproduction: Principles and Practice in Nigeria." In A. Imam, R. Pittin, and H. Omole (eds.), *Women and the Family in Nigeria.* Dakar, Senegal: CODESRIA.

Quick, P. (1972). "Women's Work." *The Review of Radical Political Economics,* 4(3).

Rufa'i, J. A. (1994). *Traditional Rights and Duties of Women: A Case Study of Nomadic Fulbe Women in Mubi.* Unpublished B.Sc. dissertation.

Sa'ad, A. M. (1988). "In Search of Justice for Nigeria: A Critical Analysis of Formal and Informal Justice in Congola State." Unpublished D. Phil. thesis, University of Sussex, England.

———. (1992a). "Queen Amina of Zaria." In B. Awe (ed.), *Nigerian Women in Historical Perspective.* Lagos: Sankore/Bookcraft Ltd.

———. (1992b). "Values, Ideology and Nomadic Education. The Case of Nomadic Fulbe." In *Proceedings of the National Workshop for Nomadic Education Supervisors.* Maiduguri: Nomadic Education Centre, University of Maiduguri.

———. (1994a). "Universal Declaration and the State of Human Rights in Nigeria." *Journal of Political and Economic Studies,* 2(3).

———. (1994b). *Focused Group Discussions with Babur/Bura Women in Biu.* Conducted for a Research on Women's Rights and Human Rights. Lagos: The Nigerian Perspective for LRRDC.

———. (1995). "Law and Justice among Gwoza Hills Dwellers in Nigeria: An Assessment of the Viability of Informal System of Justice in a Democracy." Research Report submitted to Governance and Democratisation Project, Department of Public Administration, OAU, Ile-Ife and Centre for African Studies, Florida State University, January 16.

Sa'ad, A. M., Shettima, A. G., and Babagana, I. (1994). *Traditional Institutions and Cultural Impediments to Women's Rights among the Kanuri and Babur/Bura Communities of Borno State*. Maiduguri: University of Maiduguri.

Stevens, Y. and Date-Bah, E. (1984). *Food Processing and Technological Intervention*. Maiduguri: University of Maiduguri.

Tadesse, Z. (1984). "Studies on Rural Women in Africa." In *Rural Development and Women in Africa*. Geneva: International Labor Organization.

Thomas-Emeagwali, G., Mere, A., Carter, A., and Pittin, R. (1985). *Women and the Family, Conditions of Women in Nigeria and Policy Recommendations to 2000 A.D.* Zaria: Women in Nigeria (WIN).

United Nations. (1948). *Universal Declaration of the Human Rights* (UDHR).

———. (1966a). *International Covenant on Civil and Political Rights* (ICCPR).

———. (1966b). *International Covenant on Economic, Social and Cultural Rights*.

United Nations Economic Commission for Africa (UNECA). (1974). *The Changing and Contemporary Roles of Women in African Development*. Addis Ababa: UNECA.

Vereecke, C. (1988). *Pulaaku: Adamawa Fulbe Identity and Its Transformations*. Zaria: Women in Nigeria (WIN).

Chapter 5

The *Trokosi* System in Ghana: Discrimination Against Women and Children

Abayie B. Boaten

INTRODUCTION

This chapter describes and explains the *trokosi* system, which according to its advocates and practitioners, is an African traditional religion. It also discusses how the system violates women's human rights, in contravention of Ghana's 1992 Republican Constitution as well as other international conventions, and it offers suggestions about how the system may be handled.

The *trokosi* system is based on traditional religious beliefs. It is discriminatory against women and children (Gadzekpo, 1993), and its operations violate fundamental human rights (UN, 1995). The crux of the matter is that the victims are women and children, the most vulnerable members of society. Those affected, that is, the young girls who are called *trokosis*, as well as the general public, have condemned it. However, the perpetrators and the intellectual protagonists of the practice are pleading for modification and tolerance (Dartey-Kumodzi, 1995). Nevertheless, the system is increasingly being condemned by all well-meaning Ghanaians. Women's organizations such as the National Council on Women and Development (NCWD) and the Federation of International Women Lawyers (FIDA) have proposed legislation to outlaw the system completely. Since traditions die hard, however, the process of abolishing the system and rehabilitating the victims has been slow.

THE *TROKOSI:* A CONCEPTUAL FRAMEWORK

Trokosi, which means "slaves of the gods," is an aspect of African traditional religion, a cultural practice, and a science that evolved first among the ancestors of the Ewe of North and South Tongu Districts, and then the Akatsi and Anlo Districts of Southeastern Ghana. *Trokosi* exists not only in Ghana, but also in Benin, Togo, and parts of Yorubaland in Nigeria. However, the main attributes of the *trokosi* system are the same and are intertwined. As a religion, it is practiced in shrines and is embodied in a deity or god called *tro* or *troxovi*. To the Ewe, the god *troxovi* is the god of transformation. The process of transformation usually connotes that which is good for the people. The people believe that the deity, *troxovi*, is one of the messengers of the Creator, God or *mawu*. In relation to this god, the people have developed an elaborate system of rituals and worship. As a traditional deity, it is employed to protect the people, give children to barren women, conjure blessings for the community, and serve as a source of instant justice. As an insider puts it: "Until the Police Force was introduced, fetish was the policeman, the judge and the god of goodness. The system is yet to change sufficiently to remove the need for the intervention of gods (Ahiable, 1995: 20).

The *troxovi* apparently ensures the acquisition and protection of people's properties. Crimes of all kinds are not only prevented, but the gods punish those who indulge in them. The presumed sum total of its benefits can be seen in the following: teenage pregnancy is rare, reproductive health is ensured, immorality is checked, and crime is kept under control (Ahiable, 1995). To the practitioners of this religion, the deity is a source of vitality and strength (Dartey-Kumodzi, 1995).

The following categories of persons can be identified at each shrine:

1. Those who have been spiritually called and installed, through elaborate traditional rituals, as priests or *tronua*, possess spiritual powers that they get from the *troxovi*. These powerful people actually control the system. The respect accorded them is comparable to that shown to the traditional rulers.

2. The *dorfleviwo* are individuals, both males and females, who are born into this world through the divine intervention of the *troxovi*. These privileged people may be described as the sons and daughters of the *troxovi*.

3. The *troviwo* are the biological children of the priests, the *tronua*. These offspring may be described as the "princes" and "princesses" of the shrines. They are children from properly married traditional wives. Such children are carefully looked after by their fathers, the *tronua*, and often receive some formal education.

4. The last group, known as the *trokosi*, are those vestal virgins who are sent into servitude at the shrines of the *troxovi* because of crimes allegedly committed by their senior or elder relatives such as mothers, fathers, uncles, and grandparents. These young girls enter the shrines at a tender age, between 6 and 8 years of age. The children that the *trokosis* bring forth through the relationship between them and the *tronua* are in the same underprivileged social position as their mothers, since the priests do not look after them.

There are claims that the children of the *trokosis* are special people who are destined to redeem humankind from various crimes. Nevertheless, experience has shown that so far the typical offspring of the *trokosi* have not made any significant mark even in the simple societies where the system operates. It is doubtful whether *trokosi* children born and raised under such horrible circumstances can contribute toward changing the society for the better.

The Ewe who cherish the *trokosi* system have long regarded it as their traditional religion that they have practiced for several centuries. As a seemingly preliterate society, they are unable to give the date of the origin of the religion. However, when non-Ewe ethnic groups and especially some Christian nongovernmental organizations (NGOs) learned of this practice between 1993 and 1994, people started to speak and write about it. Criticism of the system came to a head when two NGOs, International Needs and Green Earth Organization, organized a National Workshop on the *trokosi* in September 1994. Although the majority of the speakers spoke against it (Short, 1995; Boaten, 1995; Mama Asigbe, 1995), a few intellectuals tried to defend the system (Dartey-Kumodzi, 1995; Ahiable, 1995; Dzirasa, 1997).

BECOMING A *TROKOSI*

As already noted, *trokosi* is basically a matter of belief, based on the notion that things normally do not happen without a cause. This concept presupposes that the system also deals with a search for truth and knowledge, an intellectual basis of the system. The *trokosi* system is mainly recognized as an agency for punishing wrongdoers (Glover, 1993). The vestal virgins who are initiated as *trokosis* in the various shrines become *trokosis* because, as already noted, someone in their families had confessed to committing crimes that demanded reparations. It is not easy to know all the shrines since they are scattered throughout rural communities. However, the International Needs (NGO) has identified about 160 such shrines in 7 out of the 16 districts of the Volta Region, Ghana.

The offenses punishable by payment with a *trokosi* include murder, stealing, adultery, and having sexual intercourse with a *trokosi*. Indeed, the meaning of the word *trokosi* clearly shows the slave nature of the system. Etymologically, the term *tro* means gods and *kosi* means a slave girl. A *trokosi*, therefore, is a slave girl to the gods (Ahiable, 1995).

Whenever any of the above-mentioned crimes is committed, the aggrieved party approaches a priest, a *tronua*, to search for the offender/wrongdoer. The search is done spiritually through invocation of the gods. The aggrieved person demands of the priest that his deity punish the offender's family with mysterious deaths. The aggrieved person also promises the deity that should it succeed in identifying the offender, the offender should be made to pay reparations by presenting a vestal virgin to the shrine as a *trokosi*.

The deity, through its spiritual powers, will then send pestilence to the offending family, resulting in mysterious deaths. As custom demands, the affected family will also conduct a search in order to find out the cause of the family tragedy. This is what is known in the Ewe tradition as "search for knowledge" (Dartey-Kumodzi, 1995). The result of this spiritual search eventually forces the offending family to consult the shrine whose deity has been involved and then acknowledge the offense. The admission of guilt empowers the priest to inform the offending family of the necessary rituals for reparations. The most significant of the items demanded is a virgin, normally a 6- to 8-year-old girl, to serve as a slave in the shrine. The period of servitude for the vestal virgin varies from shrine to shrine and can be from three years until death. What this means is that whenever a *trokosi* dies the offending family is expected to replace her with another vestal virgin. Refusal to replace a deceased *trokosi* is supposed to result in the reoccurrence of calamities in the family of the wrongdoer.

Once the wrongdoer is able to provide a virgin to serve on his or her behalf, such a person in his or her lifetime does not become affected by the "curse." The entire "curse" is put on the innocent little girl who is provided as a sacrificial lamb, a *trokosi* (Mama Asigbe, 1995). As is often the case, a vestal virgin may not even know the family member who might have committed the crime for which she is serving in the shrine.

The *trokosi* system demands that when a girl is sent to the shrine, she serves the priest by ministering to the needs of both the shrine and the priest's personal needs. She is forced to sweep the compound of the shrine, work on the farms belonging to the priest (without having a share of the products from the farm), and have sexual intercourse with the priest as long as she remains in the shrine. The priests start to have sexual intercourse with the girls when they become teenagers. The upbringing of children who are the offspring of these sexual relationships between the priests and the vestal virgins becomes the sole responsibility of the *trokosis*. There are thousands of such "futureless" children in the shrines. In short, these children become the properties of the *trokosis*.

The adherents of this system argue that the *trokosi* is the wife of the *tro*, and therefore her spiritual role is to intercede on behalf of her family in order to prevent further calamities from befalling its members (Dartey-Kumodzi, 1995). If this assertion were true, then the *trokosi* would be powerful spiritual entities/personalities. While it is an abomination for any individual to have sexual intercourse with a *trokosi*, the priests have unlimited license to indulge in intercourse without any inhibition (Progressive Utilization, 1994: 2–6). One priest alone was said to have fathered over 400 children in his 37 years of priesthood (Okrah, 1997).

One of the most pernicious aspects of this system is the general dehumanization of the *trokosi*. Once a woman becomes a *trokosi*, she is believed to have a mystified body. As a result of this belief, such an individual becomes a curse in the society. Even her own relatives who took her into the shrine begin to shun her and her children. Her only acceptable society is her kind in the shrines. Since this happens only to the females in these traditional societies, it clearly appears that the *trokosi* system amounts to woman abuse of the highest order (Ababio, 1995).

The defenders of the *trokosi* system claim that it punishes wrongdoers and therefore deters crime. They contend that the system is so effective that if an individual offended the gods, the spirits would take vengeance on the offender. Based on these arguments, it is clear that the system is founded on retribution and fear. It is such an entrenched belief that its true adherents do not see anything wrong with it (Adda-Dontoh, 1994).

Investigations conducted with some of the girls who braved the odds and ran away from their shrines and have since been rehabilitated reveal the untold mental and emotional agony and struggle the girls experienced during their stay in the shrines. A liberated *trokosi* confided in the writer as follows:

We were living like slaves. We were made to suffer hunger. We had no soap for our bath. We did farm work under severe pressure. In the nights the priests just ordered any one of us to sleep and have sexual intercourse with him. If you felt sick, it was the responsibility of your people to give you medication. In fact, it was terrible for a human being to live in such a condition. (Personal Communication, 1996)

Another *trokosi*, a mother of two, revealed that she spent nearly 20 years at a shrine and had two children with the priest. He refused to look after the children because he did not consider the children as his own.

The experiences narrated by the *trokosi* deserters reveal that the system has a disruptive effect on family life, which is held in high esteem in African traditional religion and custom (Opoku, 1978). Once in the shrine, a *trokosi* is cared for by her family, including food and clothing, while the priest uses her as a beast of burden during the day and as a bedmate during the night but without any social obligations. The laws of Ghana regarding neglect of spouses and children do not seem to apply to those who live in those shrines. Their families that sent them there often neglect the *trokosis* who serve long sentences in the shrines. Such treatment violates the values and norms of social and family life. Those who serve life sentences as *trokosis* often offer a pitiable picture of abject poverty and neglect, especially when they become too old to work.

TROKOSI AS AN INSTRUMENT OF GENDER DISCRIMINATION

All the shrines have male priests and male shrine owners; no shrine in Ghana has female ownership. This gender imbalance in ownership explains why this system exists in its primordial form. The *trokosi* system is male dominated, and hence the tendency is to use vestal virgins instead of boys as reparation. Moreover, girls or women are more amenable to fear on which the system is based, for the priests are aware that the *trokosis* (female) cannot rebel. If the slaves were to be boys or men, the system would probably have collapsed or been highly modified. Therefore, the priests and shrine owners are safe with girls and women as their victims. Again, the vestal virgins are sent to the shrines while they are still very young and grow to accept their fate as natural. As young females, most of them are unable to offer any resistance, for example, by refusing to go to the shrines. The system does not take into consideration the fact that these vestal virgins will one day grow into adults and must therefore be trained properly in order to contribute to the good of the society. The Beijing Conference (UN, 1995: 17) stressed the importance of bringing girls up properly:

The girl child of today is the woman of tomorrow. The skills, ideas and energy of the girl child are vital for full attainment of the goals of equality, development and peace. For the girl child to develop her full potential she needs to be nurtured in an enabling environment, where her spiritual, intellectual and material needs for survival, protection and development are met and her equal rights safeguarded.

Besides, the vestal virgins are deceived by their parents/relatives when they are being taken to the shrines. The sorts of preparations initially mounted for them make them feel that they are some sort of brides. They are made to believe that they are "wives" or "brides" of the gods. They are given several pieces of cloth, white stools, new cooking utensils and such things as traditionally newly married women would receive. This deceit makes the innocent girls enter into this state of servitude willingly. It is when their parents in the shrines abandon them and as the days develop into weeks, weeks turn into months, months into years that they realize rather belatedly that they are in servitude.

The *trokosi* system is a source of discrimination against women because in the patrilineal society that puts much premium on the male, the female tends to be regarded as an "object" whose significance lies in the fact that "it" is able to produce other human forms. Since the family line is maintained through the male and a woman in marriage is, more or less, seen as the property of the man in the African context, she ceases to be a member of her first paternal kinship group, so that it is always easy to sacrifice her.

Furthermore, patriarchy regards the male as central for the defense of the traditional society, so that in terms of decision making the female plays a peripheral role in the traditional setup. The low traditional position of women in Ewe society is demonstrated by the fact that only recently have they acquired traditional female leadership. In contrast, the Twi-speaking people regard females as the ancestors of the various clans and also consider the position of the female traditional leadership as enshrined in the traditional laws and usage. Therefore, since the Ewe women have no say in the traditional society, it is easy to discriminate against them because they tend to be regarded as the weaker vessel.

Young female children are the most abused in this system because they have the least power to control their own affairs. These children, both male and female, who are the products of the *trokosi* system, are denied formal education and so cannot easily appreciate what goes on in their micro-environment and in the outside world. As a result, they live in total ignorance and take whatever experiences they encounter in the shrines as normal (Short, 1995).

SOCIAL AND LEGAL IMPLICATIONS OF THE *TROKOSI* SYSTEM

What happens in the shrines leading to the presentation of vestal virgins who become *trokosis* amounts to setting up a criminal justice system that is juxtaposed to the orthodox one (Short, 1995). When someone becomes a victim of a crime, that person consults at a shrine and promises that when the perpetrator is discovered he or she should be made to pacify the gods with a virgin.

The results of the invocations—tragic deaths and serious calamities—are subversive of the rule of law and a serious violation of human rights. This system obviously runs counter to the traditional system of law and therefore amounts to setting up a separate system of criminal justice that breeds unjustifiable suffering and often death. According to a newspaper report in *The Mirror* No. 2209 (March 27, 1997, Accra) with the title: *Trokosi* She'll Be But Mum Says 'No," a man who had allegedly stolen a cassette tape recorder many years before was now experiencing mysterious deaths in his family. A spiritual search that he conducted revealed that he needed to pay reparation with his daughter who was in primary three. When the mother, an unbeliever in the *trokosi* powers, refused to hand her child over, she was forcibly separated from her husband. The woman's refusal was unprecedented. The following discussion shows that the *trokosi* system as it operates today violates the human rights and freedom of both women and children that are guaranteed under the 1992 constitution of Ghana as well as other international human rights instruments.

Article 12 (2) of the 1992 constitution of Ghana guarantees the fundamental human rights and freedoms of all citizens. This provision requires that a person should not exercise his rights and freedoms in such a way as to violate or infringe on the rights of others. The *trokosi* system violates the rights of the vestal virgins. Yet, under the constitution the rights of this group are as important as those of their parents or guardians who send them to the shrines. According to Articles 16 (1) and 16 (2) of the constitution, a person shall not be held as a slave or be placed in a situation of servitude. Similarly, no person has the right to force another person to work for him or her.

In the shrines, however, the vestal virgins perform duties such as going to the farms to till the land, fetching fuel-wood, burning charcoal, sweeping the compound of the shrines, and undertaking all such duties as the priests may demand. The vestal virgins perform all these duties against their will. Thus, they are subjected to conditions tantamount to slavery, servitude, and forced labor. Article 19 (1) and (2) of the constitution seeks to prohibit all these activities which appear rather normal in the shrines. The Article states that any persons who commit a crime must be given a fair hearing in a law court (p. 17). Furthermore, such persons must be given the chance to defend themselves. Similarly, the *trokosi* system violates Article 15 of the Fourth Republican Constitution of 1992. This article seeks to ensure the dignity of all persons and prohibits any cruel, inhuman or degrading treatment, such as the treatment often given to the *Trokosi* which detracts from their dignity and worth as human beings.

In addition to the above constitutional provisions, Article 4 of the African Charter of Human and People's Rights provides that every human being's life and integrity should be respected (OAU, 1996). Furthermore, the Beijing Declaration at Annex 1.9 states: "Government should ensure the full implementation of the human rights of women and of the girl child as an inalienable, integral and indivisible part of all human rights and fundamental freedoms" (p. 4).

Among the many major adverse consequences of the *trokosi* system, the vestal virgins do not have the chance to go to school; rather, some of them are taken out of school and sent into servitude as *trokosis* (Mama Asigbe, 1995). This educational deprivation is passed on to the children they have with the priests. Whereas the priests' children from their properly married wives (*troviwo*) are sent to formal schools by their fathers (priests), the offspring of *trokosis* are not. The priests' refusal to send their *trokosi* children to school is illegal and equally violates Article 25 (1) of the country's constitution, which provides that all citizens of Ghana should have equal access to educational opportunities and facilities. However, because of their social status, *trokosis* and their children are denied these rights.

The United Nations Convention on the Rights of the Child provides for the right of the child to education. Ghana, as a member of the United Nations, is obliged to uphold this provision of the Convention. This point was further buttressed by the Beijing Conference (1995: 39), which stated: "the girl child should be properly nurtured and equipped with the necessary skills in an enabling environment to ensure the growth of her full potential as a normal human being." Unfortunately, the environment in the shrines is not conducive to the proper upbringing and training of the girl child.

In addition to equal access to educational opportunities, all children, no matter who their parents are, should have equal opportunity to medical care. Article 28 (1) of the UN Convention on the Rights of the Child, as well as Article 28 (4) of the Ghanaian constitution (1992), support this view. The latter stipulates that "No child shall be deprived by any other person of medical treatment, education or any other social or economic benefit by religion or other beliefs" (p. 29). Since the *trokosi* system endangers the health of the *trokosis* and denies them medical treatment, it violates the Articles just quoted.

Child sexual abuse is one of the most objectionable aspects of this system. The priests in the various shrines have unlimited sexual access to the *trokosi*. Thus, while traditionally these vestal virgins are supposed to be the wives of the *tro* and are therefore untouchable, the priests exploit them sexually and produce children who normally have no future in modern society. Some of these *trokosis* are forced to bear children at the tender age of 14 years. By the time some of the *trokosis* finish their "sentences" and are released from the shrines, they are already saddled with children whom they have no means to look after.

Traditional African society abhors the sexual abuse of children. Moreover, there are laws and usages that deal with this social misconduct (Rattray, 1929). Both Article 27 (1) of the African Charter on the Child and Article 34 (1) of the UN Convention on the Rights of the Child denounce sexual abuse. The UN Convention imposes a serious obligation on all states "to undertake to protect the child from all form of sexual exploitation and sexual abuse" (Ghana, 1993: 15).

Furthermore, the Beijing Declaration (1995: 96) is very explicit about women's rights in this respect. It stipulates that women should have the right to decide on matters relating to their sexuality, including sexual and reproductive health, free of coercion, discrimination, and violence. It further states that there should be an equal relationship between women and men in matters of sexual relations and reproduction. Paragraph 17 of the same document also states that to empower women, they should have full control over all aspects of their health as well as their fertility. However, the customary or religious practices associated with the priests in the shrines are detrimental to the health and welfare of the women. It is indeed deplorable that a single priest could "own" as many as 30 "wives" in the form of the *trokosis* without having any obligation for their welfare or the well-being of the children so produced.

The *trokosi* system not only violates basic human rights, but it also dehumanizes its victims. Article 26 (2) of the Ghana constitution prohibits all customary practices that dehumanize or are injurious to the physical and/or mental well-being of Ghanaian citizens. The seriousness of the dehumanizing aspect is demonstrated when a sick *trokosi* and/or her children are thrown out of a shrine and have to fend for themselves. This is obviously contrary to the spirit of Article 41 (d) of the 1992 constitution which stipulates: "It shall be the duty of every citizen to respect the rights, freedoms and legitimate interests of others and generally to refrain from doing acts detrimental to the welfare of other persons" (p. 41).

CONCLUSION

By and large, the *trokosi* have eluded researchers. The paucity of literature on this subject is indeed notable. Perhaps the first intellectual attempt to expose this abhorrent practice was a B.A. dissertation presented to the Department of Study of Religions at the University of Ghana, Legon (Glover, 1993). The present work is an attempt to shed more light on the *trokosi* phenomenon.

The chapter has examined the characteristics, origins, dynamics, and consequences of the *trokosi* system which can be supported neither morally nor legally. It has exposed a system that violates relevant international conventions as well as the 1992 constitution of Ghana with regard to women and children's rights (Short, 1995). The system is discriminatory and dangerous to women and children. The supporters of the *trokosi* system claim that without it the Ewe communities would have been destroyed by vice. The lameness of this argument is that not all Ewes practice this type of religion. Furthermore, the practice has not spread beyond its traditional borders, thus making it culture-specific. One curious aspect of the *trokosi* phenomenon is that, despite its apparent antiquity, only recently has it come to the attention of the Ghanaian society at large. Over the years both the practitioners and the victims of the system have remained silent on its operations.

It is incongruous that a country such as Ghana that boasts the first female high court judge in the Commonwealth would tolerate a practice like the *trokosi*. Chiefs, opinion leaders, and scholars from those areas remained silent over the practice until its exposure in 1994 by NGOs.

Since then, the public outcry against it has become loud and clear. Church groups, the Federation of International Women Lawyers (FIDA), the Commission for Human Rights and Administrative Justice (CHIRAJ), Queenmothers Associations, the 31st December Women's Movement, and the National Council on Women and Development (NCWD) have all intensified their campaign for its abolition. Some of the organizations have set up vocational institutions to enable the liberated *trokosis* to acquire some vocational skills so as to earn a decent living.

Three schools of thought have emerged regarding the *trokosi* system. The first, supported by hard-liners, notably the fetish priests, the shrine owners, and regrettably some intellectuals, contends that the system is for the good of the society and should be maintained without modification. According to some believers, the shrines also perform other functions such as giving spiritual protection to people, bestowing prosperity on others, and ensuring the fruitfulness of barren couples. These functions by the *troxovi* are considered essential in the lives of the believers, who do not think that such spiritual prowess contravenes any laws of the land. Accordingly, they do not want the system to be abolished. The second school is made up of opinion leaders, shrine owners, and some fetish priests as well as some adherents who advocate modification of the system, for example, substituting sheep, goats, or cows for vestal virgins. This group of people argues that completely abolishing the system will create a vacuum in terms of dealing with offenders. The third group is made up of the majority of Ghanaians, who consider the system abominable and reprehensible, and therefore feel that it should be abolished without reservation. The abolitionists urge that the enslaved girls be liberated, the shrines destroyed, and the recalcitrant owners and priests prosecuted in the law courts.

Recently, a bill has been tabled before the Ghanaian parliament seeking to abolish the *trokosi* system (Short, 1995). A parliamentarian from one of the districts in which the system is practiced has expressed opposition to the abolition of the system, saying that "Any resort to punishment through legislation as a means of eliminating the practice may itself create certain undesirable social upheavals" (Dzirasa, 1997: 8). He did not specify the so-called social upheavals. As a possible solution to the problem created by the *trokosi*, he suggested that the practitioners or the owners of the shrines be compensated with money, cows, sheep, or other "incentive packages."

In light of this discussion, the system should be outlawed through legislation. Both the owners and the victims should be educated to appreciate the deleterious and obsolete nature of the system. The liberated *trokosis* should be rehabilitated through vocational training, as is currently being undertaken by the International Needs (NGO). Through legislation, the *trokosi* perpetrators should be given a time frame within which to dismantle the system. After the deadline, "social upheavals" or not, the laws of the country should be allowed to take their course. An evil system such as *trokosi* should not be allowed to operate in the twenty-first century.

REFERENCES

Ababio, A. (1995). *The Legal Basis for the Abolition of the* Trokosi. *Report: First National Workshop on* Trokosi *System in Ghana* (July 6–7). Accra: International Needs.

Adda-Dontoh, R. (1994). "Tell Rawlings to Let Me Stay, *Trokosi* Girl Pleads." *The Mirror*, June 4, p. 1.

Adotey, R. (1995). Trokosi *System—A Handicap to Social Development. Report: First National Workshop on* Trokosi *in Ghana* (July 6–7). Accra: International Needs.

Agyeman, O.A.K. (1995). "First Lady, Help Abolish *Trokosi* Slavery." *The Ghanaian Chronicle*, August 17–August 20, p. 2.

Ahiable, M. (Hon.). (1995). *The Anatomy of* Trokosi *System in Ghana. Report: First National Workshop on* Trokosi *System in Ghana* (July 6–7). Accra: International Needs.

Azuma, V. (1994). "Goats Now to Replace Girls as *Trokosi* Sacrifice." *The Mirror*, April 30, p. 1.

Boaten, A. B. (1995). *The Chief as a Tool for Change in* Trokosi *System. Report: First National Workshop on* Trokosi *in Ghana* (July 6–7). Accra: International Needs.

Dartey-Kumodzi, S. (1995). "*Trokosi* or *Fiashidi*: Pillar of Africa's Survival." *Weekly Spectator*, July 15, p. 5.

Dzirasa, K. (1997). "265 *Trokosi* Slaves Freed from Bondage." *Daily Graphic*, No. 14352, January 27, Accra.

Gadzekpo, A. (May/June 1993). "Sexual Bondage." *AWO*, p. 5.

Ghana Human Rights Quarterly (January–March 1993), 1(1), p. 15.

Glover, Y. (1993). *Vestal Virgin*. Unpublished essay, Department of Religion, University of Ghana.

Mama Asigbe (Adokuwa IV). (1995). *The Role of Queen Mothers in Bringing Change in* Trokosi *System. Report: First National Workshop on* Trokosi *System in Ghana* (July 6–7). Accra: International Needs.

The Mirror (1997), No. 2209, March 27, Accra.

National Council on Women and Development (NCWD). Country Report. (1996). "Course No. J-90-03182, F.Y. Submitted." By G. Ohene-Konadu, Accra.

Okrah, L. (1997). "*Trokosi*: An Abominable System." *Green Dove*, 6.

Opoku, K.A. (1978). *West African Traditional Religion*. Accra: F.E.P. International Private Ltd.

Organization of African Unity (OAU). (1986). "The African Charter on Human and People's Rights Quoted." *Ghana Human Rights Quarterly* 1(1), January–March 1993.

Progressive Utilization. (1994). "*Trokosi*: Virgins of the Gods or Concubines of Fetish Priests." *Progressive Utilization Magazine* 1(1), 2–6.

———. (1995). *"Trokosi* Part 2." *Progressive Utilization Magazine*, 2(1), 1–6.

Rattray, R. S. (1929). *Ashanti Law and Constitution*. Oxford: Clarendon Press.

Republic of Ghana. (1992). *The Constitution of Ghana*. Accra: Government Printer.

Short, F. E. (1995). Trokosi—*Legal or Illegal. First National Workshop on* Trokosi *System in Ghana* (July 6–7). Accra: International Needs.

United Nations (UN). Assembly. (December 1948). *International Bill of Human Rights*. Quoted in *Ghana Human Rights Quarterly*, 1(1), January–March 1993.

———. (1995). *Report of the 4th World Conference on Women Preliminary Version*, September 4–15, Beijing, China.

Chapter 6

The Feminization of Poverty: Effects of the Arable Lands Development Program on Women in Botswana

Gwen N. Lesetedi

INTRODUCTION

The government of Botswana has always been committed to the development of rural areas. Programs have been formulated and implemented in order to stimulate development as well as improve the living standards of the rural population. According to the 1991 Population and Housing Census, the majority of Batswana reside in the rural areas, accounting for 54.3 percent of the total population. Of these, the majority is women who depend mostly on agriculture for their income.

Rural development, which goes as far back as 1972, is one of the major government strategies in the National Development Planning process. The strategies adopted to alleviate poverty have not been very successful. Rural poverty has deepened over the years, with the population of people living below the poverty line in rural areas increasing from 45 percent in 1974 to 64 percent in 1986 (Molale, 1995: 5).

This is not to imply that the government has been totally neglecting rural development. It is still a major government strategy of national development as evidenced by programs such as the Financial Assistance Policy (FAP), Arable Land Development (ALDEP), Accelerated Rainfed Agriculture Program (ARAP), Tribal Grazing Land Policy (TGLP), and Service to Livestock Owners in Communal Areas (SLOCA). Rural areas have experienced considerable improvements in social services provision. However, socioeconomic problems persist in rural areas, including poverty, unemployment, and rural-urban migration. The high level of poverty experienced by rural dwellers is partly attributable to the poor performance of the agricultural sector. The rural sector is not fully developed, and the rural populations, especially women, are suffering the most.

ALDEP has been selected as the focus of this study because it is one of the few programs that has tried to target women in the provision of government agricultural packages. One could dub it gender-sensitive. For instance, with respect to the zero downpayment, women are not required to put down any payment to get seeds, draught power, and so on. This is to encourage women's participation in the program. This evaluation of ALDEP seeks to assess whether the program has fulfilled its stated objectives. This chapter relies mainly on data from the Central Statistics Office (CSO) which has been authorized by law to collect, process, analyze, and disseminate data and, since independence, has conducted regular decennial censuses in 1971, 1981, and 1991. Other sources of data include the two Household Income and Expenditure Surveys (1985–1986 and 1993–1994). In combination with the census, these surveys constitute a major source of data. The limitation of these sets of data is that they were not targeted at ALDEP per se. To overcome this limitation, ALDEP evaluation reports conducted by the Ministry of Agriculture were also studied.

The chapter is divided into several sections. The first part examines the concept of poverty and the issue of feminization of poverty. Then the chapter presents an overview of ALDEP and the factors that led to its formulation. In the next section ALDEP is evaluated and its impact on poverty is assessed, which is followed by a conclusion.

THE CONCEPT OF POVERTY

Poverty is a difficult concept to define; it is defined in either absolute or relative terms. Datta (1995: 99) explains that *relative poverty* is culturally defined deprivation, measured by reference to the living standards of the bulk of the people. *Absolute poverty*, on the other hand, refers to the absence of resources to maintain a minimum standard of living. But whichever way one considers poverty, in either absolute or relative terms, it has to be adequately addressed. Statistical measures that are commonly used to define the phenomenon of poverty tend to conceal the extent of poverty, its victims, or the distribution of poverty. Poverty is, in most cases, seen in economic terms; gross national product (GNP) or per capita growth has traditionally been employed as an indicator of social welfare. But rates of GNP tend to conceal a great deal of internal variation in economic progress being made by different groups in the population. For instance, though Botswana has been experiencing rapid economic growth, rural poverty has persisted over the years. The 1985/1986 Household Income and Expenditure Surveys (HIES) estimated that

55 percent of the rural population lived below the Poverty Datum Line, and the 1993/1994 HIES estimated a percentage of 64 (Datta, 1995: 102).

Poverty does not refer merely to lack of possessions or income. It also indicates a lack of access to skills, knowledge, understanding, and empowerment (ODA, 1992: 7). Poverty may also be defined as a household's financial inability to meet its basic nutritional, education, and shelter needs (UNICEF, 1993: 77). The different definitions are an indication that poverty ideally should be looked at as a multidimensional phenomenon and not just in economic terms as is usually done.

Poverty tends to be more severe for certain groups in society, including low-income groups, people residing in remote rural areas, big families, and female-headed households. Poverty in Botswana remains largely a rural phenomenon. Urban areas have been the main beneficiaries of economic growth and development. Agricultural potential is limited due to the area's adverse climate and soil conditions. Rainfall is low and highly unreliable. The distribution of cattle, the most important farm animals, is highly skewed. In 1975, 45 percent of rural farm households did not own any cattle, a proportion that rose to 49 percent in 1991 (Datta, 1995: 102).

Apart from poverty being a rural phenomenon, we find that among those hard hit by poverty are female-headed households. They constitute the majority of the rural poor. It is even said that "poverty begets poverty." In other words, the offspring, especially females from female-headed households (FHH), will end up heading their own households characterized by poverty.

THE FEMINIZATION OF POVERTY

The link between poverty and women has been reported in many parts of the world, both in developed and developing countries. Poverty, as noted before, is more prominent among female-headed households. These households are on average younger and poorer, and yet have a high dependency burden because their families comprise mostly children. According to the 1995 Human Development Report, the situation of women is said to be getting worse, especially for those residing in the rural areas. The number of rural women living in absolute poverty rose to nearly 50 percent over the past two decades; of the estimated 1.3 billion people living in poverty worldwide, more than 70 percent are female (UNDP, 1995: 35).

The feminization of poverty is attributed mainly to factors such as the women's lack of access to economic opportunities and resources. Women have no access to agricultural land and other resources like draught power, technology, and credit. These resources are essential for the women's well-being. Furthermore, women have limited access to em-

Table 6.1
Total Number of Households by Area and Sex of Head, 1991 Census

Area	Households		Male Heads	Female Heads
	Numbers	Percentage	Percentage	Percentage
Urban	76,111	28.6	66	34
Rural	200,098	72.4	47	53
National	276,209	100.0	53	47

Source: Central Statistics Office (1995c).

ployment opportunities as compared to men. When a program to alleviate rural poverty through support to agriculture fails, it is the women who feel the impact more than the men. Therefore, program failure has more implications for women than for men.

The number of female-headed households in Botswana increased from 45 percent in 1981 to 47 percent in 1991 (Kalogosho, 1995: 189). According to the 1991 census, there were more female households in the rural areas than in urban areas. Thirty-four percent of the households in the urban areas were female headed compared to 52 percent in the rural areas. The number of households headed by females has increased because of the low incidence of marriage, rural-urban migration, prolonged absence of male partners, or through an unmarried woman setting up an independent household. The 1991 Population and Housing Census clearly illustrates the extent of female-headed households (see Table 6.1).

More households are headed by females in rural areas than urban areas. This is partly because there are more households in the rural areas than urban areas, as the majority of the population reside in rural areas. Households headed by females, whether in rural or urban areas, are generally larger than those headed by males (as shown in Table 6.2). In spite of their disadvantaged position, women carry most of the responsibilities for raising their children as well as maintaining the household.

THE ARABLE LANDS DEVELOPMENT PROGRAM (ALDEP)

Responding to conditions of poverty in the rural areas due to the poor performance of the agriculture sector, the Botswana government has initiated programs that are aimed specifically at alleviating poverty among disadvantaged sectors of the population. The government has initiated

Table 6.2
Household Size by Area and Sex of Household Head, 1991

Area	Total Average Household Size	Average Size for MHH	Average Size for FHH
Urban	3.65	3.54	3.87
Rural	5.15	4.94	5.35
National	4.73	4.45	5.05

Source: Central Statistics Office (1995c).

several programs to upgrade the living standards of the rural people, including the Arable Lands Development Program (ALDEP), Accelerated Rainfed Agriculture Program, Tribal Grazing Land Policy (TGLP), Agricultural Extension (AE 10), Service to Livestock Owners in Communal Areas (SLOCA) and Local Government 17 (LG 17).

The Ministry of Agriculture introduced ALDEP in 1982 in an effort to increase agricultural production and distribution while tackling the need for employment and income creation among rural householders. Mufune (1995: 25) has outlined the events that led to the implementation of ALDEP, notably:

1. The fact that economic growth did not lead to any significant reductions in unemployment, especially among school leavers and those engaged in small-scale agriculture.
2. The realization that despite the fact that more than 80 percent of rural dwellers were engaged in agriculture, production was still inadequate, leading to the importation of food from South Africa and perpetuating the situation of food insecurity.
3. The fact that major donors such as the World Bank were shifting emphasis to the development of small-scale holder agriculture (Mufune: 1995).

These and other factors led the government to embark on ALDEP as a poverty alleviation program. The fifth National Development Plan covered the plan period 1979–1985 and included the following objectives that the ALDEP had to fulfil.

To increase production to achieve self-sufficiency in basic grains and legumes at rural household and national levels plus export surplus for these and cash crops in all but the poorest rainfall areas; in doing so raise arable incomes (both, self-employment and waged) through improved agricultural productivity, and to optimize income distribution effects by concentrating on small-holder development;

and to create employment in lands areas to absorb underdevelopment and reduce rural-urban drift. (MFDP, 1979: 50)

The principal objective of ALDEP was to increase production, income, and employment for rural areas through technological farm investment such as draught animal power, animal-drawn farm implements (plough, planter, harrow, cultivator), and seasonal inputs (seeds, fertilizers, and pesticides). In addition, farmers would also get extension services. All these inputs were considered crucial to farming and were intended to meet the farmers' basic investment needs. The various ALDEP farm packages are designed to facilitate improvements in farming practices and, consequently, to result in higher production (Kerapeletswe, 1992).

To implement the program, the targeted group was broken up into three categories called models. Farmers were classified into different models depending on the number of cattle they owned. Model I included farmers who did not own any cattle and were the poorest of the target group; Model II were those who owned between 1 and 20 cattle; and Model III owned between 20 and 40 cattle. Farmers who owned more than 40 cattle did not qualify for assistance from ALDEP.

Initially, all ALDEP packages required a 15 percent downpayment. During the first two years of its implementation, very few women participated. According to Datta (1993: 19), less than 10 percent of the farmholders were women. This was contrary to what the program was supposed to achieve because it had been recognized that female-headed households as part of the target group constituted 54 percent of the households without cattle. In consideration of this fact, in 1983 the program was changed from a credit to a downpayment scheme. Female-headed households (FHH) were now required to contribute 10 percent toward the downpayment. This resulted in an increase in the number of FHH making use of the packages. For the period 1985–1986, 29 percent of the FHH were recorded as having made use of the ALDEP packages, and by 1986–1987 the number was 49 percent. Despite this increase, the program was still beyond the means of most FHH. In 1988, for many of the packages, the downpayment was scrapped. This meant that women did not have to pay anything to get packages. This brought about positive results because the level of participation rose to 56.5 percent in 1991–1992 (Kerapeletswe, 1992: 11). Because of the zero downpayment for FHH, the scheme was now being abused by male-headed households (MHH) who instructed their wives or daughters to take up the packages (Datta, 1993: 19). An investigation had revealed that the majority of the female beneficiaries were not family heads but dependents. Thus, instead of the women benefiting, the packages were ending up with the MHH and so were defeating the whole purpose of uplifting women's status.

Table 6.3
Male versus Female Distribution of ALDEP Packages, 1981–1982 to 1987–1988

Year	Packages by Sex	
	Male	Female
1981–1982	91	9
1982–1983	85	15
1983–1984	84	11
1984–1985	74	26
1985–1986	71	29
1986–1987	51	49
1987–1988	52	48

Source: Mayende (1990).

EVALUATION OF ALDEP AND ITS IMPACT ON POVERTY

ALDEP, one of the programs under rural development policy to address agricultural problems, is not solely responsible for the poor performance of the agricultural sector but it should have made a great impact in the alleviation of poverty. This is because its main focus was the smallholder farmers who were to be provided with technology as well as extension services. The provision of packages would enable them to increase production, which, in turn, would result in an increase in employment and income. Creating employment in the rural areas would reduce migration to the urban areas. In other words, had ALDEP fulfilled the objectives it had set out, it would have had a much wider impact than any other program under the development policy.

ALDEP has attempted to address some of the constraints faced by women such as inadequate access to draught power and technology through the provision of different packages. The distribution of packages included implements, seeds, and extension services. The distribution of packages has been very helpful. Women farmers who earlier had no access to some of these resources are benefiting from the program. There has been a significant increase in the number of women obtaining packages. Table 6.3 shows the number of applicants who have been given ALDEP packages. At the beginning of the implementation period, very few women benefited from the packages. The number has been increasing steadily, however. Notable increases were recorded in the 1984–1985

Table 6.4
Performance of the Agricultural Sectors as Compared to the Mining Sectors in the Economy

1 Components of GDP (Percentage)				
	1988–1989	1989–1990	1990–1991	1991–1992
Agriculture	5.5	5.5	5.3	5.1
Mining & Quarrying	53.5	42.3	42.3	39.3
11 Employment				
	1990	1991	1992	1993
Agriculture	3.1	2.9	2.6	2.6
Mining & Quarrying	3.9	3.4	3.7	3.7
111 Wage Earnings (Pula)				
	1990	1991	1992	1993
Agriculture	148	196	205	–
Mining & Quarrying	836	857	919	–

Note: Wage earnings for 1993 were not available.
Source: Central Statistics Office (1993).

period, which could be attributed to the fact that the downpayment for packages was 10 percent for females as compared to 15 percent for males.

This could also have resulted in a decline in the number of male applications because, in terms of downpayment, males had to pay more than the females, especially for the period 1986–1987. It was also discovered that during the period 1986–1987 some MHH were abusing the scheme by putting up their wives or daughters to take the packages (Datta, 1993: 19).

Despite the implementation of ALDEP, the performance of the agricultural sector is still poor. The mining sector, which is urban based, contributes significantly to the economy. The performance of the agricultural sector in comparison to the mining sector is illustrated in Table 6.4.

The mining sector has contributed significantly to the economy of Botswana, especially for the period 1988–1989, although now it is registering a downward trend. The contribution of the mining sector has been particularly important in terms of employment as well as wage earnings.

People working in the industry earn at least six times more than their counterparts in the agricultural sector. Agriculture's contribution to the GDP remained more or less constant for the periods 1988–1989 to 1990–1991, but declined significantly at the beginning of the 1990s.

ALDEP had also set out to stem rural-urban migration. Even though Botswana is predominantly rural, the urban population is growing at a very fast rate. The proportion of the population living in urban areas increased from 4 percent in 1964 to 9.7 percent in 1971, to 17.1 percent in 1981 and to 45.7 percent in 1991 (Campbell, 1995: 95). This growth could be attributed to the poor performance of the agricultural sector, resulting in people moving to urban areas in search of paid employment. Migration is the main factor leading to high urban growth. As ascertained from the 1991 census, rural-urban migration accounted for approximately 11 percent of total urban growth (Hope and Edge, 1996: 54). The urban areas offer a wide range of paid employment opportunities in comparison to the rural areas. The urban areas also have better social and infrastructure facilities like schools, health, water, and recreation. The recurring drought has exacerbated the situation in the rural areas, creating problems like unemployment.

The objective of increasing income among rural people has also not been fulfilled. According to the 1991 census, 79 percent of the female heads in the rural areas were economically inactive. On the other hand, 21 percent of the male household heads were reportedly inactive (Kalogosho, 1995: 194). It generally follows that fewer female heads are economically active in the rural areas; 34 percent of the females reported being economically active compared to 66 percent of the males (ibid.). About 62 percent of households headed by females have no cash-earning members compared to 38 percent of male-headed households; however, while 56 percent of the male-headed households reported having one or more cash-earning members, only 44 percent of the female-headed households had cash-earning members.

The 1993–1994 Household Income and Expenditure survey reported that male-headed households have very high cash income as compared to those headed by their female counterparts. In the rural areas (excluding urban villages) male-headed households have an average monthly disposable income of P698.43 and an average monthly expenditure of Pula P456.49 (CSO, 1995a: 6). A female-headed household only has disposable income of P558.48 and an expenditure of P297.11 on average monthly (ibid.). In addition, female-headed households have larger family sizes comprising mostly children. The male-headed households are smaller in comparison, with more adults than children.

The lower income status of female-headed households is due partly to their low level of asset ownership like cattle, land, and equipment, which are essential to rural households (Kossoudji and Muller, 1983: 831). With regard to the ownership of cattle, which is traditionally a male domain, the 1991 Livestock Crop Survey conducted by the Ministry of Agriculture found that among 79,000 households surveyed, 62 percent of female-headed households owned no cattle as compared to 32 percent of households headed by males. Cattle are a major resource and make a substantial difference to a person's livelihood. Income levels are considerably lower among the rural population in general and among female-headed households in particular. According to a UNICEF (1993) report, nearly 40 percent of women earned less than P100 per month in cash and in kind, compared to about 25 percent of the males (UNICEF, 1993: 19).

In its quest for increasing production, ALDEP, as one of its packages, had to supply animal-drawn implements such as ploughs, harrows, and planters. These implements are not appropriate for use by women. There is no appropriate technology, for instance, to ease the burden of women's tasks like weeding which is still done manually. By providing technology that is not gender-sensitive, these schemes have benefited those who are well-off in society. A woman may own a plough or a planter, but she will still need either oxen or a tractor to pull it. The men who own tractors in particular make a lot of money during the ploughing season by hiring the tractors out to people who have none. It also results in women's fields being ploughed late because they have to wait for the tractor owners to plough for themselves first.

The provision of inappropriate and inadequate technology can be traced to the colonial bureaucratic system which was largely responsible for the deteriorating status of women (Mayende, 1990: 11). Women were advised to apply traditional methods of production, while men were taught how to apply modern methods. This resulted in the neglect of the female agricultural labor force in favor of the productivity of male labor. Whereas men graduated to the use of tractors and were also participating in the cash economy, women were still using traditional implements like hoes and cultivating food for the household.

Appropriate gender-sensitive technologies are needed which women can use to ease their farming lives. Modern technology has reduced the male workload but has increased labor demands for women because appropriate labor-saving devices for women are not yet available. Women need appropriate tools in order to cultivate small hectares. A major problem facing women is their lack of access to labor. Fortman (1981: 16) shows that female-headed households have less available labor during peak agriculture activities than their male counterparts. Labor is important considering that agriculture is mostly undertaken by people using animal-drawn ploughs. Because of the adult male labor shortage fields are ploughed late, and they are not properly cared for, resulting

Table 6.5
Area Planted for Production of Crops (Sorghum, Maize, Beans/Pulses, Millet), Average Annual Rainfall and Cereal Imports, 1981–1982 to 1986–1987

	1981-1982	1982-1983	1983-1984	1984-1985	1985-1986	1986-1987
Hectares Planted (000)	290	204	229	203	211	290
Production (000) (metric tons)	58	19	16	9	20	22
Average Rainfall (mm)	577	359	346	289.1	312.5	331.0
Total Cereal Imports (000) (metric tons)	79	111	174	172	187	158

Source: Ministry of Agriculture (1991).

in low and poor yields. The shortage of adult male labor is a result of rural to urban migration.

In terms of increasing food production and achieving self-sufficiency, ALDEP has not fared well in this area either. It should be acknowledged that the arable sector in Botswana faces unconducive climatic conditions, posing adverse effects for the arable sector as, for the last two decades, the country has been facing serious shortfalls in grain production. Botswana has had to rely heavily on the commercial imports of crops like sorghum, maize, beans, and pulses. The problem has been compounded by the easy flow of goods from South Africa.

Table 6.5 shows the performance in the production of crops, average annual rainfall, and cereal imports for the periods 1980–1981 to 1986–1987. The data for cereal imports show an upward increase in the amount of cereals imported. Over the years, the government has intensified its efforts to increase basic cereal production so as to attain self-sufficiency levels by introducing programs like ALDEP at a high cost to the government. Despite such efforts, and also given the already unfavorable weather conditions, the programs have come up with extremely low yields.

Why is there so much concentration on arable agriculture when research has shown that only 6 percent of the country is suitable for arable farming? At any rate, the climate is hardly suitable for large-scale farming due to drought. Research has shown that although water is essential in crop production, it has to be there at the critical stages of plant growth, that is, during germination and flowering; "it is not uncommon for rains to disappear just when crop plants start germinating or flowering"

(MOA, 1991: 12). It is at this stage that there is a need for higher water requirements for the crops to germinate or flower. The government should come up with programs that focus on the development of water resources. Water is essential not only for agricultural development but also for industrial development.

Access to Extension staff is another problem that women face (Fortman, 1981: 18). ALDEP has tried to address this issue. Rural women generally have poor access to agricultural information and resources. Extension personnel, both male and female, tend to overlook the needs of women farmers. Agricultural training is often geared to improving export crops, whereas training with respect to subsistence crops and small livestock, where women farmers predominate, is less prominent. Most training programs for women still emphasize domestic skills rather than agricultural skills, which are equally relevant and important. This is peculiar not only to ALDEP but also to other programs. The ALDEP Extension officers have tended to focus on successful farmers, who are mostly men. According to Mayende (1990: 11), Extension workers tend to ignore women farmers because they are considered inefficient.

The Extension workers see women as poor producers in the sense that their yields are lower than those of the men, and therefore, they are regarded as "hopeless and not worth the trouble" (Mayende, 1990: 11). The Extension workers complain that too much is expected from them in that they are supposed to provide packages to people who lack the most basic means to participate in assistance programs like ALDEP. Extension workers have been trained to implement policy, that is, to provide packages to those who already have basic means. They are not equipped to deal with people who have nothing and have to be provided with basic means, and most women fall in this category. The introduction of female Extension workers has not improved the situation; they make up only a small proportion of Extension workers. Mayende goes on to say that their effectiveness is greatly undermined by their male counterparts who view them as incapable and not up to the job.

Draught power is essential for crop cultivation. Narayan-Parker (1983: 24) found that 67 percent of the women in the Southern District did not plough because they lacked draught power and implements. During the 1982–1983 drought year, about 56 percent of the households that ploughed used their own power; the rest of the households either borrowed or hired land. It was also observed that those who had draught power tended to plough more land than those without and, as a result, had better crop harvest. Although ALDEP has been providing female-headed households with draught power, this has not had much of an effect on the agricultural sector. The number of livestock has increased over the years, but the distribution, especially that of cattle, has worsened. Recent studies have suggested that at least 40 percent of rural households own no cattle; females (UNICEF, 1993: 19) head the majority of these.

CONCLUSION

ALDEP was initiated to help small-scale farmers improve their performance in the arable agriculture sector. It was expected to result in increased food production, higher employment in rural areas, and thereby reduced rural-urban migration. The implementation strategy was to be through provision of farm investment packages, that is, implements (ploughs, planters, harrows, and cultivators) and water tanks.

ALDEP has failed to achieve its objectives. Instead, the plight of the rural areas, especially in the female-headed households, has worsened. The program has not taken into consideration issues like the status of women, cultural factors, and the role of the implementers. In other words, ALDEP did not consider the role of the beneficiaries, that is, poor rural masses as well as the implementers—the Extension workers.

Women have an important role to play in alleviating poverty owing to their strategic position in the household. Women's projects usually center on home-related tasks like baking, dressmaking, and knitting. These projects are not very profitable compared to animal husbandry, for example. What is needed is the gender approach to development, premised on the knowledge that since development affects both men and women, economic growth can be achieved through the participation of both. Development projects should be targeted to benefit both male and female farmers, thus actually moving away from policies that service cattle production, which has proved to be more biased toward male farmers. Female-headed households, living in poverty, are poor for many of the same reasons as their male counterparts. Even though they should be treated as a separate category when targeting them for development programs, this should not be done at the expense of men. Otherwise it will result in abuse of the program such as occurred when men still accessed ALDEP packages through their female relatives.

There is a tendency to focus on rural people as a homogeneous category through which women are treated as a single group with the same needs. They might have something in common in that all are victims of poverty. At the same time, there are female-headed households that function very successfully both socially and economically. It is not that all women are victims of poverty, but what one should bear in mind is that the successful female-headed household represents a very small proportion.

ALDEP tended to assume that the problems rural dwellers such as women faced are agricultural. There should be a diversification in the programs. While other programs like FAP often result in diversification,

ALDEP does not. The government should offer packages that improve the status of women in the rural areas instead of simply offering them livestock and implements. The government packages could include provision of shelter at a minimal cost. ALDEP's main focus has been on crop production without considering the poor climatic conditions and infertile soils that would not be able to sustain arable agriculture. An effective irrigation system should be developed, which would be an addition to the other packages offered.

For a program or policy to be effective, all the different actors should be included. The target group, often the rural dwellers, should be consulted. This group should be involved in analyzing their own problems, proposing solutions, and consequently taking collective action. This approach was not taken in the formulation of ALDEP; if it had, then those piece-meal additions to ALDEP would never have been proposed. The scheme started off as a loan subsidy, but this form had to be changed due to poor response from the farmers who lacked the collateral to back up the loan. During 1983, the downpayment grant scheme was introduced (Datta, 1993: 19). When it was discovered that female farmers were not fully participating, the zero downpayment was introduced for them. Proper consultation with the target group would have shown that most females were not in a position to pay a deposit.

For a program to be effective, not only the beneficiaries, but also the implementers should be involved. They should be involved during the planning stages as well as during other aspects of project implementation. In the case of ALDEP, the implementers who had direct access and contact with the beneficiaries did not understand the objectives of the program. The result was misinterpretation of policy guidelines and misconceptions (Kerapeletswe, 1992: 6). For a program to be effective, cultural factors should also be considered. For example, cattle ownership and rearing have traditionally been a male domain. Women are seldom involved in this sector, but now through ALDEP the cattle sector is open to them. This seems to have increased the women's burden, despite the shortage of labor that has affected them so severely that they now have to look after livestock in addition to their everyday chores.

While focusing on rural poverty, it is also necessary to examine poverty in urban areas. The women in urban areas are just as badly off as those in rural areas. Usually a link exists between households in the two areas. Although ALDEP has not been particularly successful in alleviating poverty, compared to other programs it has fared relatively better. Despite its limitations, ALDEP has had a greater impact on women than similar programs designed to promote productivity and reduce poverty among small-scale farmers in Botswana. The program is currently under review, which, hopefully, will result in the implementation of strategies to deal with its shortcomings, such as its failure to reduce the country's massive reliance on food imports from South Africa.

REFERENCES

Braimoh, D. (1995). "Integrating Women into Rural Development in Africa by Participatory Research." *Development Southern Africa*, 12(1), 127–133.

Brown, B. (1980). *Women's Role in Development in Botswana*. Gaborone: Ministry of Agriculture.

Brydon, L. and Chant, S. (1989). *Women in the Third World: Gender Issues in Rural and Urban Areas*. Aldershot, England: Edward Elgar.

Campbell, E. K. (1995). *Population Distribution and Urbanization*. Report of the 1991 Population and Housing Census Dissemination Seminar, May 1–4. Gaborone: Government Printers.

Central Statistics Office (CSO). (1993). *Botswana in Figures*. Gaborone: Government Printers.

———. (1995a). *Household Income and Expenditure Survey 1993/1995*. Gaborone: Government Printers.

———. (1995b). *1991 Population and Housing Census: Summary Statistics on Small Areas Volume 1*. Gaborone: Government Printers.

———. (1995c). *1991 Population and Housing Census: Technical/ Administrative Report*. Gaborone: Government Printers.

———. (1996). *Population and Housing Census Dissemination Seminar, 1–4 May 1995*. Gaborone: Government Printers.

Chambers, R. (1983). *Rural Development: Putting the Last First*. New York: Longman.

Datta, K. (1993). *Research on Women in Economy and Its Impact on Policy Making in Botswana*. Gaborone: National Institute of Research (NIR), University of Botswana.

———. (1995). *Rural Poverty in Botswana in National Rural Development Planning Workshop*. Gaborone: NIR.

Egner, B. E. and Klavsen, A. L. (1980). *Poverty in Botswana*. Gaborone: NIR.

Food and Agriculture Organization (FAO). (1990). *Women in Agricultural Development: FAO's Plan of Action*. Rome: FAO.

Fortman, L. (1981). *Women's Agriculture in a Cattle Economy*. Gaborone: Rural Sociology Unit, Ministry of Agriculture.

Hope, K. R. and Edge, W. A. (1996). "Growth with Uneven Development: Urban-Rural Disparities in Botswana." *Geoforum*, 27(1), 53–62.

Kalogosho, D. (1995). *Household Perspective of Women and Men in Botswana*. Report of the 1991 Population and Housing Census Dissemination Seminar, May 1–4. Gaborone: Government Printers.

Kerapeletswe, C. K. (1992). *Program and Impact Assessment of ALDEP 1982–1992*. Gaborone: Ministry of Agriculture.

Kiros, F. G. (ed.). (1985). *Challenging Rural Poverty*. Trenton, NJ: Africa World Press.

Kossoudji, S. and Muller, E. (1983). "The Economic and Demographic Status of Female Headed Households in Rural Botswana." *Economic Development and Cultural Change*, 31(4).

Mayende, P. (1990). *Rural Development Policy and Women. The Case of ALDEP in Botswana*. Hull, England: University of Hull.

Merafe, Y. B. (1986). "Policy Implications on the Role of Women in Agricultural Development." Paper presented at a Workshop on Policy Implications on the Role of Women in Agricultural Development. Lusaka, Zambia, August 6–10.

Ministry of Agriculture (MOA). (1991). *Botswana Agricultural Policy: Critical Sectoral Issues and Future Strategy*. Gaborone: Ministry of Agriculture.

———. (1993). *ALDEP Quarterly Progress Reports on Package Distribution*. Gaborone: Ministry of Agriculture.

Ministry of Finance and Development Planning. (1979). *National Development Plan 5: 1979–1985*. Gaborone: Government Printers.

Ministry of Finance, UNICEF and UNDP. (1993). *Planning for People a Strategy for Accelerated Human Development in Botswana*. Gaborone: Ministry of Finance, UNICEF and UNDP.

Molale, E. (1995). "Population Growth Poverty Alleviation and Rural Development in Botswana." Paper presented at the National Conference on Population Policy, Gaborone.

Momsen, J. H. (1991). *Women and Development in the Third World*. London: Routledge.

Moser, C.O.N. (1993). *Gender Planning and Development: Theory and Practice*. London: Routledge.

Mufune, P. (1995). "Comparing Land Policy and Resource Degradation in Botswana and Zimbabwe." *Botswana Journal of African Studies*, 9(2), 71–89.

Narayan-Parker, D. (1983). *Cattlemen, Borehole Syndicates and Privatisation in Kgatleng District of Botswana*. Unpublished Ph.D. Thesis, Boston University.

Oakley, P. and Marsden, D. (1990). *Approaches to Participation on Rural Development*. Geneva: International Labor Organization.

Overseas Development Administration. (1992). *Poverty Reduction in Developing Countries*. Sussex, England: ODA/IDS Workshop.

Seisa, S. (1995). "Gender, Population and National Development." Paper presented at the Gaborone National Conference on Population and Development, November.

United Nations Children's Fund (UNICEF). (1993). *Children and Women in Botswana: A Situational Analysis*. Gaborone: UNICEF.

United Nations Development Program (UNDP). (1995). *Human Development Report*. New York: Oxford University Press.

United Nations Educational, Scientific, and Cultural Organization (UNESCO). (1969). *Evaluating Development Projects*. Paris: UNESCO.

Chapter 7

Prostitution, Patriarchy, and Marriage: A Zimbabwean Case Study

Ishmael Magaisa

INTRODUCTION

Prostitution is a controversial issue in Zimbabwean society. Despite the fact that Zimbabwean law prohibits soliciting and despite expressions of disgust from some moralists, prostitution continues to flourish in many parts of the country. Its practice reflects, albeit in an extreme way, the antagonistic gender relations that pervade Zimbabwean society today. In Zimbabwean society, for most women security lies in marriage. Thus, the unmarried, divorced, and widowed with no source of income are literally pushed to the margins of society where they resort to the sale of sexual services for their economic survival. Zimbabweans are generally reluctant to openly discuss sexual issues. However, since prostitution now includes girls as young as 12 years and is linked with AIDS and baby-dumping, this means that there is need to examine sex work and its place in society.

Although prostitutes have featured in many social discourses in Africa, ranging from moral issues to AIDS infection, the literature is concerned less with prostitutes themselves than with a general account of the problem. Cases in point are the works of Moyo (1991) and Gaidzanwa (1987). By focusing on the origins and causes of prostitution, and by citing colonialism as the main culprit, Moyo relies too heavily on theory at the expense of empirical reality.

Gaidzanwa (1987) concentrates on the gender imbalances that force women to live in ways that society considers undignified. Although her gender approach is useful in any analysis of prostitution, she, too, fails to make the voices of women prostitutes heard. Mushanga (1976) assesses the relative merits and demerits of prostitution. Generally, the literature on prostitution in Africa either overemphasizes the economic aspects of prostitution or oversexualizes sex work. Since the beginning of the AIDS pandemic in Africa, the literature on prostitution has increased dramatically. However, such literature is often written by medical sociologists and anthropologists interested in the role prostitutes play in contributing to AIDS infection rates (see Wilson, 1990; McFadden, 1992; Day, 1988). This preoccupation with the economic, sexual, and health aspects of prostitution has resulted in women prostitutes being seen as deviant, immoral, and dangerous. Although the various works cited above contribute to our understanding of prostitution in Africa, they fail to see prostitutes in their nondeviant roles—as people struggling for gender equality. Pfohl (1985: 125) tells us that the story of deviance is always a story of resistance to power, regardless of whether the resistance is deliberate or inadvertent.

From a feminist perspective, prostitution can be seen as a manifestation of gender antagonism. Its practice reflects conflict between men and women over limited resources and a struggle over the sharing and distribution of social and economic power in Zimbabwe during the 1990s. This chapter therefore focuses on the gender conflict that arises when prostitutes take on other identities as wives of their clients in order to demonstrate that prostitution is not only sexual deviance but also an active rebellion against the conventional customs and obligations of women in Zimbabwe. Bearing in mind that an adult woman in Zimbabwe gets full social recognition primarily through marriage and the bearing of children, we can see prostitution as cultural defiance in that it challenges patriarchal demands for one-sided monogamous unions as the basis of socially approved female sexuality. Male double standards of affording themselves greater sexual freedom, thereby dividing women into girls for sexual pleasure and girls for marrying, might explain why Zimbabwean prostitutes have a hostile attitude toward marriage. The Legal Age of Majority Act 1982 (LAM) gave African women 18 years of age and above majority status for the first time in Zimbabwean history, but many traditionalists discount LAM and continue to treat women as legal minors (Stewart et al., 1990: 170). Thus, the position of Zimbabwean women as social minors and the heavy patriarchal constraints under which they live result in marital arrangements that do not satisfy a sufficient section of the female population. As a result, resistance to marriage by female prostitutes should be seen in the context of both a cultural and a political struggle against perceived injustices within the marriage contract. In such a case, marriage is examined as an intersecting point of gender conflict, manifested in a complex network of relations between prostitutes and their clients and based on their identities as prostitutes.

METHODOLOGY

Since the intention of this chapter is to present the views and concerns of women prostitutes in Zimbabwe, use has been made of a research strategy guided by the interactionist perspective and feminist analysis. The following discussion is based on observations of, and informal-in-depth interviews, with women prostitutes who solicit for clients in the bars and nightclubs of Harare, the capital of Zimbabwe, with a population of 1.5 million people (Zimbabwe, 1992). The girls were sampled through snowballing, a sampling method that uses the respondents' social networks to access other respondents with similar characteristics in the social network. My initial acquaintance with three prostitutes produced referrals to others. The interviews and field observations were conducted over a period of 18 months during 1993 and 1994 with 12 women prostitutes whose ages ranged from 18 to 40 years. In the study, prostitution was defined as an income-generating activity using one's sexual organs. These women prostitutes were divided into three major categories: poverty girls (very poor women relying exclusively on prostitution for their survival); adventure girls (young, educated, but unemployed women who get more money through their sexual adventures with men); and supplementing women (women with low-paying jobs who supplement their incomes through prostitution).

Based on prostitutes' attitudes toward marriage, it can be argued that in Zimbabwe, the processes of becoming wife and prostitute are analogous in that both involve social adjustments to fit the new status, but the prostitute and the married woman make these adjustments in two different ways. In patrilineal Africa, married women are disempowered by the marriage contract that reduces them to *property* owned by their husbands. This is not to say that married women in Zimbabwe are totally disarmed by the marriage contract, for it may well be that they wield some power in their subordination. Although a prostitute may have certain obligations toward her clients, evidence based on my observation and interviews with Zimbabwean sex workers suggests that prostitution can be empowering in that the woman prostitute is neither socially nor legally attached to a particular man who may claim ownership over her. Prostitution is problematic in two ways. First, in a society in which every woman is not only expected, but also strongly encouraged, to belong to a man through marriage, independent and unattached women are treated with suspicion. This is not because they are a problem per se but because without male control, society is not sure of their behavior (Heidensohn, 1985). Second, prostitution appears to be a viable alternative to marriage and serves as an example to other women that one can have sexual autonomy (Delacoste and Alexander, 1987). To begin with, the types of marriages found in Zimbabwe are briefly outlined. Thereafter prostitutes' attitudes toward marriage are examined, followed by an analysis of why prostitutes and their clients behave like wives and husbands. Finally, some case studies of informal marital arrangements by prostitutes and their clients are presented and the reasons these marriages do not work are examined.

TYPES OF MARRIAGES IN ZIMBABWE

Marriage in Zimbabwean society is understood as a sexual union between a man and a woman for purposes of procreation. There are basically two types of socially recognized conjugal unions in Zimbabwe, civil and customary marriages. A third type, called *mapoto*, lies somewhere between recognition and condemnation. Civil marriage (Chapter 237) is a marriage before a magistrate and is strictly monogamous. It was initially meant for white settlers and other related nonindigenous people, but since independence in 1980, people of various kinds can register under this marriage act if they wish. The advantage of a civil marriage is that in the event of marital discord, arbitration can be sought in the courts and each partner can be compensated accordingly. The second type of marriage is the customary, which is potentially polygynous (African Marriages Act, Chapter 238). It may have a legal certification if solemnized in court, but usually it is based on social recognition rather than on legal certification. The validity of customary marriages is dependent on the consent of the father or guardian of the girl and the fulfillment of some traditional social procedures and requirements in particular, the payment of bride wealth.

In fact, all the above marriages involving black Zimbabweans must include bride wealth if they are to be socially approved. Bride wealth is increasingly becoming big business in Zimbabwe, with some parents charging as much as U.S. $1,000 (about 10,000 Zimbabwean dollars) plus five or more cattle for an educated girl. Daughters, then, can be considered as assets by their parents. Since the introduction of the Legal Age of Majority Act, parents have no legal right to demand bride wealth for a girl over 18 years, but, of course, socially things are different. Many girls like it this way and feel cheap if they are not paid for. Nevertheless, it is important to note that insistence on bride wealth as the basis for validating a marriage makes female sexuality a commodity and reduces women to sexual objects, with very limited rights and privileges as compared to their husbands who pay in order to marry them. Conjugal unions in which the man has not paid *lobola* are denigrated and referred to as *mapoto*, a type of marriage historically associated with the system of labor migrancy.

In the past, men would leave their wives in rural areas and go to work in mines and farms where they would get a temporary wife for whom no *lobola* was paid. However, the *mapoto* type of marriage is becoming very common and is getting limited recognition because parents no longer have full control over the marital decisions of their sons and daughters. As a result, marriage has become a matter of individual choice rather than a customary or a cultural requirement.

PROSTITUTES' ATTITUDES TOWARD MARRIAGE

Attitudes toward marriage largely coincide with my earlier classification of prostitutes, and they are also dependent on age, level of education, and marital status prior to beginning prostitution. Generally speaking, attitudes toward marriage are ambivalent and sometimes contradictory. Poverty and supplementing girls still assume that marriage and having children are the appropriate goals for women, even though they might not achieve them because they are "spoiled"—because they are no longer virgins, because they have babies, or because they are known to have had too many boyfriends. For the majority of poverty girls, marriage is an ideal worth striving for. This can be explained by the need to have somebody to take care of them just as husbands take care of their wives. Since prostitution is a transitional period for most Zimbabwean women, some actively seek marriage as an attempt to get out of prostitution. Supplementing girls with tertiary education often argue that "my job is my husband." Yet behind these words lies a deep wish to get married in order to have the social honor and respectability associated with marriage.

The adventure girls, on the other hand, who are generally young and educated, have a negative attitude toward marriage. Although they gave no particular reasons, the most common response was "marriage does not pay." This negativity may be the result of the high demand for young prostitutes. Young girls between the ages of 15 and 24 are "hot cakes" as men call them on the sex market. Clients generally believe that younger girls are not HIV infected. As such, young girls dominate the market, and their economic rewards are higher than those of older women. Marriage then is generally seen as a less lucrative option. Also, marriage is seen as reducing one's freedom and sexual autonomy. In such cases, marriage is viewed as oppressive and exploitative.

Older women (30 to 39 years) are divided over the marriage issue. Their responses seem to be based on a subjective assessment of one's chances of getting married. Those who do not see the likelihood of a happy marriage and those who have had a bad marital experience are both negative. Women who have been divorced, assuming exploitation was the reason, are very bitter about the exploitative aspects of Zimbabwean marriages. The widowed are divided depending on whether the husband was good and responsible or bad and irresponsible. Those who have never married but have children think that men cannot be trusted to the point of marrying.

The attitudes of poverty girls can be explained by their social ontology. This is a category of downtrodden prostitutes whose humiliating experiences explain their desire to get married. Poverty makes them so desperate that they become targets of male abuse. Tendai, one of the poverty girls, reported that clients force her to engage in various sexual acts that she would not agree to if she had other alternatives. Such prostitutes tend to think that they could avoid such treatment if they were married. For these women, prostitution is not emancipating but a form of sexual slavery whereby women are used as sexual objects. Marriage is seen as advantageous in that it provides social, economic, and emotional security. It is also less labor intensive than prostitution in which they have to provide sexual services to hundreds of men. Tendai was surprised that married women cannot satisfy their husbands sexually, especially when dealing with one man. She criticizes married women for failing to realize that the most important aspect in marriage is sex. In her view, women are not married for child care or to cook and clean but to provide their husbands with sex whenever they demand it.

This investigation found an apparent contradiction between the prostitutes' attitudes toward marriage and their actual behavior. Contrary to the expressed attitudes, most prostitutes and their clients tend to behave like wives and husbands. Like their counterparts with a positive attitude toward marriage, prostitutes with a negative attitude also behave like wives and sometimes get married. The stories of Chipo, Brenda, and Susan (not their real names) in the following sections illustrate these apparent contradictions between action and thought. Susan and Chipo, for example, had spoken strongly against marriage, yet they both entered into semimarital arrangements with their clients. Brenda, on the other hand, had positively valued marriage. But when she married one of her clients, she acted otherwise. This can be explained by the fact that their attitudes reflect a general disposition toward marriage rather than a principle-guiding behavior. Behavior, unlike attitudes, is always dependent on the context, situation, circumstances, and interests as perceived by the actor at a particular point in time. Thus, a theoretically antimarriage prostitute may get married for certain strategic reasons without necessarily abandoning an ideology against marriage.

BEHAVING LIKE WIVES AND HUSBANDS IN PROSTITUTION

To illustrate these arguments, let us look at the relationships between bar prostitutes and their clients. Although money is central to prostitution, relations between prostitutes and their clients are not purely economic. Economic considerations are important in the initial stages of the affair, but depending on how well the initial sexual encounters go, relationships tend to be normalized. A normalized relationship is a relationship that begins as a sexual transaction between a prostitute and customer, but later on, the economic aspect of the relationship is muted and the prostitute–client relationship assumes that of boyfriend and girlfriend or that of husband and wife. The following case study illustrates this process.

Chipo, one of the *supplementing* girls, met Peter in a bar and that very same night, they slept at Peter's place. Peter gave Chipo $50 for the sexual services rendered. The next day, they had a date in the same bar. This went on for days until they started staying together, in a *mapoto* type of marriage. Chipo was providing sexual services and performing other wifely duties such as cooking and laundering, yet Peter was not paying much, probably only something in the form of food and accommodation. The relationship lasted six months but ended after a series of disagreements and a bitter struggle between the two.

The normalization of a commercial relationship depends on the frequency of face-to-face interactions between bar prostitutes and their clients, which tend to create long-lasting social relationships that are further cemented through regular sexual relations with the same girl or man. This leads to the division of clients into the "loved" ones and the strictly business ones. The loved clients may be exempted from using condoms and are commonly referred to as husbands, while those for business are referred to as "my catch." However, men rarely refer to these women as their wives. When men talk among themselves, the women are referred to as *hure rangu* (my prostitute), but, when in the company of these women, "my girlfriend" is used. Referring to client–boyfriends as husbands is not entirely irrational. These are the informal conjugal unions, characteristic of the *mapoto* type of marriage. The advantage is that such husbands or boyfriends usually take some limited responsibility for the welfare of these girls. Some wealthy clients pay rent for their girls, which is a major expense; given that there are accommodation problems in Harare, such financial help is a major plus in a relationship. The more enterprising prostitutes actually gain a great deal out of these pseudo-marriages. Given the status of a wife, they have easier access to the man's resources, thereby making it easier for the girls to steal from their unsuspecting husbands. One prostitute managed to withdraw all of the husband's money from the bank and disappeared. Others sell the men's property, and in the event of a pregnancy, they can claim maintenance. Usually, they do not get maintenance, especially if the "husband" is uncooperative. Generally, Zimbabwean men are not prepared to look after children of whose paternity they are not sure.

Normalized relationships are sometimes very exploitative. Some client–boyfriends can capitalize on these relationships and have sex for free, only to dump the girls at a later stage. This is not the plight of prostitutes alone. Nonprostitutes are sometimes cheated into believing that they have found "Mr. Right," only to be abandoned when the man gets tired of the girl. What makes the prostitute's position worse is that client–boyfriends who pretend to normalize the relationship often want to possess their prostitute girlfriends and demand that they only cater for their sexual needs, something that is inconsistent with the nature of sex work. This monopolization of the prostitute is no different from how ordinary men monopolize their wives in marriage. A major difference between married couples and a normalized relationship is the legal protection of wives, whereas such prostitute wives are legally unprotected. Also in a normalized relationship, the wife-prostitute can be hired in the presence of the boyfriend and sometimes with his active participation under a special arrangement in which the exercise is seen to be of mutual benefit. For example, this happens when the new client interested in the girl is known to have a lot of money that can be shared between them. Such client–boyfriends turn out to be pimps. In a normalized relationship, while girls are required to behave like good wives who do not engage in extra sexual relationships, the men are also required to behave like good husbands who regularly provide their girlfriends with money, security, food, and sometimes house rent. In reality, however, the balance of exchange is tilted in favor of client–boyfriends who often violate the verbal contract at will, as is shown in the case of Susan.

Susan, an *adventure girl* has a client–boyfriend who pays her rent. In the terms of the agreement, the boyfriend was to warn Susan in advance when coming to spend the night with her. As it turned out, Susan was never warned. On one occasion, Susan's boyfriend had come only to find her in bed with another client. The boyfriend demanded that the other man leave; she refused and to her disappointment, the boyfriend sat on her bed the whole night quarreling with her. These untimely visits to Susan's place and at awkward hours have paralyzed her income-generating project, and yet the boyfriend who claims rights over her does not take the full responsibilities of a husband toward her.

There is a problem here. If prostitutes survive through selling sex, why then do they agree to enter such exploitative relationships that temporarily jeopardize their business? As already noted, such calculated maneuvers are based on an instrumental rationality designed to maximize one's profits. Prostitutes utilize a variety of resources and strategies to secure for themselves relatively good deals with their clients. None of the girls considers prostitution to be a permanent occupation, and entry into prostitution, especially for the very poor, is an act of desperation rather than a carefully planned career path. Hence, most prostitutes consider their business to be temporary, which can be abandoned at the earliest convenient time, and so they are not committed to their trade. Insecurity within the trade leads to the development of a "you never know" attitude in case one of the clients may prove to be useful in the future. This type of attitude makes prostitutes take chances and so become involved in unstable and exploitative relationships.

Prostitutes with a negative attitude and those with a positive attitude toward marriage always try to behave like good girls, that is, to behave like nonprostitutes when in fact they are prostitutes. Their determination to uphold societal values, even when it is not necessary, explains why very few prostitutes are successful in their business. Zimbabwean society has instilled in women the importance of pleasing men regardless of whether or not it is beneficial to them. On one hand, prostitutes are workers; on the other hand, society expects them to be good wives and mothers. Failure to solve this contradiction between societal demands and the view of themselves as sex workers is responsible for prostitutes' inability to carry out their business in a professional way. Nonprostitute women also fail to advance professionally because of this apparent contradiction between their aspirations and what society expects of them.

THE MARRIED PROSTITUTE

Some prostitutes do marry, but, as the following case study illustrates, these marriages are characterized by gender conflict that often appears in the form of a struggle for equality and the elimination of various forms of gender oppression. Brenda is one of the *poverty girls* who desired marriage, but her story as a married prostitute illustrates the apparent contradictions between the concepts of marriage, prostitution, and freedom for women.

Brenda got married formally to Taruvinga, a soldier and one of her clients with whom she had been going out for five months. Brenda was introduced to Taruvinga's parents and relatives in the rural areas, who did not hesitate to accept her as Taruvinga's wife. Although Taruvinga took the normal steps in marrying Brenda, he did not pay *lobola* because Brenda had no parents to claim *lobola* from Taruvinga. Brenda's mother died, and her stepfather disowned her because she was a prostitute. She had some stepbrothers whom she did not particularly like because they criticized her for prostituting. In the traditional Shona society, it was assumed that the person who receives money paid as *lobola* would take responsibility for that girl in the event of a divorce or separation. Many men take the dollars but fail to look after the interests of the girls. Brenda had the sense not to let them get involved in her marriage plans, and so the marriage remained essentially a *mapoto* type.

In Zimbabwe, when a girl is married, she is expected to make certain social adjustments commensurate with the new status. Such adjustments normally include good public relations with the husband's relatives, and in the case of rural communities, the wife should be hardworking, generous, and sociable. Brenda successfully demonstrated these qualities required of a new wife. But these very same characteristics for which Brenda got praised, namely, sociability and generosity, proved to be counterproductive and cost her the marriage that she valued very much. Taruvinga became unhappy with her sociability and accused her of infidelity. He further complained that Brenda was excessively generous, giving out food, clothes, and money to friends. To make matters worse, Brenda continued to drink beer and to associate with other prostitutes. In fact, as soon as Taruvinga left for work, Brenda would also leave for the bar where she would spend the whole day boasting to her groupmates in prostitution that she was married. Sometimes she would come home late, drunk, and with a group of prostitutes whom she would have invited to come and see how successful she had become. There is nothing particularly wrong with this kind of behavior since many Zimbabweans like to display their achievements. What went wrong in Brenda's case, however, is that her friends, through peer pressure, forced her back into prostitution. Furthermore, when faced with financial hardship, she was unable to resist the temptation to get money through the sale of sexual services. Former clients and boyfriends continued to offer her money and to demand their share of sex. Matters became worse when Taruvinga tried to impose the discipline of a married woman on her. She resisted strongly, arguing that since the husband had not paid *lobola* he was not within his rights in trying to domesticate her. Brenda further argued that Taruvinga knew in advance that she was a prostitute and that he married her knowing the risks involved. It appears that Brenda was not prepared to give up her independence. She also pointed out that she had noticed, on several occasions, that Taruvinga was being unfaithful to her, and she argued that there was no reason why he should stop her from doing what he was doing. Tit for tat.

Although attitudes toward marriage are ambivalent and contradictory, prostitutes are ideologically united, and their behavior is the same both within and outside marriage. Brenda uses the same arguments as those used by her counterparts who reject marriage. Getting married should be seen more as a matter of convenience than as a commitment to the values of marriage. Even those who get married continue to practice prostitution, rationalizing this behavior by arguing, perhaps unreasonably, that since their clients agree to marry them well knowing that they are prostitutes, then the clients have accepted them as they are. In reality, however, the transition from prostitution to marriage is a painful exercise for the prostitute because it involves adjustments that contradict her daily experiences in prostitution. The process of adjusting to marriage involves a radical transformation of the prostitute's personal identity as well as her whole outlook on life. The movement from a relatively independent woman to that of a disempowered housewife entirely dependent on one man for survival presents a role strain for most prostitutes. As in the case of Brenda, she found the role of being wife incompatible with her previous experiences, and so she failed to adapt to her new status as a wife.

MARRIAGE—OPPRESSIVE AND EXPLOITATIVE

In contrast, *adventure girls* view prostitution as a more respectable trade than marriage. Prostitution is seen as a woman's emancipation from both male domination and the traumas and nightmares of marriage. This view is even stronger among prostitutes who had previous marital experience before entering the trade. From this group came one of the most relentless attacks on the institution of marriage ever heard. The adventure girls see marriage as an evil institution designed to imprison women and limit their capabilities. They have no respect for marriage, and they do not wish to remarry. Mary described how she sometimes gets clients who want to marry her, but the moment she knows that, she starts avoiding the men by not keeping appointments. Mary further argued that a man is yours when he is in bed with you, but when he is on the street, he belongs to every woman who wants him. Contrary to popular opinion, the girls do not see themselves as sexual objects because they determine when to have sex and with whom to have it. This situation is in contrast with that of married women who are forced to provide sex to their husbands even if the wives do not want to. Accordingly, married women are the ones who are actually used as sexual objects. Mary related how in her previous marriage, she was forced to have sex with her husband even when he had a sexually transmitted disease. She could not refuse because the role of a Shona wife is to be submissive to her husband. In marriage, men may use violence to get their own way. Mary proudly declared that now that she is a prostitute, she is master of her own body.

I am the owner of my body and I have power over it. I have the right to use it the way I want, to have sex whenever I have the sexual feelings. There is a lot of oppression in marriage. Married women are restricted in movements, yet men go wherever they want including coming to us prostitutes. Prostitution is what many women want, but they are denied the opportunity and oppressed by the so-called societal values which are nothing but a male moral code that should not apply to women. Women are deprived of *kunakidzwa* (sexual pleasure) because they are married, yet our clients are mostly married men. Is that fair? If you get a husband with a small penis, you will die without enjoying sex. We prostitutes are privileged because *hombe nediki hapana yatisingazivi* (we have tasted both big and small). Married women also like a big penis, but they cannot complain because they want to behave like good girls. They are just passive because they are afraid of being seen as prostitutes, but we, *makumbo tinovhura zvebasa* (we do sex as we like). That is why married women resort to extramarital affairs. Having one partner is suppressing one's sexual desires.

This prostitute is addressing fundamental issues that are often ignored and yet are crucial to the survival of modern marriages in Zimbabwe. The male double standard is clearly evident in her statement. Prostitution is, as argued earlier, an active political resistance to patriarchal control. Both married women and prostitutes provide sexual services to men, the former for economic, social, and emotional security and the latter for financial gains (Davis, 1961; Day, 1988). Married women have their sexual services paid for in advance in the form of *lobola* while prostitutes charge men as they come. The hostility generated toward prostitutes is related mostly to the fact that they directly charge men themselves, whereas in marriage the money is paid to men. Prostitution is an economic loss for Zimbabwean men, who as fathers and brothers usually gain a lot through the social management of women. When a girl becomes a prostitute, there are no economic rewards (bride wealth) to the parents—hence, in part accounting for the hostility generated toward prostitutes. Using women as objects of exchange for the benefit of males is quite common in many social situations that do not involve prostitution. In *roora (lobola)* men pay to marry women, but the money goes to other men (fathers of the girls). Men are the traders while women are the traded objects.

In a society in which men generally control women through marriage, the unmarried woman presents a serious threat to the established male order. Prostitutes are a contradiction in a male-dominated society; that is why prostitutes become the subjects of ridicule and targets of attack. While some prostitutes like Mary claim to belong to a category of emancipated women who have rights over their own bodies, a right that is denied to Zimbabwean married women, this research suggests that both prostitutes and some married women are oppressed by men. But while wives take it passively, the prostitutes are fighting back. Anger is expressed against men in these prostitutes' lives, and we also hear ambivalence to marriage; they want the benefits of marriage, yet they cannot find it because they do not trust men and do not want to lose their independence and sexual autonomy. Experience has taught the prostitutes that the majority of men they encounter are untrustworthy. Prostitutes are not against marriage per se but against aspects of marriage that are dehumanizing, especially a marriage that involves a rigid, unfaithful, and domineering husband. While previously married prostitutes may be speaking from their experience of the dehumanizing aspects of marriage, there is no doubt that the more educated prostitutes may be speaking under the influence of the current wave of feminism that is sweeping across the country. For their ideas are not new; they have long been expressed in feminist literature (see Kitzinger, 1987; May, 1983). Obviously, these women have little access to feminist literature because prostitutes often have little education. However, Zimbabwean women's anger is often evident in their conversations as they try to make sense of their own experiences. This is not theory but day-to-day description of events, and from these shared ideas, they draw conclusions about life, the nature of male–female relations, marriage, and various other matters pertaining to their lives.

Both married and single clients of prostitutes also expressed dissatisfaction with certain marital arrangements in Zimbabwe. Men's attitudes toward prostitutes should therefore be seen in the context of those satisfactions that marriage fails to provide, which create a high demand for prostitutes. Sixty percent of the male respondents argued that they seek the services of prostitutes because prostitutes are experts in sexual performance, doing it in different fascinating styles. Prostitutes satisfy men's sexual curiosity and fantasies by doing those things that married women and decent girls do not do for fear of being labeled prostitutes and yet that would greatly please their husbands and boyfriends (Mushanga, 1976: 96–97). Male respondents pointed out that sexual aggressiveness displayed by women prostitutes during sexual encounters, the way they dress, sit and talk, are all very appealing. There is an interesting contradiction here. Men would not normally want their wives and girlfriends to dress in miniskirts as prostitutes often do, and neither would they want them to be sexually aggressive, yet these are the very characteristics admired in prostitutes. A lot of divorce issues in Zimbabwe are related to conflict over double standards and the fight for freedom between husbands and wives.

CONCLUSIONS

This chapter has examined the relationships between bar prostitutes and their clients. It has also highlighted the complementary nature of prostitution, marriage, and normal courtship. Normalization may follow when a man wants to redeem a woman from prostitution, one who gives him sexual satisfaction, and when the woman feels accepted as she is. With the impending emancipation of women and their empowerment through education and employment, there is need to reassess relationships between men and women in Zimbabwean marriages. These prostitutes are questioning patriarchy and its denial of female sexuality. This issue is quite disturbing to many married women, many of whom are afraid to discuss it with their husbands. It can be said that the prostitutes' attitudes toward marriage illustrate the problems of cultural recontextualization of marriage and attempts at negotiating satisfactory sexual relations between men and women. Women enjoy sex just as much as men do, but problems arise when women do not respond to those desires men consider as axiomatic. Thus, if a woman claims her rights, she becomes unmanageable and unmarriageable, a plight that torments most women in "the women's rights movement." Evidently, marriage is an unsatisfactory institution that society insists on for reproduction, ignoring women's desire for sexual expression and satisfaction. So prostitution survives in order to guarantee the survival of the institution of marriage.

Although women prostitutes in Zimbabwe can be seen as cultural protesters and not merely as deviant women, their quest for sexual autonomy and independence cannot be achieved without economic empowerment. Depending on men for their "wages," women prostitutes are in a vulnerable position; as a result, they end up in unstable relationships that lead to further exploitation, oppression, and disease. In particular, the normalization of relationships between prostitutes and their clients leads to further problems such as failure to use condoms in sexual encounters, resulting in AIDS infection and unwanted pregnancies, which makes them even more dependent on their clients. There is therefore a need to professionalize prostitution in Zimbabwe so that prostitutes can avoid playing the role of the good girl. However, the legalization of prostitution may be far away, considering the fact that Zimbabwean society is sexually conservative and that the country has no organization representing the interests of prostitutes.

REFERENCES

Davis, K. (1961). "Prostitution." In R. Merton and R. Nisbet (eds.), *Contemporary Social Problems: An Introduction to the Sociology of Deviant Behavior and Disorganization* (pp. 262–288). New York: Harcourt.

Day, S. (1988). "Prostitute Women and AIDS Anthropology."*AIDS*, 2(6): 421–428.

Delacoste, F. and Alexander, P. (1987). *Sex Work: Writings by Women in the Sex Industry*. San Francisco: Clers Press.

Gaidzanwa, R. B. (1987). *Pornography: A Review of Pornography in the Zimbabwean Context*. Harare: College Press.

Heidensohn, F. (1985). *Women and Crime*. New York: New York University Press.

Kitzinger, C. (1987). *The Social Construction of Lesbianism*. London: Sage Publications.

McFadden, P. (1992). "Sex, Sexuality and the Problems of AIDS in Africa." In R. Meena (ed.), *Gender in Southern Africa* (pp. 157–193). Harare: SAPES Trust.

May, J. (1983). *Zimbabwean Women in Customary and Colonial Law*. Gweru: Mambo Press.

Moyo, S. (1991). *The Prostitution Question: With Special Reference to Zimbabwe*. Harare: Zimbabwe Institute of Development Studies.

Mushanga, T. M. (1976). *Crime and Deviance*. Nairobi: Kenya Literature Bureau.

Pfohl, S. (1985). *Images of Deviance and Social Control*. New York: McGraw-Hill.

Stewart, J. et al. (1990). "The Legal Situation of Women in Zimbabwe." In J. Stewart and A. Armstrong (eds.), *The Legal Situation of Women in Southern Africa* (pp. 165–241). Harare: University of Zimbabwe.

Wilson, D. et al. (1990). *A Health Education Pilot Study for a Program to Reduce Sexual Transmission of HIV among Commercial Sex Workers in Zimbabwe*. Harare: Department of Psychology, University of Zimbabwe.

Zimbabwe (1992). *Census Statistics*. Harare: Central Statistics Office.

Chapter 8

Unequal Opportunities and Gender Access to Power in Nigeria

Roseline C. Onah

INTRODUCTION

The relative position of women in society vis-à-vis their male counterparts has emerged as an important issue of concern in the global social arena. The prevailing view among numerous authors on the subject (Harrison, 1981; Leacock, 1972; Guillaume, 1956; Tade and Ademola, 1992) is that there is subordination of female to male gender in societies worldwide. Stewart and Winter (1977: 531) chose to use the concept of female suppression, describing suppression as "the interlocking complex of lower status and limited opportunities for women, as compared with men, in the sphere of law, education, the economy and social power." They posit that female suppression is widespread and pervasive in many cultures. The subordination, exploitation, and oppression women suffer are manifest in the roles they play in the society at large, ranging from the family through the society to government.

The situation is even worse in developing countries, as can be inferred from the following comment made by Paul Harrison (Egonmwan, 1991: 382).

The lot of women in the Third World is a hard one. They are the poorest of the poor, doubly oppressed by national and international injustices, and by family systems that give husbands, father and brothers the whip hand. . . . Men enjoy greater privileges, women bear greatest burdens. The unfair sexual distribution of power, resources and responsibilities is legitimized by ancient tradition, socialized into women's own attitudes, often enshrined in law, and can be enforced, where necessary, by male violence.

In fact, Harrison's comments summarize everything that can be said about the gender power relationship in Nigeria.

Instances of this unequal gender access to power both within and outside Nigeria abound. In Zambia, as Osei-Hwedie's chapter (Chapter 9) in this book illustrates, representation in decision making at all levels is very low. In the case of Nigeria in 1994, only 1 percent of councilors, 5 percent of members of parliament, and 8 percent of cabinet ministers were women (NGOCC, 1995: 4). As of March 1994, women accounted for only 8 percent of Ghana's members of parliament, and there were only 2 women out of 19 cabinet members (*West Africa*, May 8–14, 1995: 709). Out of the 21-member Executive Council in Nigeria as of January 1992, not one was a woman (Iromba, 1992: 13). On a brighter note, though still quite unsatisfactory, out of the present 36 members of the Nigerian Executive Council, 3 are women. These statistics lend credence to Harrison's statements about gender power relations in the Third World.

GENESIS OF UNEQUAL GENDER ACCESS TO POWER

Various authors (Kolb, 1978; Rowe, 1969; O'Barr, 1984) have defined power as the ability to influence another's behavior to one's advantage. In order to be able to influence the behavior of another, the power wielder must possess some resources, which can be used in a variety of ways. These resources include (1) legal authority; (2) prestige; (3) knowledge, information and expertise; and (4) wealth or varied forms of economic resources (Kolb: 41–48).

The law accords governments the authority to create and allocate various values, which are ordinarily cherished by most people and thereby influence people to support government and to obey its laws. Legal authority also affords government the right to use coercive instruments to influence behavior. People tend to respect the opinions of those with prestige and their supposedly superior views on what is just, rational, or in the public interest. Prestige as a power resource can flow from many sources. It may be rooted in the traditions or culture of a society.

Knowledge, information, and expertise are important resources of influence over and within governments. Contemporary governments need expert information in various specialized fields of economics, politics, and social affairs, and have become increasingly dependent on experts in such fields. Wealth or varied economic resources such as land, property, and, most importantly, money, can be used in a variety of ways to confer or deny needed or desired values on individuals or group targets and to influence their behavior.

This chapter discusses how women's limited access to these power resources has led to unequal gender access to power in Nigeria, a situ-

Table 8.1
Percentage of Females in Educational Institutions

	1988	1989	1990	1991	1992
Primary	42.4	45.0	43.2	43.8	44.1
Secondary	41.2	42.0	43.0	41.0	45.0

Source: Central Bank of Nigeria (1993).

ation that has put women in a disadvantaged position. Our immediate focus, however, is on tracing the genesis of unequal gender access to power within the country.

Access to Education

According to Ijere (1991: 7), in the past, women's education in Nigeria was calculated to achieve two objectives: to make good wives and mothers of women and to enable them to run the affairs of the home. The Nigerian woman participated fully in rural life, her role being delineated by custom. House and road sweeping, mediation among the men in times of conflict, and general regulation of the home belonged to women. Consequently, the preparation given to women for adult life in parts of the country revolved around giving them tuition in home management and etiquette, food preparation, and cultural training like dancing.

Right from the inception of modern education in the formal sector, women's education also faced considerable handicaps. Girls were sent to school after boys, and whenever problems arose over financing the children's education, the first dropout victim was always the girl. Girls were sometimes withdrawn from training and married off to support the boys for further studies. Women were considered to be inferior to men in status, and the role of women was considered to be in the domestic sphere (Ijere: 7–8). Child marriages were prevalent in many parts of the country, thereby denying girls educational opportunities. These unequal opportunities also manifested themselves in access to training facilities. When vocational centers like the Akure and Wusasa (Zaria) training centers were established, the girls were offered only domestic science subjects. Even when separate grammar schools were built for boys and girls, the curriculum differed, with science being omitted in most of the girls' secondary schools.

Statistics from the Central Bank of Nigeria (1993: 119) show that females also lag behind in school enrollment as shown in Table 8.1.

As Table 8.2 shows, the gender imbalance in education provision is

Table 8.2
Percentage of Female Student Enrollment in Polytechnics in Nigeria

	National Diploma (ND)			Higher National Diploma (HND)		
	Total	Female	Female as % of Total	Total	Female	Female as % of Total
1987–1988	26,992	8,450	31.3	8,717	1,971	22.6
1988–1989	40,187	14,721	36.6	1,009	2,651	24.0
1989–1990	42,053	14,359	34.1	30,404	3,033	10.0
1990–1991	45,728	14,009	30.6	14,685	4,102	27.9

Source: Federal Office of Statistics (1993): 163, Table 8.114.

even noticeable at the tertiary level, as reflected in the lower percentage of female enrollment in the polytechnics.

Access to Employment

In the Nigerian traditional setting, the man is the absolute breadwinner responsible for the whole of his family. A woman is responsible for domestic duties and helps with farmwork if the husband is a farmer. The Purdah system, which is both a cultural and a religious practice common among Muslims, forbids a woman in Purdah to go to work (Olotu, 1980: 994). Purdah is an Islamic practice that confines women to the home; if they go out they must cover all parts of their faces except their eyes. The above constraints put women in a disadvantaged position as regards access to employment. This disadvantage is reflected in the percentage distribution of female employees compared with the total, as shown in Table 8.3.

Table 8.3 shows that the highest percentage of female employees in total employment is 29.94, which is registered under local government. This is followed by 23.37 percent in state civil service employment. Only 5.61 percent of employees working under joint ownership by federal and state governments are female.

It is even more disheartening to realize that in secondary schools and teacher training colleges, which are supposed to be dominated by women, the female gender still lags behind (see Table 8.4).

As Table 8.4 shows, only in Anambra State Teacher Training Colleges did female teachers make up more than half (51.3%) of the total staff. No other state registered up to 40 percent female employees.

Table 8.3
Distribution of Employed Females Compared with Total Employment by
Type of Employers in Nigeria, 1986

Type of Ownership	All Employed Persons	Employed Females	Females as % of Total Employment
Federal Government Civil Service	146,403	30,786	21.03
Federal Government Parastatals	105,975	11,785	11.12
State Government Civil Service	297,428	69,496	23.37
State Government Parastatals	101,204	21,185	20.93
Local Government	95,863	28,697	29.94
Joint Ownership by Federal and State Government	22,136	1,241	5.61
Joint Ownership by Government and Private Interest	71,622	7,185	10.03
Purely Private Enterprise	235,422	27,976	11.88
Voluntary Agency	7,652	1,724	22.53
TOTAL	1,083,705	200,075	18.46

Source: Federal Republic of Nigeria (1989).

Access to Income

The cultural and religious factors that inhibit women's access to employment also impact on their access to income. Generally, more men are employed in the mining, construction, transport, communication, and banking sectors, which attract higher wages and other benefits. For instance, only 7.48 percent of the total employees in mining and quarrying in 1986 were women. The figures for manufacturing and processing; financial, banking, and insurance; and transport and communication were 9.28 percent, 14.72 percent, and 12.00 percent, respectively (Federal Republic of Nigeria: 61). The level of education and training possessed by both sexes often dictates this pattern of employment. In addition, con-

Table 8.4
Percentage of Female Employment in Educational Institutions in Select States in Nigeria, 1984–1985

	Vocational and Technical Colleges			Secondary Grammar and Commercial Schools			Teacher Training Colleges		
	Total	Female	% of Female to Total	Total	Female	% of Female to Total	Total	Female	% of Female to Total
Anambra	232	36	15.5	8,937	3,077	34.4	926	475	51.3
Bauchi	—	—	—	1,416	337	23.8	685	173	25.3
Bendel	597	166	27.8	11,275	3,190	28.3	746	228	30.6
Benue	178	17	9.6	3,328	514	15.4	432	60	13.9
Imo	307	78	25.4	11,360	3,684	32.4	331	89	26.9
Ogun	96	11	11.5	5,555	1,589	28.6	298	98	32.9
Plateau	98	4	4.1	2,277	564	24.8	429	136	31.7
Rivers	194	22	11.3	4,667	713	15.3	89	27	30.3
Sokoto	86	9	10.5	1,012	253	25.0	682	152	22.3

Source: Federal Office of Statistics (1985): 75, 78, 81.

struction and transportation are regarded as too rigorous physically for women and are therefore viewed as areas exclusive to men.

The dual careers—wage earning and motherhood—undertaken by women also inhibit their access to income, particularly among women who are not on salaried income such as petty traders and daily-paid wage earners. Procreation is detrimental to the economic position of women who are not on salaried income. For at least three months after having a new baby, a nursing mother cannot carry out commercial activities that will generate income. Even when she is deemed fit to engage in commerce, she faces the problem of who will take care of the baby. Consequently, the woman with a young baby often settles for less demanding and less income-yielding ventures, for she has to carry her baby while she does her business. Therefore, Nigerian women generally earn less income than their male counterparts.

The Structural Adjustment Program (SAP) has worsened the plight of Nigerian women. Among the structural adjustment measures adopted by Nigeria are reduction in government expenditure and removal of government subsidies on some commodities. For instance, the removal of government subsidy on electricity resulted in an over 600 percent rise in the electricity tariff (Onah, 1995: 116). The price increase has had the effect of raising household expenditure on electricity and hence reducing the disposable income that would otherwise have been available for spending on other goods and services.

The removal of government subsidies also has resulted in a higher price for a liter of petrol from 70 kobo to Naira 3.25 and then to Naira 11.00 (Onah, 1995: 117), and kerosene, which ought to be the cheapest cooking fuel, from 50 kobo to Naira 2.75 and then to Naira 6.00. This increase in the price of kerosene impacts more on women who are traditionally responsible for obtaining fuel for cooking.

For most women, adjustment programs mean longer hours of work, both paid and unpaid. More time is spent on maintaining a household as a result of reduced resources. Women have to spend more hours shopping for food and other needs of the home. Sometimes they may have to travel many kilometers in search of cheaper products in view of their limited resources. Cooking, washing, and other household chores have become more cumbersome, as inferior facilities are now utilized for these tasks. This situation is worse among rural women who are also essentially poorer and unable to procure some household gadgets that aid urban women in their household tasks. Thus, recession and structural adjustment influence women's access to power because economic difficulties make it harder for women to participate in public activities so that they can have access to positions of power and decision making.

THE INFLUENCE OF RELIGION

Religion has generally contributed to relegating women to a secondary status. For instance, Islam contains an ideology of gender and embodies assumptions about women. The positive elements of this ideology include the extension of basic legal rights in marriage, divorce, and property. However, it excludes women from holding formal office in the governing structures of the religious community. Thus, even though Islam ensures basic rights, it does not necessarily guarantee equality since each of these rights is limited when compared with those of men (Strobel, 1992: 94).

Women under Purdah cannot exercise their franchise since the system does not permit them to vote along with other people. As noted above, women in Purdah are not supposed to be seen by men other than their husbands. Moreover, lower class women are less bound by the propriety demanded by Purdah than are upper class women, who are more likely to aspire to positions of power. This point supports the inhibiting nature of the system.

Similarly, the spread of Christianity reinforced gender differences. Christian missionaries brought with them to Africa strong beliefs in the "separate spheres" of male and female activity. The role of women was that of mother and wife, whereas politics and the running of the church belonged to the world of men. Hence, in most Christian denominations, women generally occupied a secondary position.

Women also occupy secondary positions within the African traditional religion. They have important roles to play in activities relating to women such as being ritual specialists or belonging to the spirit possession cult. However, where such cults are hierarchically structured, females are subordinate to men. In most cases, they cannot play the role of priests. Even food used for the worship of some idols is taboo for women. Therefore, by relegating women to secondary status, all the various religions practiced in Nigeria constitute obstacles to women's access to power.

WOMEN AND POWER POSITIONS

A cursory look at the gender makeup of the important positions of the Nigerian political setup portrays gender bias. Right from its emergence as a country, Nigeria has neither had a female president/head of state nor a vice president. No woman has been the chief executive of any of the regions or states. Out of the 95 members of Nigeria's Senate during the Second Republic (1979–1983), none was a woman, while only 3 of the 450 members of the House of Representatives were women (King-Akesode, 1980: 818).

During the attempt to establish a Third Republic, which was quashed with the annulment of the June 12 presidential election in 1992, 11 women vied for the governorship of their various states, but none of them won (Nkemakolam and Ebonugo, 1991: 22). As regards appointed posts, Nigeria registered its first women federal ministers/members of the Federal Executive Council under the Abacha regime, as already mentioned. Out of these female ministers, two were ministers of state, equivalent of junior ministers. The one individual fully in charge of a ministry was responsible for the Ministry of Women Affairs and Social Services. At the state level, women commonly serve as commissioners to nonsensitive departments such as Health, Education, Information, Youth, Sports, and Culture. No woman has ever been made the commissioner for Finance, Works, Commerce, Industry, or other ministries whose tasks pose greater challenges.

TOWARD IMPROVING WOMEN'S ACCESS TO POWER: POLICIES AND PROGRAMS

The existence of gender imbalance in access to power is nationally recognized. Various policies adopted by regimes in Nigeria to ameliorate the situation have been carried out under various ministries and agencies.

Federal Ministry of Social Development, Youth, and Sports

One of the earliest official institutional frameworks for policy outputs directed toward the development of women in Nigeria is the Federal Ministry of Social Development, Youth, and Sports. Women development policies of the various states of the Federation are informed by national policy direction from this ministry. However, the Federal Ministry of Social Development, Youth, and Sports receives input from the states' Department of Community Development.

Programs for development of women at the state level, therefore, fall under the purview of the Community Development Directorate of the Ministry of Social Development, Youth, and Sports. Prominent among such activities is home economics, including day care center management, which according to official declaration is "designed to enlighten women in rural areas on modern methods of home keeping and child care" (Bendel State Government, 1982: 118). Program objectives include improvement of family living conditions, nutrition, health, and sanitation, and improvement in the literacy rate. The sum of 2 million Naira was allocated for the women's development program in the Bendel State Fourth National Development Plan (1980–1985).

The Federal Ministry of Education

This ministry is the official channel of promoting activities for the development of women. These activities are carried out under the women education program of the ministry. Under this program, the ministry has a blueprint on every aspect of women in both the non-formal and formal setup for its guidance. The Adult Education Program of the ministry also represents policy instruments for enhancing women's development. An extract from the 1989 capital budget submissions of the Bendel State Ministry of Education shows that the federal government had set up the National Adult Education Agency. It subsequently directed all state governments to set aside 5 percent of their capital budget on education for the Agency (Egonmwan, 1991: 390).

Another overt policy, which the Federal Ministry of Education has formulated for improving the educational situation of women, is the establishment of a scholarship scheme for interested female candidates who excel in science, technology, mathematics, and other science-related subjects. Two technical colleges have been devoted to enhancing women's development in the country (*Daily Times*, May 31, 1989).

Under its nonformal education scheme, the Federal Ministry of Education has established model centers in Lagos and other cities in the country for the teaching of science, technology, and mathematics in elementary forms (*Daily Times*, June 12, 1989). This scheme was designed to put women on a sound footing in their various businesses in addition to integrating the rural women, in particular, into the social and economic mainstream of the country.

The Better Life Program for Rural Women (BLP)

The Better Life Program for Rural Women (BLP)—also discussed in Chapter 4 in this book—is by far the most ambitious program mounted in Nigeria for the improvement of females. This program was set forth in 1987 under the auspices of the wife of the then president, Mrs. Maryam Babangida. The objectives of the program, include the following (Federal Republic of Nigeria, 1992: A 361).

1. To stimulate and motivate rural women to achieve better living standards and to sensitize the rest of the Nigerian population to the problems of women.
2. To mobilize women collectively in order to improve their general lot and ability to seek and achieve leadership roles in all spheres of society.
3. To educate rural women in simple hygiene, family planning, and the importance of child care and to increase literacy rates.

4. To raise consciousness about the rights of women, the availability of opportunities and facilities, and their social, political, and economic responsibilities.
5. To inculcate the spirit of self-development, particularly in the fields of education, business, the arts, crafts, and agriculture.

The organization of the program was hierarchical, with the wife of the president at the apex as the chairperson. The National Organizing Committee (NOC), which was also the think-tank of the BLP, assisted her. At the state level, the wife of the governor was the chairperson and the state committee assisted her. The third level of organization was the local government in which the wife of the local government chairman was the program's chief coordinator. She, in close consultation with the state committees, was to mobilize women leaders and the bulk of the women in the local government, ward, village, and community levels (NOC, 1991: 4).

The strategies laid down for attainment of the objectives include the following:

1. Enlightenment campaign, study tours, and visits.
2. Radio broadcasts and television discussions educating women and the general public about BLP's objectives.
3. Organizing seminars and workshops.
4. Field days—BLP fairs and cultural displays at both the district and village levels, aimed at generating interest.

National Commission for Women

The National Commission for Women (NCW) was established by Decree 42 of 1989 (Federal Republic of Nigeria, 1992: A 361). This was in line with the resolution marking the United Nations Decade for Women (1975–1985) that member states should seek to establish a national machinery for integrating women in national development. The commission is charged with carrying out the aims and objectives of the BLP, which have already been discussed. Other functions of the commission include the following:

• To stimulate actions to improve women's civic, political, cultural, social, and economic education.
• To encourage the sense and essence of cooperative societies and activities among women in both urban and rural areas and to stimulate in them creative entrepreneurship in the field of cottage industries.
• To work toward the total elimination of all social and cultural practices tending to discriminate against and dehumanize womanhood.

• To support the work of governmental organizations and to play a coordinating role between government and the Nigerian women's organizations.

Other Programs

Certain institutions have no direct or statutory relationship with the development of women but carry out activities that positively impact on the enhancement of the status of women. Such institutions include the Directorate for Social Mobilization (MAMSER) and the Directorate of Food, Roads, and Rural Infrastructure (DFRRI). MAMSER was created by the government in 1987 to promote new sets of attitudes and culture for the attainment of the goals and objectives of the Nigerian state. The Directorate also had to establish an appropriate framework for the positive mobilization and education of all Nigerians toward economic recovery and development, and a new social and political order (Directorate for Social Mobilization, 1987: 2).

In order to achieve the above objectives, the Directorate had to engage in mass mobilization, political education, and mass education. These activities were aimed at generating greater productivity, creating a new and positive political consciousness among the masses, and promoting mass literacy. The National Orientation Agency (NOA) has now replaced MAMSER and performs similar activities to the Directorate.

As the name implies, the activities of DFRRI are directed toward the uplift of life in the country by assisting in the provision of food, roads, and rural infrastructure. To attain these set objectives, the Directorate (Ezeani, 1995: 46) has initiated various programs. These are general programs that are expected to be of benefit to the entire Nigerian populace, including women. DFRRI therefore elicits women's participation in its numerous programs, including those of political development and social mobilization.

During the 1995 Federal Executive Council reshuffle, a Ministry of Women Affairs and Social Services was established. A woman, Ambassador Judith Atta, headed this agency. This ministry was expected to concern itself with all matters that affected the welfare of women in the country. In addition, the wife of the then head of state, Mrs. Maryam Abacha, introduced the Family Support Program (FSP). The introduction of FSP, which then replaced the BLP, was perceived essentially as a political action aimed at creating the impression that the president's wife had a new program to her credit. The FSP was expected to perform similar activities as the BLP. However, according to the initiator of the program, it was supposed to be more encompassing than the BLP. It was designed to focus on the family as a whole (including the father and children), both rural and urban, and not just rural women. The Family Support Trust Fund has already been launched in every state capital and in Abuja. The hierarchical organization of FSP is similar to that of the BLP.

POLICY EVALUATION

The numerous policy and program responses designed to enhance opportunities for greater women participation in national affairs, and hence their greater empowerment, have been highlighted. These represent bold attempts to improve the women's situation in Nigeria. Next, a critical assessment of the real impacts of these policies and programs is provided.

Social Development and Education

As already mentioned, the Ministry of Social Development, Youth, and Sports has embarked on activities directed toward enhancing the socioeconomic status of women and their access to power. In connection with this endeavor, by 1983, the former Bendel State Women's program had successfully turned out 59,200 rural women who participated in the 6-week to 12-month training program organized for rural women. The program facilitated the establishment of 38 day care centers and 115 women's community development centers, manned by 500 trained female frontline workers (Egonmwan, 1991: 394).

Both women's and the adult education programs of the Ministry of Education have been directed toward developing and expanding the intellectual base of women, which as a result of the past social apathy to women's education had afforded them less opportunity than their male counterparts. The Ministry of Education has embarked on mass adult education, as is reflected in Table 8.5, which shows the adult literacy enrollment percentages in Nigeria.

The table shows that in no year did female enrollment reach 50 percent. This is a disturbing situation because by 1989 only 37 percent of African women were literate as against 56 percent of the men (Snyder, 1990: 9). Even though the current literacy ratio for both sexes in Nigeria is not readily available, the situation will not be very different from the rest of Africa. This lower response emanates from the harsh economic situation in the country, which makes it difficult for women to participate, and the uncooperative attitude of men toward their wives' participation. Such men feel that since their wives would not get a salaried job through literacy classes, the idea is a waste of time.

The Better Life Program

Various attempts have been made to evaluate the Better Life Program (Okoye and Ijere, 1991; Egonmwan, 1991; Central Bank of Nigeria, 1993;

Table 8.5
Females as a Percentage of Adult Literacy Enrollment in Nigeria, 1987–1991

Year	Total	Female	Female as % of Total
1987	520,376	182,042	35.0
1988	724,939	288,774	39.8
1989	618,830	281,044	45.4
1990	674,954	298,659	44.2
1991	620,296	253,240	40.8

Source: Federal Office of Statistics (1993): 163, Table 8.114.

Nwosu, 1989). The consensus opinion is that the BLP has made remark-able achievements and has therefore been a success. For instance, the Central Bank of Nigeria (CBN) has a checklist of facilities provided under BLP, including cooperative societies, maternity clinics, vocational train-ing centers, livestock farms, and cottage industries (CBN, 1993: 115–119). Specifically, the CBN pointed out that the number of cooperative socie-ties established under BLP rose from 5,479 in 1991 to 9,044 in 1992. (This latter figure differs from that of NOC, which is 9,492.) In agriculture, about 481.9 tons of seeds and 79,860 bundles of cassava cuttings were distributed to women farmers in 1992. Livestock farms increased from 194 in 1991 to 282 in 1992 (CBN, 1993: 115). Okoye and Ijere (p. 180) highlight the fact that just about two months after the launching of the BLP, the United Bank for Africa (UBA) came up with a credit scheme for rural women, by which loans would be given to them for farming, poultry keeping, piggery, and trading. The Afribank has also developed a Female Credit Scheme for similar purposes as that of UBA.

Enlightenment and awareness campaigns were important strategies adopted by the BLP toward the attainment of its objectives. To this end, two BLP fairs were organized in Lagos in 1989 and 1990, respectively (NOC, 1991: 9). These fairs were aimed at providing new market outlets and economic links for women. They were also meant to create a forum for interaction, cooperation, and joint ventures between rural women and urban entrepreneurs. Better Life markets were also established and lo-cated in state capitals, the Enugu Better Life Market being a case in point. Although these fairs and markets may have been well intentioned, their locations made them counterproductive. After all, how many rural women actually went to Lagos for the fairs? Implicitly, the beneficiaries of the fairs were essentially urban women. The BLP also worked closely with MAMSER toward the sensitization and mobilization of women. Through the use of jingles and songs, information was transmitted to the people via the mass media (radio and television), creating a lot of awareness among the women.

Although these statistics on the achievement of the Better Life Program may sound very plausible, they are not without snares. For instance, the above-mentioned bank credit schemes have stringent conditions attached to them that make it very difficult for most women to benefit from them. The Afribank scheme requires a minimum financial base of Naira 12,500. In addition, a feasibility study must be conducted on the project, while it must also be self-financing in terms of servicing the loan. These are by no means easy conditions for the average Nigerian woman to satisfy.

Most of the organizers and participants of the BLP were not committed, as is evidenced in the amount of dishonesty exhibited by its members. On many occasions, the supposed multipurpose cooperative societies never really carried out any serious commercial or business activities. They were there as showpieces to attract loans and funds whenever opportunity arose. There were cases of members of farming cooperatives planting their own sign posts against farms belonging to individuals in the event of a visit to their zone from a higher body of the BLP. In addition, goats were collected from individuals and presented as belonging to the society.

The general organization of the BLP left much to be desired. The fanfare and flamboyance that accompanied the activities of the BLP right from its launching in 1988, through the two fairs, cast doubt on the real motives of the entire program. The categories of women that occupied various offices of the program at all levels and thus dominated the activities of the BLP were highly elitist. This elitism is also reflected in the site of the two fairs held in Lagos and those of the Better Life markets. The rural nature of the program was not reflected in the hierarchy, even at the local government level. This is why the program acquired the derogatory name of "Better Life for Urban Women." Offices in the BLP were also highly politicized, and people lobbied heavily for them. Consequently, personal interest overrode that of the organization, and officials took to personal aggrandizement. The above lapses limited the effectiveness of the BLP as an instrument for empowering Nigerian women.

Writers on DFRRI (Muoghalu, 1992) have highlighted the achievements of DFRRI in the areas of construction and extension of rural feeder roads, rural water, rural electrification, food, and agriculture. DFRRI is also said to have been able to supply a continuous flow of information to the general public on the Directorate's activities. However, some of the DFRRI's claims to success have been criticized as unfounded.

There have been cases of false claims of road construction by the Directorate and also of its taking credit for tasks performed by other bodies. Whatever the success of DFRRI may be, as already mentioned, the Nigerian woman benefits only as a member of the generality of the Nigerian rural population.

MAMSER (now NOA) has done a lot to make Nigerians aware of their rights, especially in the political arena. Through drama, jingles, and talks on the radio and television, MAMSER has created a great deal of political and economic awareness. Posters (such as those illustrating the proper use of the naira or currencies) were also utilized to deliver the message. However, apart from assisting the BLP in the mobilization process, MAMSER does not have a statutory relationship with women's development.

NIGERIAN WOMEN AND ACCESS TO POWER: THE WAY FORWARD

The genesis of gender imbalance in access to power in Nigeria has been traced to social and economic factors. These have created situations that have greatly limited female access to power resources. Official policy responses toward ameliorating this social problem have also been discussed. Based on the information available, it has been argued that these policies have not had much impact because they have been essentially elitist. Consequently, they have not been made accessible to most Nigerian women who live in the rural areas, at the grassroots.

Women's Education

The most expedient approach to women empowerment is through enhancing their education. In the words of Morna et al. (1993: 15). "When women learn, everyone benefits." Literacy has also been described as a springboard that will enable women to become active and informed participants in all areas of development—hence the adage that "knowledge is power." Education imparts knowledge and therefore, empowers the individual. Education will enable women to understand and appreciate their handicaps and therefore join in efforts to ameliorate their situation.

The enhancement of women's education as proposed in this chapter should start with ensuring the education of the female child. The education offices at the local government councils should collaborate with community organizations and social groups to ensure that no child of school age is denied education by its parents. The federal government should also initiate legislation making it an offense, punishable under the law, for parents to offer their female children who are below 18 years old for marriage. This would at least ensure that such children would complete their secondary school education before marriage. Such a law should be strictly enforced through the traditional rulers of various communities. Any breach of the law should be immediately communicated to the local government headquarters for the law to take its course.

The scholarship program established for the support of female candidates who excel in science and technology is a step in the right direction. The program should be expanded so that at least one female student benefits from it in the terminal class in every secondary school in the federation. With regard to functional education for women, more special science schools for girls should be established. It is important that these colleges not be concentrated in the urban areas but rather should also be located in rural areas. This will ensure adequate female participation, since the economic situation in the country has made it extremely difficult for the average Nigerian to be able to maintain a child in a boarding school. A similar situation exists in Jordan, where schools were segregated by sex and parents were unwilling to allow their daughters to travel far to school. The policy reaction was to build smaller and more dispersed vocational schools for girls which were located near their homes (Warren and Stokes, 1985: 489).

The on-going adult education program run by the Ministry of Education is quite commendable and should be pursued with greater vigor. The enrollment figures as presented in Table 8.5 are impressive. Adult education should be seen as a welfare scheme and should therefore be heavily subsidized by the government through the provision of books and other necessary materials. More centers should also be established, especially in the rural areas.

Toward the Proper Self-Concept

Nigerian women need to be motivated and mobilized to develop the right self-concept. The self-concept, as Harry Sullivan once said, is composed of the "reflected appraisals" of others (Maduewesi, 1980: 872). Through learning the opinions, attitudes, and expectations of others, the person, beginning from childhood, learns who he or she is. Nigerian women have not received positive appraisal by men and have been made to believe that they are second-class citizens. The role of women has been limited to the domestic sphere. This has influenced the kind of education and training they have been given, which in turn is reflected in their self-concept. Nigerian women have perceived their role in society as inferior and as supportive of men's position. This fact has been re-echoed from a wider perspective: Frantz Fanon (1967: 217) observes that "The woman in an undeveloped society, and particularly in Algeria, is always a minor, and the man—brother, uncle or husband—represents first of all a guardian. The young girl learns to avoid discussions with the man, not to 'aggravate the man.' "

This negative self-concept must be shed, and Nigerian women must be sensitized to its undesirability, for it contributes to the lack of support for women aspirants, even from members of their own sex. This is where the FSP can take up from where BLP left off. Enlightenment talks and drama aimed at raising the self-esteem of women should be organized both in the media and in the various rural localities. The FSP should guard against elitism which militates against the goal attainment of BLP. It should also make itself available to the women by meeting them in their natural habitat and should make use of mobile schools and demonstration teams. The message should be clear: Women must join together to raise the image of womanhood; women must support other women.

Once women are fully sensitized, nongovernmental organizations such as the National Council of Women Society (NCWS), Women in Nigeria (WIN), and other women-oriented organizations will have fertile ground for operation. They can, as in the case of NCWS (King-Akesode, 1980: 822), fight for the abolition of government laws that deny a woman the "full right to sign contracts and to be considered in her own right as a fit and proper person to stand surety for herself in her own cognizance or for others." Similar demands as that made by Alhaja Hajia Gambo Sawaba for the liberation of women bound by Purdah for their active participation in politics (King-Akesode: 822) could be pursued with greater vigor in collaboration with the FSP. Legislation should also be sought against the improper treatment of widows in the name of tradition in different parts of the country. The Nigerian Association of Women Lawyers should emulate the International Federation of Women Lawyers (FIDA) in Ghana, which has been operating a legal service program since 1985 (*West Africa*, May 8–14, 1995). Under this program, women are educated as to their legal rights and responsibilities, and free legal representation for needy women is provided. Since 1985 FIDA has handled 2,347 cases including child maintenance and intestate succession.

"Gender Touch" and "Human Face Strategy" for SAP

In view of the adverse effect of the Structural Adjustment Program (SAP) on the entire population and on women in particular, the program should be modified to give it a "human face" and a "gender touch." This approach requires greater selectivity in public expenditure cuts, the removal of subsidies, and greater self-reliant food production. If user charges are introduced for social services, these charges could be differentiated. Greater increases in charges for electricity, water, and sanitation services could be introduced for those living in wealthier urban areas compared to low-income areas. Fees for university students could be increased instead of fees for secondary schools. In a country like Nigeria, where most secondary schools are under the control of state governments that have limited resources, the federal government should increase state allocations in that sector. This will help forestall exorbitant rises in school fees, which contributes to the dropout of girls at this level.

Governments should also be selective in removing subsidies on petroleum products. There should be only a minimal increase in the price of petrol since it generates a chain effect that invariably leads to price rises in every segment of the economy. Kerosene is the cooking fuel for the low-income earners. Removal of the subsidy on kerosene (hence leading to a price rise) will always have a more devastating effect on the poor, especially women who are traditionally responsible for cooking fuel. Subsidies on kerosene should therefore not be removed. In addition, cuts in government expenditures should be gradual and spread over a period of time so that the average citizen can absorb the shock.

Emphasis should shift to self-reliant food production instead of export crop production as often advocated by the World Bank, which has been unable to produce the desired effect (Elson, 1989: 73). Emphasis on self-reliant food production entails increasing the productivity of small-scale women cultivators who are less dependent on imports and who grow foods that are staples for poor groups, like cassava, maize, and rice. Policy reforms to this effect include directing more inputs and support services to women cultivators. Furthermore, the land tenure system should be reformed to give women the right of ownership and access to land.

CONCLUSION

This chapter has attempted to establish the existence of gender imbalance in the position of power and decision making in Nigeria. The origin of the imbalance has been traced to the African (hence Nigerian) tradition and culture, which has subordinated women to men. Consequently, women have been socialized into accepting the fact that their role in the society is domestic and that they are supporters of men, and therefore receivers, rather than makers of policy. Because of this wrong perception of women's role in society, Nigerian females have been denied equal access to education and training, which would have afforded them the chance to compete with their male counterparts for employment and positions of authority on an equal footing. Women, therefore, generally have less access to positions of power.

Policy measures adopted by various Nigerian governments to ameliorate the problem have not been very effective because of their elitist character. The programs have not been sufficiently geared toward rural women, who constitute more than 50 percent of the total rural population (Egonmwan, 1991: 405), and of course a greater percentage of Nigerian women. It has been recommended that these policies be made more goal oriented. Most importantly, more resources should be channeled toward enhanced female education.

Kenneth Little (1973: 16) credits women with being less responsive to offers of place and office and less open to corruption. It is common knowledge that one of the greatest problems facing Nigeria is the abuse of office mainly in the form of bribery and corruption. Based on the above premise and Little's observation, it follows that Nigeria will benefit immensely from an increase in the number of women who occupy positions of power. These women can serve as important role models for the male counterparts and other women, demonstrating the need for honesty and uprightness on the part of public officers and competence that has hitherto been ascribed mainly to men.

In view of the potential benefits from giving women increased access to power, governments should use the following indicators in planning to ensure adequate female representation.

• Percentage of women in the total membership of legislatures.
• Percentage of women in the top four levels of the civil service ministries, including departments, commissions, and boards.
• Percentage of women in private sector senior management.
• Women as a percentage of all illiterates.

These indicators should be frequently updated for the purpose of planning and policy making.

REFERENCES

Bendel State Government. (1982). *Bendel State 4th National Development Plan, 1981–85*. Benin City: Official Document No. 3.

Boserup, E. (1970). *Women's Role in Economic Development*. New York: St. Martin's Press.

Bullough, V. L. (1973). *The Subordinate Sex: History of Attitudes Towards Women*. Urbana: University of Illinois Press.

Central Bank of Nigeria (CBN). (1993). *Annual Report and Statement of Accounts for the Year Ended 31 December 1992*. Lagos: Central Bank of Nigeria.

Daily Times. (1989). Lagos, May 31.

———. (1989). Lagos, June 12.

Directorate for Social Mobilization. (1987). *MAMSER Handbook*. Lagos.

Egonmwan, J. A. (1991). *Public Policy Analysis: Concepts and Applications*. Benin City: S.M.O. Ada and Brothers Press.

Elson, D. (1989). "The Impact of Structural Adjustment on Women: Concepts and Issues." In Onimode Bade (ed.), *The IMF, the World Bank and the African Debt: The Social and Political Impact* (pp. 56–74). London: Zed Books Ltd.

Ezeani, E. O. (1995). "The Directorate of Food, Roads, and Rural Infrastructure (DFRRI) and Rural Development in Nigeria." *Nigerian Journal of Public Administration and Local Government,* 6(2).

Fanon, F. (1967). *A Dying Colonialism.* New York: Grove Press.

Federal Government of Nigeria. (1989). *Four Years of Babangida Administration.* Lagos: Federal Government Printer.

Federal Office of Statistics. (1985). *Social Statistics in Nigeria.*

———. (1988). *Social Statistics in Nigeria.*

———. (1993). *Annual Abstract of Statistics.*

Federal Republic of Nigeria. (1989). *Report of the Survey of Nigeria's Manpower Stock and Requirements, 1986.* Lagos: National Manpower Board.

———. (1992). *Supplement of Official Gazette Extraordinary,* 40(79). Lagos: Federal Republic of Nigeria.

Guillaume, A. (1956). *Islam.* Revised ed. Baltimore, MD: Penguin Books.

Harrison, P. (1981). *Inside the Third World.* Harmondsworth: Penguin Books.

Ijere, M. O. (1991). "Mobilizing Women Power for Nigeria's Economic Development." In M. O. Ijere (ed.), *Women in Nigerian Economy* (pp. 7–21). Enugu: ACENA Publishers.

Iromba, A. E. (1992). *Past and Current Affairs in Nigeria.* Enugu: Vickson Press.

King-Akesode, M. C. (1980). "Women and the Political Process in Nigeria." In F. I. Omu, P. K. Makinwa, and A. O. Ozo (eds.), *Proceedings of the National Conference on Integrated Rural Development and Women in Development,* Vol. 2 (pp. 816–828). Benin City: Center for Social, Cultural, and Environmental Research (CENSCER).

Kolb, E. (1978). *A Framework for Political Analysis.* Englewood Cliffs, NJ: Prentice-Hall.

Leacock, E. (1972). Cited in Leith Mullings (1976), "Women and Economic Change in Africa," in N. J. Hafkin and E. Bay (eds.), *Women in Africa.* Stanford, CA: Stanford University Press.

Little, K. (1973). *African Women in Towns.* London: Cambridge University Press.

Maduewesi, E. (1980). "Self Esteem: A Psychological Dimension of Female Socialisation." In F. I. Omu, P. K. Makinwa, and A. O. Ozo (eds.), *Proceedings of the National Conference on Integrated Rural Development and Women in Development,* Vol. 2 (pp. 877–885). Benin City: Center for Social, Cultural, and Environmental Research (CENSCER).

Morna, L. C., Chola, M., Issoufou, B. K., Kelimwiko, L., and Safo, M. (March 1993). "When Women Learn, Everyone Benefits." *African Farmer,* 15–21.

Muoghalu, L. N. (1992). "The Task Force Approach to Rural Development in Nigeria: An Evaluation of the Directorate for Foods, Roads and Rural Infrastructure." In M.S.O. Olisa and J. I. Obiukwu (eds.), *Rural Development in Nigeria: Dynamics and Strategies* (pp. 297–312). Awka: Mekslink Publishers.

National Organizing Committee (NOC) of Better Life Program. (1991). *Four Years of the Better Life Program.* Lagos.

Newswatch. (1995). Lagos, April 3.

Nigerian Institute of Social and Economic Research. (1988). *Social Impact of the Structural Adjustment Program*. Ibadan: NISER Monograph Series No. 1.

Nkemakolam, J. and Ebonugo, M. (April 1991). "Politics of the Weaker Sex." *Platform*.

Nongovernmental Organization Coordinating Committee (NGOCC). (1995). *Expose and Eradicate Gender Discrimination*: Lusaka: United Nations Fourth World Conference on Women, Beijing.

Nwosu, I. E. (ed.). (1989). *History and Achievements of the Better Life*. Enugu: Office of the State Coordinator.

O'Barr, J. (1984). "African Women in Politics." In M. J. Hay and S. Stichter (eds.), *African Women South of the Sahara*. New York: Longman Group Ltd.

Okoye, C. U. and Ijere, M. O. (1991). "Role of the Better Life Program in National Development." In M. O. Ijere (ed.), *Women in Nigerian Economy* (pp. 175–183). Enugu: ACENA Publishers.

Olotu, B. (1980). "Impediments of Women's Labor Participation in Nigeria." In F. I. Omu, P. K. Makinwa, and A. O. Ozo (eds.), *Proceedings of the National Conference on Integrated Rural Development and Women in Development*, Vol. 2 (pp. 994–1000). Benin City: Centre for Social, Cultural and Environmental Research (CENSCER).

Onah, R. C. (1995). "The Socio-Political Implications of Privatization and Commercialization in Nigeria." *Nigerian Journal of Public Administration and Local Government* 1, 105–125.

Rowe, E. (1969). "Modern Politics." In *An Introduction to Behavior and Institutions*. London: Routledge and Kegan Paul.

Snyder, M. (1990). "Women the Key to Ending Hunger." *The Hunger Project Papers* (8).

Stewart, J. A. and Winter, D. G. (1977). "The Nature and Causes of Female Suppression." *SIGNS, Journal of Women in Culture and Society*, 2(3), 531–553.

Strobel, M. (1992). "Women in Religion and in Secular Ideology." In M. J. Hay and S. Stichter (eds.), *African Women South of the Sahara*. London: Longman.

Tade, A. A. and Ademola, T. S. (eds.). (1992). *The Challenge of Sustainable Development in Nigeria*. Ibadan: Nigerian Environmental Study/Action Team (NEST).

Warren, C. B. and Stokes, M. T. (1985). *Investing in Development: Lessons of World Bank Experience*. Oxford: Oxford University Press.

West Africa. (1995). London, May 8–14.

Chapter 9

Constraints on Women's Participation in Zambian Politics: A Comparative Analysis of the First, Second, and Third Republics

Bertha Z. Osei-Hwedie

INTRODUCTION

This chapter analyzes the role of Zambian women in politics since independence. The study of women's political role is important because, first, they make up the majority, 51 percent, of the Zambian population (Republic of Zambia, 1995: 1), and consequently the majority of the electorate. Second, political parties and politicians readily mobilize women for political support; therefore, women are more visible in political activities in terms of attendance at political rallies, demonstrations, and voting. Third, the degree of their involvement in politics is reflected in the nature of the government's policies. Where women occupy a considerable number of policy-making positions in government, there is more likelihood that policies will reflect their interests. Underrepresentation of women in positions of authority is likely to result in inadequate apportionment of government resources, such as jobs and finances, to them as a group. The United Nations acknowledges the importance of involving women in decision making in order to promote equality between men and women, provide opportunities for realization of their potential, and formulate appropriate policies for the fulfillment of the goals of development, especially on issues that affect them (Graham and Jordan, 1980).

The first section of this chapter provides a theoretical analysis of women in politics in Africa. The second section examines Zambian women as political actors. The precolonial and colonial situations are analyzed because they determine the nature of women's political participation in the post-independence period. This is followed by a review of the role of women in the First, Second, and Third Republics. The primary focus is on the latter two periods because only limited data are available for the First period. Women's participation as voters, candidates, decision makers, and pressure groups shows the extent of their role and the nature of gender relations in Zambia. Attention is also given to identifying the type of women who have been active participants in politics since independence. In addition, government policy on gender is explained. The third section of the chapter examines the constraints on women's effective role in Zambian politics. Lastly, a short conclusion is provided with some recommendations.

The political role of women in Zambia is best understood by analyzing the country's political development, which is divided into three periods. The first period extended from independence in 1964 to 1972, when Zambia had a multiparty system. The United National Independence Party (UNIP) was the dominant, ruling party, with the African National Congress (ANC) the opposition party. The second period was the One Party Participatory Democracy from 1972 to 1991. From 1964 to 1991, President Kenneth Kaunda and his party, the UNIP, ruled Zambia. The Third Republic began in 1991 with the reintroduction of multiparty politics, based on the principles of liberal democracy. In that year President Frederick Chiluba and his party, the Movement for Multiparty Democracy (MMD), was voted into power with a landslide victory. The 1996 presidential and parliamentary elections returned President Chiluba and the MMD to power in elections boycotted by some opposition parties, including the UNIP, because of alleged constitutional and electoral irregularities.

WOMEN AND POLITICS IN AFRICA: AN ANALYSIS

Although the chapter focuses on Zambian women's participation in politics, its observations can be generalized to the rest of Africa, especially Southern Africa. This is because most African countries share common characteristics, such as a patriarchal culture. In general, women in African, and developing countries, operate in the same political environment controlled by males. Therefore, this section presents definitions and a generalized theoretical analysis of women and politics in Africa. According to Hague et al. (1992: 156), political participation is "activity by individuals formally intended to influence who governs or how they do so." In short, political participation encompasses citizens' involvement in politics to influence the choice of public policies, administration of public affairs, and choice of national or local leadership of government (Weiner, 1971).

The most common form of women's participation is voting. Women in most of Africa make up the majority of the population, 51 percent

(United Nations, 1995). Therefore, they have been an important source of electoral support for politicians since independence. However, analysis of the women's vote reveals that their vote is manipulated and mobilized by men through political parties to elevate themselves to power at the expense of women. McFadden's (1990–1991) analysis of women in Botswana, showing that, politically, men have used the women's votes to acquire power positions, aptly applies to the rest of the African continent.

Analyzing the representation of women in decision-making positions, Parpart and Staudt (1989: 8) have observed that "women occupy minute numbers of decision-making positions in all African states," both democratic and nondemocratic. Data for the mid-1980s indicate that women represent only 6 percent of legislative members in Africa. There are even fewer women in executive positions such as cabinet ministers. "Half of the states in Africa have no women in the cabinet at all" (Parpart and Staudt, 1989: 8). The few women cabinet ministers are confined to lowly placed ministries like community development. For example, currently Botswana has one woman minister out of a total of 10. The 1990s did not witness a radical improvement in women's political position in Africa in spite of democratization.

African women have not passively accepted their disadvantaged political position. According to Gordon (1992), one option open to women has been to form organizations to collectively pressure for change through articulation of their needs, demands, and problems. The 1970s experienced an increase in the number of women's organizations, especially after 1975, the International Women's Year. It was during this period that international organizations and donor agencies "began to promote women's groups in the hope of improving women's economic, political, and social positions" (Gordon, 1992: 213). However, women's organizations have had limited success in promoting gender equality in the political arena.

Furthermore, most of the African states have adopted some mechanisms to redress gender inequalities in politics through adoption of gender-sensitive policies and special machinery for women. Such approaches were adopted partly as a result of local and international pressure to include women in the overall process of development (Gordon, 1992). Policies include provision of maternity leave, equal employment opportunities, and equal property rights (Afshar, 1996). Suggestions were also made that policies be established regarding women's access to land, capital, technology, training, and other productive resources (Gordon, 1992). African governments, including Cameroon, the Gambia, Botswana, Lesotho, Zambia, and Zimbabwe, created special women's units, bureaus, ministries, or committees to deal with women's issues (Gordon, 1992: 214). In addition, Afshar (1996) has observed that many political parties in African countries, especially one-party regimes, formed women's wings. Gordon (1992: 214) argued that some African states, like Tanzania, adopted another approach to increasing women's political participation in government by setting aside 10 seats in the legislature for women.

Different explanations have been given as to why women's efforts to change political inequality between men and women have yielded little results. Feminist and Marxist theories, as a single framework, offer the best explanation of gender inequalities. Feminist theories explain that gender inequalities are caused by the "patriarchal structure of society and its institutions" (Taylor et al., 1987: 224)—that is, "male dominance of the family, the economy, the government and other important institutions in society" (pp. 224–225). Marxist theories see gender inequality as a product of a capitalist economy, with attendant class divisions and property ownership that oppress women who make up the majority of the working class (Barrett, 1980; Taylor et al., 1987; Little, 1994). Parpart and Staudt (1989: 8) point to the lack of higher education and wage employment to explain why there are few women at the top of the decision-making hierarchy. Without substantial income or any other resources, due to low-wage jobs and economic dependence on husbands as heads of the family, women find it hard to compete effectively in politics and to exert political influence.

With regard to women's policies, Afshar (1987: 3) notes that the problem is that African governments "do not have coherent policies about women, nor do they usually have structural facilities for coordinating their decisions." Furthermore, the existence of national machinery, for example, bureaus, has not brought more women into positions of authority because such institutions are there primarily to control women's participation and to mobilize women's support and votes rather than to advance women (Afshar, 1996). Gordon (1992) argues that the problem with the women's bureaus is that they have not been given adequate power and financial resources to carry out their functions effectively. She argues further that bureaus, as government organs, "cannot be highly critical of government policies and push for radical change" (Gordon 1992: 214). Thus, the "greatest problem is that women and women's groups do not challenge the fundamental gender roles that subordinate them to males and extol the sexual division of labor that gives wealth and power primarily to men" (Gordon, 1992: 213). This, according to Gordon (1992), is partly attributed to the control of women's organizations by educated middle-class women who accept Western and African views that a woman's place is in the home. The constraints on women's participation in politics in Africa in general, and in Zambia in particular, are discussed further below.

Political analysts are optimistic about the future prospects for women in spite of the ineffectiveness of women's organizations in overcoming gender inequalities in politics. Gordon (1992: 214) observed that women's organizations are "expanding women's consciousness and building self-confidence and leadership skills that will be necessary for bolder and more effective political activism in the future."

WOMEN AS POLITICAL ACTORS IN ZAMBIA

The Precolonial and Colonial Context

The situation of women in the precolonial and colonial periods strongly determined their role in the post-independence period. In the precolonial period, there was a marked sexual division of labor between men and women, and on the whole, men predominated in all spheres of life. However, women were allowed to occupy political positions such as "headmen" among the Tonga of Zambia, and they made decisions about women's affairs in most precolonial societies (Gordon, 1992: 203). Some women inherited the chieftainship among some matrilineal African tribes. The advent of British colonialism ended women's influence in politics. The colonial state, based on indirect rule and the Western notion of gender relations, relied on male chiefs and headmen and gave preference to males in the economic sphere as well, thereby marginalizing females in all spheres of life—a trend that has changed relatively little in the post-independence period. The independence struggle reactivated the role of women in politics. However, except for a handful of women (four, according to Ferguson et al., 1995: 2) who were actively involved in political organization, Zambian women played a minimal, indirect role during the independence struggle. While men, mobilized by both the ANC and UNIP, were at the forefront of civil disobedience, women mostly played a passive role by morally supporting their spouses and relatives who were engaged in confrontation with the British colonial administration.

Women in Politics in the Post-Independence Period

Political independence meant that all citizens had the right of the franchise. For women this meant they could engage in several activities, including choosing political leaders, influencing public policies through petitioning and lobbying, contesting public office, joining and working for political parties, attending public meetings, and contributing to campaigns. Such acts are designed to support and make demands on government (Weiner, 1971). Women's impact in the political arena is felt through the exercise of their voting power. Although election results are not analyzed on a gender basis, it is assumed that women make up the larger number of voters since they constitute the majority of the population. Presidential and parliamentary elections in Zambia offer the electorate the opportunity to participate in the political process by choosing between competing political parties during the multiparty era, and choosing between rival candidates during the one-party system. Therefore, women as voters, contribute to the popularization and legitimization of leaders.

Through the vote, women determine the composition of government, including the president and members of parliament (MPs). The turnover of MPs and the president since independence illustrates the power of the voters to choose or eliminate political leaders. Closer analysis, however, reveals that the Zambian women's vote is manipulated and mobilized by the men through control of the political parties to elevate themselves into power at the expense of the females. This generalization is valid for both pre- and post-1991 periods.

Women also serve in leadership positions. However, there are only a few women in positions of political authority, either as leading members of parties or as members of government, for both elective and appointed positions. This is because few women contest elections, and even fewer women candidates are named by the parties, which are dominated by males. Moreover, few women win parliamentary seats. For example, the 1964 elections brought in three female MPs, as did the 1968 elections (Government of Zambia, 1968). There were no women ministers from 1964 to 1968, and there have never been more than eight female MPs and members of the Central Committee (MCC) of UNIP since the attainment of independence and during the one-party state, respectively. The MCC was the supreme policy-making organ of the party and hence of the state.

A comparison of the three periods in Zambian political history suggests an increase in the number of women elected as MPs, with more women MPs in the Third Republic. During the First Republic, voting choices were made on the basis of party affiliation rather than on the individual merit of a candidate. The candidates elected to parliament on both the UNIP and ANC tickets tended to be full-time local party members (Chikulo, 1988). Since few women were actively involved in the ANC and UNIP, it follows that very few were selected as candidates by either party, hence the figures: three women MPs in 1964 and in 1968. Being an MP was the only decision-making position open to women.

The Second Republic saw more women in political leadership positions than the previous one. This was partly due to political appointments and to the creation of positions and institutions by the UNIP which never existed in the First Republic, including the Central Committee, provincial political secretaries, district governors, district political secretaries, and district Women's League chairpersons. One would have expected greater participation by women as candidates during the Second Republic, primarily because under the one-party system, based on participatory democracy, the character and qualification of a political candidate determined his or her success at the polls (Chikulo, 1988). Every candidate had a common platform, the UNIP. Therefore, the electorate chose the one who responded favorably to their interests and needs as well as made frequent visits to the constituency.

However, the criterion of individual personality did not enhance women's chances of winning elections as the election results of the Second Republic indicate. After the elections in 1973, 1978, and 1983, females made up 3 percent, while males comprised 97 percent of all elected MPs. There was a slight improvement in 1988 when females accounted for 5 percent of all elected MPs (Government of Zambia, 1973, 1978, 1983, 1988). The data show that the role of women as parliamentary candidates and MPs is marginal: Few were selected as candidates by the UNIP, and on average less than half of those who stood in elections were successful.

The same pattern of few women presenting themselves and being selected as candidates for parliamentary elections continued into the Third Republic. The percentage of women candidates increased from a low of 1 percent in 1978 to 4 percent in 1991. Females made up 5 percent of all elected MPs after the 1991 elections, and the ratio of women to men MPs improved slightly from 1:34 to 1:20 (Government of Zambia, 1978, 1991). Therefore, political liberalization, following the 1991 elections, has been no panacea for women's underrepresentation in parliament. By-elections held since the 1991 elections marginally increased the number of women MPs from the original eight (seven elected and one nominated) to nine. The 1996 elections also saw an increase in the number of women candidates who won parliamentary seats totaling 16, or 11 percent of all elected MPs. Of the 16 elected, 12 (75%) were for the MMD, 2 (13%) for the Agenda for Zambia (AZ) party, and 2 (13%) independent. However, since the MMD won more seats in 1996 (131) compared to 125 in 1991, one would have expected women to win more than the 12 seats (9% of total seats) under the MMD.

There has been a change in the type of women who contest parliamentary elections. In the First and Second Republics, women who contested parliamentary elections had a low level of education, whereas those who did so in the 1991 elections under the MMD were well educated (including university graduates), professional, salaried, and allied with a business class (Ferguson, Ludwig, et al., 1995). The same trend of educated women contestants was reflected in the 1996 general elections. However, a breakdown of the 16 women MPs by ethnic group shows the predominance of Bemba speakers numbering eight (50%), followed by five (31%) Lozi speakers, two (13%) Nyanja speakers, and one (6%) Tonga speaker. The distribution also represents major tribes of Zambia in politics just as in the previous government of Kaunda. Therefore, it is safe to assume that those tribal considerations and the interests of their constituencies rather than representation of gender interests in government would primarily guide such women. This assumption is strengthened by the fact that women's issues and gender equality have never been part of the political debate during electoral campaigns by either the women candidates or the MMD party. However, there is a strong belief among women in government that "women bore the major responsibility for articulating these (women's) interests in debates and policy formulation" as "men were not likely to do so" (Ferguson, Ludwig, et al., 1995: 19).

The local government elections held in 1992 also supported the view that women refrain from presenting themselves for elections and that the party leadership dominated by males discriminates against prospective women candidates. For example, of the 86 candidates running for local government offices in Ndola, only 2 were women standing on the UNIP ticket. Other parties, including the MMD, failed to adopt women candidates during primary elections due to discrimination against them as aspiring candidates. The 1992 MMD primary elections in Ndola failed to select a woman who had polled more votes than her male colleagues as the MMD candidate for local government elections in preference for a male (Sunday Times of Zambia, November 8, 1992). Thus, even at the local level there is unequal power sharing between men and women. For example, there were more male mayors (22) than female (1) and more male councilors (1,113) than female (16) in 1994 (Republic of Zambia, 1995: 19).

Women fared worse in the cabinet appointments made following the 1996 general elections. President Chiluba appointed only one woman minister and four women deputy ministers. Again, of the five, three (60%) are Bemba speakers, one (20%) is a Lozi, and one (20%) a Tonga, again reflecting Bemba dominance in national politics. Five women permanent secretaries have retained their positions. In addition, after the 1996 elections, President Chiluba appointed four men and no women to parliament. Compared to the First and Second Republics, women appointed to government in the Third Republic are well-educated and of the middle and upper classes.

One would expect women to fare better in political appointments to decision-making positions in government and political party structures. Ideally, political appointments to government and ruling party posts are expected to reflect a wider representation of the population. This was supposed to be the norm under the one-party system as the party was supposed to represent mass interests, including those of women. However, tribal rather than gender balancing was the underlying determinant of political appointments. Tribal considerations were reflected in the appointment of women to leadership positions as follows: three Bembas, one Nyanja, and one Lozi in the MCC in 1988. This mirrors the dominance of Bemba males in politics and raises the question of whether women appointed on such a basis would promote gender interests rather than tribal ones. The most glaring facts about the political role of women during the Second Republic are:

1. Women were relegated to lower level political positions, primarily at the district level.
2. Few women were found in important leadership positions such as minister, MCC, ambassador, or high commissioner. For example, from 1978 through 1991, there was no woman minister.
3. Women were confined to women's positions, for instance, district Women's League chairpersons. The majority of women (i.e., 59 in 1980) were in this category (Party and Government of the Republic of Zambia, 1985).

The trend toward male dominance of females in parliamentary and ministerial positions continues into the Third Republic. It would appear that a liberalized political atmosphere associated with democratization does not necessarily lead to more representation and participation in decision making by females. President Chiluba, like his predecessor, has not utilized his power of nomination of MPs to boost the number of women in the National Assembly, for he nominated only one woman MP as opposed to three men in 1991. Similarly, after the 1991 elections, President Chiluba's first appointments included no woman cabinet minister and only four women deputy ministers. This was worse than the situation under the Kaunda government, which had two women in the cabinet in the 1970s. However, after the resignation of some ministers, including one woman deputy minister and the cabinet reshuffle of April 1993, women deputy ministers were elevated to full ministerial posts. There were only 2 women cabinet ministers out of a total of 23 ministers and 1 woman deputy minister out of a total of 32 deputy ministers. In addition, there were five women permanent secretaries and three women in charge of foreign missions credited to Germany, France, and Kenya. In 1994 the number of females in the Foreign Service was reduced to two due to resignation and the closing of one of the embassies. Nonetheless, women are still underrepresented in decision-making structures in the MMD government and administration, thus perpetuating the traditional dominance of men in positions of authority. President Chiluba's appointment of women to the cabinet and foreign missions reflected tribal preferences, just as Kaunda before him. Although the president claims to be oblivious to tribal balancing, women were drawn from each of the major tribes dominant in politics: four Bembas, two Lozis, and one Tonga, by 1994.

Government Gender Policy

The marginalization of women in politics can be explained by lack of proper and effective government gender policy. Gender policy and practice can be analyzed at three levels: overall national policy on women; policy on women in development; and sectoral policies targeted at women. With regard to a national policy on women, neither the UNIP government nor the MMD government has developed an explicit government policy on women targeted at promoting gender equality in all spheres of life—such as legal, administrative, social, and economic. The MMD's position is a radical departure from democratic principles which it espouses and its 1991 Manifesto which, in the section on Women in Development, portrayed itself as a champion of gender equality as part of its election promise (Movement for Multi-Party Democracy [MMD], 1991: 10). This may raise the suspicion that the MMD merely intended to attract the vote of women and had no serious intention of fulfilling its election promises.

A national policy on women would be in line with Chapter 1 of the Arusha and Nairobi Forward Looking Strategies (FLS) and the United Nations Convention on Elimination of All Forms of Discrimination Against Women which the UNIP government ratified in June 1985 (ZARD, 1994: 12). Unfortunately, neither the UNIP nor MMD government has formulated a national policy to mirror the policies of the regional and international conventions on women. However, there is an implicit government policy on women which dates back to 1985 (UNIP era) and continues under the MMD government. This implicit policy restricts itself to reforms of some laws that overtly discriminate against women. Thus, the government has revised several laws to end legal discrimination against women in the areas of employment, age of retirement, widows' inheritance, personal income tax, right to citizenship of foreign spouses, and protection of women against discrimination on the basis of sex as per the 1991 constitution formulated by UNIP (ZARD, 1991: 12, 20–21). It should be noted, however, that such legal reforms have been cosmetic in that they have not substantially affected gender discrimination.

The second level of analyzing gender policy and practice focuses on government policy on women in development. The UNIP government had a policy on Women in Development (WID) contained in the Fourth National Development Plan (FNDP), 1989–1993, but the MMD government conveniently failed to adopt it in 1991, for no reference was made to it in the party manifesto or in the development programs, including successive budgets. Consequently, at present, there is no policy on gender and development. Under the UNIP government, Chapter 25 of the FNDP, focused on WID. Such a focus was designed to allow for total participation and integration of women in the development process with a view to improving their socioeconomic conditions (Republic of Zambia, 1989: 441). The focus on Women in Development in the FNDP was apparently in line with national, regional, and international programs, including UNIP's Women League Program of Action, 1987–1995; Arusha and Nairobi FLS for Advancement of Women Beyond the UN Decade for Women to the year 2000; Africa's Priority Program for Economic Recovery and Development (UNPAAERD), 1986–1990; and the Convention on Elimination of All Forms of Discrimination Against Women (Republic of Zambia, 1989). In the absence of data and the UNIP's fall from power in 1991 (two years after the start of the FNDP), it is difficult to assess the practical impact of the Women in Development policy on the economic condition of women. However, the fact that the emphasis was on integration of women into the development process rather than on gender equality in access to economic resources meant that it was limited in objective and fell short of the requirements of regional and international conventions, but were more in line with the objectives of the Women's League.

The liberalized economic policy of the MMD government since 1991 meant the abandonment of centralized planning. Consequently, the FNDP and centralized planning on gender and development were abandoned, too—a big step backwards for women's development. However, the MMD government inherited the Women in Development (WID) Department of the National Commission for Development Planning (NCDP). The WID Department, which under UNIP was responsible for coordinating and monitoring women's development projects, has been reduced to data collection on the situation of women by the MMD government since 1991 (ZARD, 1994).

Lastly, lack of an explicit national policy on gender also means lack of a gender-based approach at sectoral and provincial levels. Under the government of UNIP, the FNDP provided for sectoral planning for women in all sectors and fields of the economy. Therefore, each ministry, department, and unit (i.e., Provincial Planning Units) had to have objectives, strategies, and investment programs for implementation (Republic of Zambia, 1989: 443). But with the coming to power of the MMD, the initiatives of the UNIP government fell away. In their place is a decentralized, selective approach by each ministry and province. Consequently, very few ministries and provinces have anything resembling a policy. According to ZARD (1994: 4), the Ministries of Health and Water Development "recently produced draft policy statements." Similarly, the Luapula Provincial Planning Unit (PPU) "has established a Gender Oriented Development Policy." The gender policy followed by the Luapula PPU is based on UNIP's policy on women's equal access to productive resources. However, the gender-based policy formulated by the Ministry of Education and Luapula Province were heavily influenced by donor agencies funding programs there (ZARD, 1994: 14). As long as donor agencies make gender equality a condition for financial assistance to various ministries, departments, and provinces, there is a likelihood of a positive development in sectoral and provincial policies on women.

The nonexistence of a national policy on gender has meant lack of national machinery devoted to gender issues in the MMD government. However, this appears to be changing. President Chiluba found it worthwhile to create two special desks at the State House for religion and youth immediately after the 1996 elections (*The Post*, December 3, 1996). Although he did not do the same for women at that time, in early 1997 he appointed a permanent secretary for women's affairs. Thus, although democratization has not meant that women's issues occupy a high position on Zambia's policy agenda, it appears that the basis of a special machinery for women has been created. At least under the UNIP government the party established national machinery in the Women Affairs Committee as the Ninth Committee of the Central Committee. The Women Affairs Committee was responsible for presenting and promoting women's issues to the party and government (Party and Government of the Republic of Zambia, 1985; ZARD, 1995: 15). Unfortunately, the Women Affairs Committee failed to lobby the party and government for equal sharing of power between men and women. But it was influential only in securing paid maternity leave for working women, a very limited impact, though beneficial to working mothers.

In the MMD Manifesto of 1996 (MMD, 1996: 16–17), the government claims that it "has developed a comprehensive policy for Women in Development which embraces full and equal rights to women in all aspects of life." However, in reality, the MMD government only has rudiments of WID policy because the Manifesto is a checklist of what the government intends to do for women from 1996 onward. The checklist promises to form the basis of what Moser (1994) calls the equity approach to WID.

Women's Organizations as Political Pressure Groups

The foregoing discussion on the marginalization of women in politics and the lack of an explicit national policy on women has shed light on political participation by women. This participation can be looked at from two viewpoints: participation circumscribed by the political party as in the case of the Women's League of UNIP; and an independent, self-generated participation through voluntary women's organizations like the Zambia Association for Research and Development (ZARD), the National Women's Lobby, and the Non-Governmental Organizations Coordinating Committee (NGOCC). These and other women's organizations, unwilling to accept the marginalization of women and lack of government policy and action, initiate action to promote gender equality. Thus, this section compares the political role of women's organizations in the Second and Third Republics since there were no women's groups in the First Republic. Women's nongovernmental organizations (NGOs) are supposed to promote the interests of women by exerting pressure through petitioning and lobbying both government and ruling parties, the UNIP and the MMD.

In 1975, the Women's League was created as the political organ of the UNIP. Originally, it was known as the Women's Brigade. Created by the male leadership of the party, the Women's League became an instrument for mobilizing and coopting the support of women (Ferguson, Ludwig, et al., 1995: 3) and for showing that the party had provided an avenue for participation by women. This in turn shaped the nature of the League's membership and role in politics. Since its inception, League membership has been small and has been drawn from older, urban women, primarily wives, with little or no formal education, and petty traders. Therefore, it failed to attract the support of the majority of Zambian women.

The role of the League was reduced to the mobilization and political education of women, support for male politicians, and entertainment of male leaders with dances at political rallies and airports. This meant that the League upheld the women's traditional role as mother, wife, and supporter of males in politics without challenging the predominance of males in the decision-making structures of the party and government. Ferguson, Ludwig, et al. (1995: 3) candidly sum up the situation: "Men created the Brigade, directed its organization, policies and activities and appointed its officials." "Brigade members were not intended to seek power for themselves. . . . Women's political role was 'backstage' and this was 'natural'." The same was true for the League.

Geisler (1987: 59) illustrates the marginalization of women in the League and decision making on gender issues. In 1985, when the League requested the establishment of a special women's commission to identify laws that discriminate against women on the basis of sex, the minister of legal affairs, a man, turned down the request. Similarly, in 1986, women headed only two of the five ad hoc committees of the Women Affairs Committee of the Central Committee. Instead of allowing the League to address women's issues, UNIP confined it to nonpolitical issues like moral and behavioral issues, especially the wearing of wigs and miniskirts, and prostitution among urban women. These "immoral" acts were seen as the root cause of economic decline in Zambia (Geisler, 1987: 48); Ferguson, Ludwig, et al., 1995: 3). President Kaunda's government discouraged the League from addressing the problem of gender discrimination, while neglecting national problems like discrimination based on religion and creed. In view of its constrained role, it is no wonder that the League was unable to push for a higher number of women in positions of authority. There were two women cabinet ministers during the early 1970s, and during 1984–1985, there were no women cabinet ministers, only four women MCCs, two women ministers of state, and two MPs (Geisler, 1987: 60). This situation improved relatively little by 1988.

A few attempts by the League to address gender issues proved futile. For example, as stated above, the male leadership of the party spurned its request for a special women's commission and for 50–50 representation in parliament and the Central Committee of UNIP (Geisler, 1987: 48, 59). However, the League was useful for lobbying government and the party to promote the interests of its members, especially petty traders, and it served as a springboard for the advancement of its members into positions of authority (Geisler, 1987: 46, 57), although only a handful of them were appointed to government positions.

The League's inability to address gender issues alienated it from the majority of women, both urban and rural, and determined its credibility as a champion of women's issues and its membership. The League's attack on "immoral" acts of the urban women and support for banning unescorted women in hotels and bars after 18 hours as well as its aversion to educated women incurred the wrath of these women. Similarly, its support for a proposal to encourage rural women to increase output to feed the nation demonstrated its lack of appreciation of the difficulty rural women faced in growing food for household consumption and its blind adherence to party policies. Such a stance by the League, guided by its belief in the women's traditional role, meant that the few young, educated, and professional women were left out of the League and consequently out of politics. Such women turned to alternative women's organizations to articulate their interests. Religious, research, and professional NGOs readily accommodated them. Formation of NGOs, including women's organizations, was restricted under the one-party state because UNIP required all important issues to be addressed within the legal party structures. In the case of women's NGOs, they were either to be cleared by or affiliated to the League, which in effect restrained open discussion of gender issues by such women's organizations. This explains why very few women's NGOs existed in the Second Republic, numbering 10 in 1980 and increasing to 17 in 1985 (ZARD, 1994: 15). Nevertheless, in the absence of total control of every organization by UNIP, women's NGOs were able to address gender issues as welfare issues.

ZARD, a nonpolitical organization, was formed in 1984. Unlike the League, it has been able to address gender issues. With a high membership estimated at 500, it is composed of educated, elite women (ZARD, n.d.). Its mission is to carry out "participatory, action-oriented and gender-sensitive research and undertake consultancy, publishing and networking aimed at empowering women" (ZARD, n.d.). Thus, it is geared to the advancement of the position and interests of women through advocating gender equality in party and government posts, employment opportunities, distribution of economic resources, and the general welfare of women. ZARD's success has been evident in numerous publications designed to provide data on, and publicize, the socioeconomic situation of women, including laws, housing, education, inheritance, and political participation. ZARD has channeled its dissatisfaction with women's position through seminars and the media, and it has urged governments to improve women's position. ZARD's ability to conduct research and publish its works is largely due to financial assistance from international donor agencies like the Norwegian Agency for International Development (NORAD), the Royal Netherlands Embassy, and the United Nations Development Program (UNDP).

ZARD's efforts to promote gender equality are best understood as a collective effort with other women's NGOs. For example, together with other women's NGOs, ZARD lobbied government to ratify the UN Convention on the Elimination of All Forms of Discrimination Against Women. In addition, it was due to heavy lobbying of MPs by ZARD, NGOCC, and other women's NGOs that the redrafted bill on Wills and Inheritance became law to provide widows with legal rights to property. Two Acts were passed—the Intestate Succession Act No. 5 of 1989 and the Wills and Administration of Testate Act No. 6 of 1989. The first applies when the deceased has left no will, and it provides for sharing property among the widow or widower (20%), children (50%), parents (20%) and dependents (10%). The second act is administered based on the will left by the deceased (ZARD, 1996: 63–64).

Although women's NGOs, including ZARD, have been accused of being elitist in orientation, they have tried to promote the general interests of women of different social backgrounds. Under UNIP, ZARD's efforts had limited success primarily because gender issues had not been a priority for UNIP's leadership. This did not deter ZARD and other women's NGOs. They have continued their struggle for gender equality into the post-1991 regime.

In spite of resistance from the male political leadership, the Third Republic has witnessed greater activity by women's NGOs. This is partly attributable to the liberalized political atmosphere that allows for freedom to form associations, partly because of women's greater awareness and determination to promote gender equality in all spheres of life. Yet another contributory factor has been the increased level of donor funding. Thus, by 1994, there were 34 women's NGOs devoted to the promotion of women's issues (ZARD, 1994: 15). But again, as was true in the past regime, the success of women's NGOs is constrained by the paternalistic state they are challenging, which has tended to resist their demands.

The following discussion focuses on the National Women's Lobby, NGOCC, and other women's NGOs as they collectively initiate pressure on the MMD government. The Women's Lobby was formed in 1991 during the transition to multiparty politics and continues to exert pressure on government, together with other organizations like ZARD and NGOCC. Its major objectives are mobilizing women to actively promote gender issues; lobbying government to appoint more women into public offices; promoting equal power sharing between men and women; and encouraging all women candidates to stand for public office, regardless of party affiliation. Other objectives include pledging financial assistance and skills training to all women candidates; mobilizing women voters to rally behind women candidates; and reorienting attitudes of the general public toward women (*The Weekly Post*, January 22–28, 1993). In 1995, the Women's Lobby made submissions for equal rights for women to the Constitutional Review Commission responsible for drafting the constitution. Despite the fact that the 1996 constitution provides for "equal worth of men and women in their rights to participate" (Government of Zambia, *Act No. 18*, 1996: 637), the provision for "succession to property and assets" remains a contentious issue, and women's interests are still inadequately addressed. The Intestate Succession Bill of 1996, meant to repeal and replace the Intestate Succession Act of 1989, was withdrawn from parliament after protests from women's NGOs. This was because, among other things, the bill has contradictory provisions and loopholes, and it is unfair to women as it assumes that all property (i.e., a house) belongs to the husband. Moreover, it does not provide for the consent of the surviving spouse in appointing an administrator of the estate. For the 1996 elections, the Women's Lobby mobilized election funds for women candidates through Support Women Campaign Fund, but it was unable to generate sufficient resources.

Efforts by women's NGOs to lobby and pressure the MMD government have proved to have very limited effect. For example, as discussed earlier, after the 1991 elections, President Chiluba, to the amazement of women's NGOs, failed to appoint a woman to the cabinet. Consequently, "a broadly based NGO Petition was presented to the President at State House" (ZARD, 1994: 9). Six months later in a cabinet reshuffle, three women were promoted to ministers in a cabinet of 23, which was a very small victory for women's NGOs. However, the efforts of women's NGOs from 1992 through 1994 to pressure the MMD government to adopt a national policy and machinery for advancement of women had been futile. In March 1992, a delegation from five NGOs presented a petition to President Chiluba demanding fulfillment of election promises for gender equality and establishment of a national machinery to implement election promises on gender equality. The lack of a positive response from the president prompted women's NGOs to try a different approach. In August 1992, women's NGOs formulated a blueprint of organizational options for the establishment of national machinery for women. Both the NGOCC and the WID Department at the NCDP submitted proposals and policy options to the MMD government on how to establish national machinery for women's advancement. These proposals were discussed by a joint consultative meeting between the president's special assistant for the press, the WID Department of the NCDP, the MMD WID Committee, and the NGOCC. Instead of the president's special assistant accepting the proposals, he requested that the NCDP, MMD, and NGOCC submit revised proposals detailing how the proposed machinery would assist the grassroots women (ZARD, 1994: 16).

In October 1994, the NGOCC delegation presented the president with its revised proposal for national machinery for promotion of women's interests. President Chiluba merely promised that his advisers would study the proposals, but no commitment was made (ZARD, 1994: 17) which reflects a lack of gender sensitivity in formulation and implementation of policy. However, in spite of the failure by women's NGOs to influence the government on policy and to develop a special machinery for women, at least they have shown determination and zeal to improve their situation and impact on the government in spite of resistance by the male leadership. It can only be hoped that the current efforts by women's NGOs would bear fruit in the future.

HINDRANCES TO WOMEN'S PARTICIPATION

A combination of patriarchy and a lack of resources are the primary obstacles to women's participation in politics, such that the other two factors—type of state and lack of women's commitment or unity—can be explained in relation to patriarchy. Therefore, the underlying explanatory factor is patriarchy. The factors are discussed below in descending order of importance.

Culture of Patriarchy

Gender relations are the products of male dominance over females based on patriarchal culture. Parpart (1989: 9) argues that it is the ideology of patriarchy which constrains women's political role. Male dominance over females in all spheres of life, both private (i.e., family) and public (i.e., politics, the workplace) demonstrates the powerlessness and oppression of women (Little, 1994: 24). Dominance by males is reinforced by Zambian cultural values and customs, which stress the father and husband as the "head" or power-holder, with women subservient to them, and gender role specialization. Males, seen as the "breadwinners" for their families, have various roles both inside and outside the household, whereas women are confined to household and motherhood roles. Both females and males have been socialized to accept their assigned roles (Little, 1994: 20). The diffusion of Western culture in Zambia since colonialism widened the scope of male dominance beyond the family into what is called public patriarchy (Little, 1994: 25). However, it simultaneously opened up opportunities for women beyond the home, at the same time that it fostered discrimination against them on the basis of sex, thereby encouraging gender inequalities.

Inadequate political participation by women is explained by patriarchy and functional specialization based on gender, and it accounts for two major features in Zambia. First, the majority of women shun political jobs, preferring less controversial and more "feminine" jobs, like nursing and teaching. The small number of women candidates contesting parliamentary elections since independence exemplifies this preference, making it difficult for them to win. Interviews conducted by Ferguson, Ludwig, et al. (1995: 14) indicate that sexual discrimination accounts for the few women in politics in the Third Republic. Second, very few women have been appointed to positions in government and party, especially top positions like MCC, minister, or ambassador/high commissioner in the entire independence period. This is because of the general belief by both women and (especially) men that politics is the man's domain and that women do not make good politicians or leaders (Ferguson, Ludwig, et al., 1995: 12).

Lack of Resources

That women lack resources is partly explained by patriarchy rooted in precolonial Africa, reinforced in colonial Africa, and perpetuated into the post-independence period. Women generally lack resources, especially financial, educational, self-esteem, and leadership skills which would enable them to compete with other candidates, primarily male, in the political arena. Such a situation arises from both the predominant position of the male/husband and the institution of ownership, especially that associated with capitalism. This is called the dual systems theory (Little, 1994: 22). Both male dominance and economic (class) position determine women's access to resources and power. Marx (1983) attributes lack of personal independence, oppression, alienation, or lack of political power of any individual or group to lack of control of the means of production, as one's economic position determines one's political position. Barrett (1980: 153) argued that the oppression of women under capitalism should be understood in terms of the linkage between "division of labor at work and in the home."

Electioneering requires substantial amounts of funds for campaigns. It is a valid assumption in Zambia and Africa in general that women depend on their spouses for financial support, except when they are heads of households or earn more than their spouses. In the Second Republic, UNIP assisted candidates, both male and female, with funds for elections, but most parties in the Third Republic do not. Data on sources of financial support for women candidates in the Third Republic indicate that parties are not an important source of financial support because the majority of candidates mobilize their own funds either from personal income or from relatives and friends (Ferguson, Ludwig, et al., 1995: 10–11). Financial dependence constrains the use of funds and leaves little room for investment in politics. This might help to explain why there are more divorced or single women than married ones in government (p. 9).

Furthermore, politics requires vigor, stamina, self-esteem, and aggressiveness as basic leadership skills to be able to enlist the support of voters and compete with the males. It is generally assumed that most women in Zambia and Africa, because of both limited education and cultural constraints, lack the requisite characteristics and drive crucial for effective political competition and excellence. Although it is generally assumed that one does not need high levels of education to participate in politics, a complete lack, or little of it, constrains women's participation. Access to education, especially high-level education (secondary school, college, and university), gives women the requisite skills, such as leadership skills, self-confidence, analysis of issues and candidates, and a broader perspective on the role of women in society. Unfortunately, women's educational opportunities in independent Zambia have been hampered by the tradition of giving priority to the education of boys, by its inadequate educational institutions, and by the expulsion of girls who get pregnant at school. This explains why Zambia has fewer women than men with the skills for political competition.

Although all women are subject to male dominance, they do not all suffer from lack of resources. While the majority of women belong to the working class and peasantry, and are therefore poor, a few upper- and middle-class women have access to economic resources and high-paying jobs. Therefore, these few have the resources to finance elections, but they can only enter politics with the help of male relatives. Fatton (1989: 49) describes African politics candidly: "In general a woman's access to state resources and hence to class power hinges upon her male linkages." This in effect means that "women . . . lack the political and material autonomy that transforms individuals into full citizens" (Fatton, 1989: 49). Ferguson, Ludwig, et al. (1995: 9–10) reveal that the majority of women in government had relatives who were active in politics or were chiefs and chieftainesses and who encouraged and financially supported their entry into politics. Because of the relatives' strong influence on women's careers in politics, it is difficult for them to promote (women's) interests other than those of their backers, largely male.

Lack of resources affects individual women as well as women's NGOs. Women's organizations, such as the Women's Lobby and ZARD, depend heavily on donor agencies for financial and material assistance, which has severe consequences. Donors in turn depend on the good-will of the state to allow them to assist women's NGOs. This means that donors are constrained in their efforts to assist women's groups by the need to maintain cordial relations with the host government lest they are accused of interference in a host country's domestic affairs. This is the explanation offered by the donor's inability to release K1 million pledged to the Women's Lobby to finance the campaigns of women candidates during the local government elections of November 1992 (*Sunday Times of Zambia*, November 8, 1992). The importance of the government's acceptance of donor funding to NGOs came to the fore in 1996. After the elections, President Chiluba threatened to regulate the operations of NGOs through legislation and the monitoring of their financial sources because of the belief that they were being used by "external forces" to discredit the government. These threats arose after the local NGOs monitoring elections failed to declare the 1996 elections free and fair as anticipated by the MMD government (*The Post*, December 3, 1996).

Furthermore, in instances where donors, like NORAD and SIDA, prefer to channel resources through the NGOCC, the coordinating body, rather than directly to individual organizations, delays in disbursement of resources are a likely result. The organizational capacity of the NGOCC and its relationship to particular women's organization determine the expediency with which the NGOCC releases the aid. Where relations are cordial, an organization has easy access to its share of the donations; the opposite is true in the case of lukewarm relations.

Type of State

The nature of the government in power, particularly its ideological orientation, determines the nature of women's participation in politics. A one-party state, as under UNIP, is supposed to be an all-inclusive system allowing participation by all segments of the population, both male and female. It is generally assumed that a government guided by a socialist ideology is more committed to political emancipation and participation of women (O'Barr, 1984) than one based on other ideological orientations. The socialist ideology rests on egalitarian values emphasizing the equality of all citizens regardless of sex or any other differentiation.

The UNIP government, guided by the philosophy of Humanism since

1967, was against all forms of discrimination based on sex, tribe, color, or creed. Even the 1991 constitution protected women against discrimination. Therefore, the Zambian ideology of Humanism (Zambian version of socialism) emphasized equal participation of both men and women in all spheres of social life, including the political process. But the reality was different. Although President Kaunda portrayed himself as having a positive attitude toward gender equality, he appointed very few women to leadership positions and had very few women parliamentary candidates during his rule. Moreover, the quality of most of the women appointed to ministerial positions and the Central Committee of UNIP made a mockery of such appointments as they had little education, while denying the educated ones the opportunity to serve in public office.

Similarly, a liberal state under the MMD, which inherited and broadened gender-neutral constitutional provisions, is expected to be accommodating of group interests, including women's for the sake of representation and accountability, hallmarks of democracy. But Chiluba's government, like its predecessor, has not embraced equal power sharing between men and women, and there are very few women in positions of authority. Therefore, it makes no substantial difference to women's political status whether the government is a one-party or multiparty government because in both types of regimes women have remained underrepresented and downtrodden. Zambia, therefore, fits in neatly with Fatton's (1989: 48) conclusion that "state power is conspicuously male power, and this in turn implies that African women have been marginalized."

The lack of resources issue can also be analyzed from the point of view that Zambia is a developing country with limited resources. Available resources are devoted primarily to overcoming problems of development (economic, political, and social) for the betterment of all population groups in society. Gender equality is not a salient political issue, and women do not have sufficient political clout to pose any danger to the stability or well-being of society as a whole. It would be naive to expect an underdeveloped Zambia to devote much attention to gender issues when even the most developed countries are still characterized by gender inequalities in politics. However, donors' external pressure on government might direct its efforts to ameliorating the wide discrepancies between men and women but not necessarily eliminating them.

Lack of Commitment and Unity among Women's NGOs

In the Second Republic, women's lack of commitment to the promotion of their political status coupled with disunity among their groups, as well as the existence of many women's NGOs, partly account for gender inequalities in politics. The UNIP League's affiliation to the party necessitated 'toeing' the party line, which prevented radical demands for gender equality. It is argued, however, that the biggest obstacle to women's advancement was not so much its affiliation to the ruling party but its lack of commitment to gender equality in politics and leadership orientation to the traditional role of women. To paraphrase O'Barr (1984), alignment or nonalignment to the ruling party does not determine the contribution of women's organizations but women's commitment to their cause.

In addition, divisions symbolized by the existence of numerous organizations advancing divergent and sometimes similar interests of women; and the diversity in membership with some groups consisting of semieducated women (i.e., Women's League of UNIP), while others have educated professional women (i.e., ZARD), have prevented development of a united stand in relation to the government. In the Second Republic, the different activities and orientations of the League and ZARD drove a wedge between them, preventing a coordinated strategy for advancement of women. Similarly, a proliferation of women's NGOs in the Third Republic has fostered diversity of goals, with no common agenda and strategy due to different agendas. This applies to the Women's Lobby (promotion of women candidates and appointment to public office), ZARD (research and publication), the YWCA (promotion of literacy training, income-generating projects, and prevention of domestic violence), and Women for Change (improvement of rural women). The result has been competition as each organization promotes its own goals, although they have at times coalesced under the umbrella of the NGOCC. More important is the lack of a cordial working relationship between women's NGOs and women in government, making it difficult for them to influence government policy. Consequently, women's NGOs have been accused of not supporting women in government and of isolating "themselves from other women, even MPs," as well as "advancing themselves" (Ferguson, Ludwig, et al., 1995: 24–25). Indeed, some women have used women's NGOs (e.g., the Women's Lobby) as a gateway to positions in government (e.g., as a permanent secretary), while some women have used women's NGOs (e.g., ZARD) to gain access to resources, through research funds. Because of divergent and conflicting interests, women's NGOs might find it difficult to legitimize their claims or successfully pursue their legitimate goals.

Furthermore, at times, politicians have tried to promote disunity among women to weaken their resolve to achieve gender equality. For example, the Women's Lobby might be frustrated in its efforts to mobilize women by politicians dissuading them from supporting it. In an attempt to discredit the group, some politicians once labeled it a group of unmarried women with nothing else to do (*The Weekly Post,* January

22–28, 1993). Women's organizations have generally been believed to be composed of single women (which is not necessarily true) because husbands are unwilling to let their wives join such organizations. Such misconceptions have led the authorities not to take the views of such organizations seriously.

CONCLUSION

Constitutionally, both men and women in Zambia are accorded equal political rights and freedom as citizens. However, in practice, the Zambian woman's role in politics is dictated by patriarchy and limited access to resources such that the few women who have been able to enter into politics since independence have done so at the pleasure of the males, hence their marginalization. Efforts by women's organizations to exert pressure on the governments in the Second and Third Republics have managed to publicize the plight of women but have produced only limited results. This is due to resistance to the promotion of gender equality by males who control state power, the absence of a single, well-articulated strategy among women's NGOs, and the promotion of interests of a few, educated women as opposed to the interests of all women.

The change of government from a one-party to a multiparty system has not radically improved women's position, for no demonstrable effort has been made toward equal power sharing in spite of democratization of the political process—again a confirmation of the predominance and continuation of the ideology of patriarchy. This has several implications. Women's political situation has reached a stalemate, with no solution in sight to the problem of insufficient participation. Thus, women face great obstacles to their effective participation in politics, and women's NGOs lack political clout to effectively pressure for equal political appointments and resource allocation. Therefore, prospective women candidates and women's NGOs, composed primarily of educated, elite women, need to review their strategy in order to mobilize the majority, low-class women of workers and peasantry, as voters for women candidates and supporters of the women's cause. Actually, then, women candidates and women's NGOs have to reorient themselves away from personal and elitist gains toward serving all women's interests as the basis of women's unity against male supremacy in politics. In addition, the women's groups' pressure on the government and the ruling party should be intensified to promote gender equality. However, the challenge to male control of power is not likely to produce significant results in the short term, although it might bear fruit in the long run because it is not easy to change a patriarchal culture.

REFERENCES

Afshar, H. (ed.). (1987). *Women, State and Ideology*. London: Macmillan.

———. (1996). *Women and Politics in the Third World*. London: Routledge.

Barrett, M. (1980). *Women's Oppression Today*. London: Verso.

Chikulo, B. (1988). "The Impact of Elections in Zambia's One-Party Second Republic."*Africa Today*, 35(2), 37–49.

Fatton, R. (1989). "Gender, Class and State in Africa." In J. Parpart and K. Staudt (eds.), *Women and the State in Africa* (pp. 47–66). Boulder, CO: Lynne Rienner Publishers.

Ferguson, A., Ludwig, K. et al. (1995). "Zambian Women in Politics: An Assessment of Changes Resulting from the 1991 Political Transition." Michigan State University (MSU) Working Paper No. 13 on Political Reform in Africa, September 3.

Geisler, G. (1987). "Sisters under the Skin: Women and the Women's League in Zambia." *Journal of Modern African Studies*, 25(1), 43–66.

Gordon, A. (1992). "Women and Development." In A. Gordon and D. Gordon (eds.), *Understanding Contemporary Africa* (pp. 201–221). Boulder, CO: Lynne Rienner Publishers.

Graham, N. and Jordan, R. (1980). *The International Civil Service*. New York: Pergamon Press.

Hague, R., Harrop, M., and Breslin, S. (1992). *Political Science: A Comparative Introduction*. New York: St. Martin's Press.

Little, J. (1994). *Gender, Planning and Policy Process*. Oxford: Pergamon Press.

MacKinnon, C. (1989). *Toward a Feminist Theory of the State*. Cambridge, MA: Harvard University Press.

Marx, K. and Engels, F. (1983). *Selected Works in Three Volumes*. Moscow: Progress Publishers.

McFadden, P. (December/January 1990/1991). "The Impact of Gender Analysis on African Development." *Southern African Political and Economic Monthly* (*SAPEM*), 4(3), 39–42.

Moser, C. (1994). *Gender Planning and Development*. London: Routledge.

Movement for Multi-Party Democracy (MMD). (1991). Lusaka: MMD.

———. (1996). *MMD Manifesto '96*. Lusaka: MMD.

O'Barr, J. (1984). "African Women in Politics." In M. Hay and S. Stitcher (eds.), *African Women: South of the Sahara* (pp. 140–155). London: Longman.

Parpart, J. (1989). "Introduction." In J. Parpart (ed.), *Women and Development in Africa* (pp. 3–18). London: University Press of America.

Parpart, J. and Staudt, K. (eds.). (1989). *Women and the State in Africa* (pp. 1–19). Boulder, CO: Lynne Rienner Publishers.

The Post. (1996). December 3.

Sunday Times of Zambia. (1992). November 8.

Taylor, M., Rhyne, L., Rosenthal, S., and Dogbe, K. (1987). *Introduction to Sociology*. New York: Macmillan.

United Nations. (1995). *1993 Demographic Yearbook*. New York: United Nations.

The Weekly Post. (1993). January 22–28.

Weiner, M. (1971). "Political Participation: Crisis of the Political Process." In L.

Binder et al. (1974), *Crises and Sequences in Political Development* (pp. 159–204). Princeton, NJ: Princeton University Press.

Zambia, Government of. (1996). *Act No. 18.* Lusaka: Government Printers.

Zambia, Party and Government of the Republic of. (1985). *Zambia's Report to the World Conference of the United Nations Decade for Women: Equality, Development and Peace, Held in Nairobi, Kenya, 15–26 July.* Lusaka: Government Printer.

Zambia, Republic of. (1964, 1968, 1973, 1983, 1988, 1991). *Presidential and Parliamentary Elections Results.* Lusaka: Government Printer.

———. (1989). *Fourth National Development Plan (FNDP), 1989–1993.* Lusaka: Government Printer.

———. (August 1995). *Gender Statistics Report.* Draft. Lusaka: Central Statistical Office.

Zambia Association for Research and Development (ZARD). (n.d.). Booklet.

———. (October 1994). *NGO Shadow Report on the Situation of Women in Zambia during the Decade 1985–1994.* Lusaka: Non-Governmental Organizations Coordinating Committee (NGOCC).

———. (March 1996). *Zambia Today: A Gender Perspective.* Lusaka: ZARD.

Chapter 10

Street Children: A New Liberation Movement?

Arnon Bar-On

INTRODUCTION

Since the early 1980s, much attention, often very emotive, has been given to children in developing countries who make their livelihood on the streets, largely because of the violence members of the enforcement arm of the criminal justice system do to some of them. Many humanitarian organizations have begun to take ameliorative action to assist these children, and it was only a question of time before researchers began to take similar interest and produce a growing body of literature on the "street child." In both cases, people were spurred not so much by the "discovery" of child streetism, but by the perception that there is an acute problem, a challenge, to be addressed.

On closer examination, however, this literature reveals a strange phenomenon, though not unheard of in advocacy research: that with singular exceptions (e.g., Apteker, 1991; Oliveira, Baizerman and Pellet, 1992) its authors systematically ignore their own findings whereby most street children's maturation process, albeit undoubtedly harsh, is not adversely effected by their circumstances—in favor of the predetermined conclusion that streetism is invariably harmful to children and so must be eradicated. In the light of this phenomenon, this chapter seeks first to highlight some of the facts on street children that are commonly neglected and to explain why they are neglected. The main conclusion drawn from this discussion is that most writers assess street children by criteria that are inappropriate to their particular circumstances, namely, by criteria that derive from Northern, middle-class mores rather than by criteria that reflect the real world the street children inhabit. Finally, several recommendations on helping street children are presented that are influenced by the "social equality" movement (Mishra, 1995) and feminism in particular. Most of these recommendations deviate from those that the caring professions usually champion.

This material is based mainly on three previously unpublished studies of street children in Africa—two by the late Peter Taçon (1991a, 1991b) and one by Van Ham, Blavo, and Opoku (1992)—with additional sources of information drawn from similar studies around the globe. Together, the African studies included 2,100 randomly selected interviewees in Ghana (1,000), Namibia (300), and Zambia (800).

GENERAL BACKGROUND

Child streetism identifies children in the South who regularly engage in gainful economic activity in geographical areas designated for the use of the public, such as parks, shopping malls, and street intersections. In contrast, in the North, children with similar characteristics are more often-called homeless, runaways, or delinquents, which in common discourse connote quite different meanings. At the turn of the 1990s, it was estimated that the number of street children stood at around 5 percent of the South's total child population (Taçon, 1992). This number, however, is probably much exaggerated, given that child streetism is solely an urban phenomenon and that except for the Latin American and Caribbean region, over half the South's population is rural (IFAD, 1993: 1). A more realistic figure, therefore, calculated from a survey of street children in Kampala that places their number at one out of 380 residents (Herbert, 1996b), would be just over half of 1 percent of their age group. This calculation is based on the assumption that, as in the rest of Uganda, at least half of Kampala's population is under 18 years of age.

The existence and prevalence of child streetism can be attributed directly to macro and micro poverty. At the macro level, it primarily reflects the inability of many families to meet the cost of even their most basic needs and government's inability to support these families in child rearing or, in some cases, their ideological reluctance to provide such support. For example, in Botswana, social assistance is provided at a flat rate per family, regardless of the family's size, which is done not out of financial constraints but to encourage interfamily responsibility. Another macro-level reason is the poverty of the scholastic system that fails to act as a channel of upward mobility. In part, this is attributable to a chronic shortage in school places (especially, but not only, beyond primary education). It is also due to the phenomenon—even where places are available—of teachers abandoning their students to work elsewhere to supplement their low wages, partly because they are often unpaid for months (Herbert, 1996a). Other important school-related factors are the irrelevance of much of the curricula that try to emulate the North rather than fit the local environment, and the insistence of educators that children attend school in uniforms and pay other nontuition fees, which their families can ill afford.

At the personal level, on the other hand, poverty contributes to child streetism more indirectly. This is because poverty generally weakens the capacity of adults to cope with daily contingencies, which, in turn, increases the value they place on their children's obedience and maintenance of the home (McLoyd and Wilson, 1991). Some children find these pressures difficult to withstand and seek, therefore, greater freedom and sustenance elsewhere. It needs to be pointed out, however, that contrary to popular perception, research has shown that at least with regard to most street children, this desire for freedom is secondary to their own and their families' economic predicaments (Dewees and Klees, 1995; Rizzini and Lusk, 1995).

Unlike other groups of children, who might be classed, for example, by their physical or mental abilities, street children cannot be described by precise criteria. Rather, "street children" is a generic term that denotes young people with a special relationship to the street, to their families, and to the public at large.

The overwhelming majority of street children belong to a category that is usually called "children in the street" (Glauser, 1990). These are young people who spend a significant part of their time on the streets because this is where they work and socialize, having carved out for themselves niches in the lower rungs of the informal or so-called black economy. Most often, this work consists of easy-entry occupations that allow considerable autonomy and require little or no capital. Typical examples of these occupations are street vending and simple personal services, such as portering, running errands, and washing cars as well as less prepossessing activities such as begging and recycling garbage. Contrary to the popular perception, however, *none* of the children in this category are runaways or abandoned: they all have homes to return to, and they typically maintain daily, or almost daily, contact with their immediate families or with other relatives (Rizzini and Lusk, 1995). Indeed, it is usually their parents who provide them with the start-capital they require to set up their "businesses" (Ghana National Commission on Children, 1991).

In contrast, only a small number of street children—usually only 2 to 7 percent—have severed all, or most, contact with their biological families (Blanc, 1991; Taçon, 1991a, 1991b.) These children are called "children *of* the street." This is because they both work and frequently live in the streets. However, even among this group, many children shelter with informal guardians, and some 40 percent continue to contribute occasionally to their immediate families' budget (Blanc, 1994). The children of the street are usually older than their counterparts *in* the street (Lusk, 1992).

Yet, probably the most significant characteristic of street children is their relationship to the public. Instead of using the street and other public arenas chiefly as channels of conduit between private pursuits, as most people do, street children spend much of their time in these places and so are publicly visible much of the time. This public visibility challenges bourgeois society, which, because of the importance it places on private property, distinguishes sharply between the public and the private domain, and governs itself so that children intrude as little as possible on the adult world. The major consequence of this position is that the dominant elite generates strong pressures that street children "disappear from view" rather than be helped.

Besides these basic relations of child streetism to mainstream society, it is distinguished by three additional attributes. First, it is an exclusively urban construct. Children in rural areas who are similarly placed are not identified as such, including children in rural villages. Nor, for that matter, are children in other traditional groupings, such as fishing communities, even if they live in cities. Second, street children belong to the middle to late childhood age groups. For example, in the Ghanaian survey (Van Ham, Blavo, and Opoku, 1992), whose findings have been replicated elsewhere (for example, Chatterjee, 1992; Natale, 1992; Rizzini and Lusk, 1995), 51 percent of the children were 13 to 15 years of age, and 34 percent were 7 to 9 years old. Only 4 percent of the children were younger (4 to 6 years of age). This distribution of age apparently reflects the fact that the youngest age at which a child can work on the street is around 5, and can survive—if alone—when 6 or 7 years old, while older children leave the street in search of more profitable, socially rewarding, and stable forms of employment (Rizzini et al., 1994). Third, most street children are male. Girls make up no more than a quarter of street children and typically far less. For example, in Namibia and in Botswana, they account for less than 5 percent of this population. This much lower participation rate for girls is usually attributable to cultural constraints and to families' insistence that girl children help with the housework, a duty from which boy children are generally excused.

PERCEPTIONS VERSUS FACTS

The typical depiction of street children by the media invariably connects them with physical deprivation, inadequate nutrition and hygiene, and the skirting of the law. It also portrays children as being vulnerable to adult (particularly male) exploitation and to environmental hazards. These and other negative traits are supposedly evidenced in the street child's poor health, inadequate clothing, and alienation that percolates down to feelings of personal insecurity, resultant emotional disabilities, and destructive behavior. All this reflects the fact that these children spend much of their time away from adult support (Kotlowitz, 1991).

Yet, the empirical evidence is quite different. Many street children earn, on average, as much as the adults in their vicinity (Dewees and Klees, 1995) and often up to one and a half times the minimum wage of most of these adults (Blanc, 1994; Porio, Moselina, and Swift, 1994). For example, in Gaborone, Botswana, where a maid usually earns P20 for eight hours of work, few street children would spend 15 minutes to clean a car for less than P5. Their income, therefore, is generally sufficient to meet the cost of decent and nutritious meals (Taçon, 1991a, 1991b). Indeed, for many, food is far less plentiful at home, if available at all (Burling, 1990a; Munyakho, 1992). For this reason, too, a good outfit is usually not beyond their means, although they often ignore middle-class views of decency in preference of worn-out clothes, or, if engaged in begging, then they wear tattered clothing and wash only weekly, to increase their earnings potential (Herbert, 1996a).

In the same vein, research regularly shows that most street children are predominantly healthy (Apteker, 1989) and that when they are ill, they are usually looked after by a relative. Thus, in Accra, only 14 percent of the 1,000 street children interviewed claimed that they looked after themselves in times of illness. Nevertheless, 42 percent reported that, like many of their elders, they often resorted to self-medication purchased from traditional drug peddlers or over-the-counter, which is a phenomenon common to much of the underdeveloped world.

Another misconception about street children is that they are highly individualistic or that they are driven to individualistic behavior by their circumstances. Research shows, however, that they are more likely to live and to operate in groups, where solidarity extends from sharing food so that "everybody at least gets something" (Burling, 1990a, 1990b) to providing emotional support. These groups are also highly organized: they usually have a recognized leader, whose position is rarely based on harassment, while other members treat each other as equals. Indeed, it is as if they create for themselves new "families." For example, Vittachi (1989) describes a group of children in Chile who lived under a bridge. Every morning they drew up shopping lists and distributed tasks, and while the older members went to work, the middle-aged children cared for the youngest. Similarly, but demonstrating a measure of far greater institutionalization, a Kotokoli street girl in Accra reported that she regularly contributed part of her earnings to a Kotokoli "mutual aid association" of street children that looked after its members when they were unable to work (Van Ham, Blavo, and Opoku, 1992).

This last facet of child streetism suggests that its members live largely in a "children's society." However, at one and the same time, most street children (including those *of* the street) are rarely cut off from "positive" adult influence. This is because, like their resilient, family-anchored counterparts in Werner and Smith's (1982) famous study in Hawaii, they often attach themselves to adult "mentors" or are temporarily "adopted" by adults in times of trouble (Apteker, 1989). This is especially so in Africa, where in spite of the weakening of the traditional responsibility of adults to direct the conduct of children—whether or not their parents—this practice persists. For example, the person one street child in Accra liked best was the secretary of the local fishermen's association, not only because he gave him food and money, but more importantly, advice (Van Ham, Blavo, and Opoku, 1992). Similarly, several of the researchers who undertook this Ghanaian study noted that their greatest obstacle to interviewing street children were other adults on the street, who prohibited the children from answering their questions for fear that the children might come to harm. It was only after these adults were put at ease that they allowed the children "in their charge" to be interviewed.

Finally, and again in contrast to popular perception, most research shows that few street children are actively involved in crime, although given that some of their activities, such as begging, are regulated by law, they are often "attended to" by the police. For example, although in both Windhoek and Bombay two out of five children reported that they were at times arrested, 80 percent were never incarcerated (Taçon, 1991a; Blanc, 1994). Similarly, in Botswana, 75 percent of the children who were detained by the police were found to be criminally "clean" (Okello-Wengi, 1994), and in Zambia Taçon (1991a, 1991b) was unable to trace a single street child who was ever brought to court. Instead, it would appear that most detentions of street children are driven chiefly by so-called clean-up campaigns in the belief that their presence affects tourism adversely (Dorfman, 1984; Porio et al., 1994). Other reasons are that informal trading competes with established enterprises and deprives governments of the revenues they can generate from issuing trading permits.

DECONSTRUCTION

In delineating some of the differences between the popular perceptions of street children and reality, this chapter by no means intends to romanticize the street child. Nor is it designed in any way to ignore the fact that street children are at risk and that their life is extremely harsh. But to say that street children are vulnerable is not to say much; so are many other children in developing countries who receive far less attention. Moreover, as harsh as the life of street children undeniably is, it is wrong to uphold that it is invariably distressed. For one, work provides most of these children with a measure of material security and its advantages that few of their nonworking siblings have. For example, they are able to take advantage of opportunities, like going to a concert or visiting an amusement arcade, that is denied to most of their peers. But more importantly, work gives these children a purpose away from the daily drudgery of poverty, which typically involves relative idleness for boys and hard domestic labor for girls, and often can lead to troubled family relations. In fact, most street children report that their relations with their family much improved after taking to the streets. For example, they are punished less frequently than their nonworking siblings are (Rizzini et al., 1994).

Even if we were to appraise the street child's life by more stringent standards, such as those of the middle class, it is questionable whether such commonplace and sweeping pronouncements like "what the street teaches, none of us would want our children to learn!" (Palaparti, 1995: 2) are justified. For example, Oloko (1991), who studied street children in Nigeria, shows that they excel in the attributes of leadership, while Apteker (1989), who worked with street children in Colombia, found that they were no less emotionally functional than other children. They were also, on average, more socially competent than the average school-going child, and they were more resourceful and persevering. Hence, as one street child put it (echoing the entrepreneurial culture that all governments are currently strongly espousing): "I'll be a good businessman because I have learnt to look after myself" (Agnelli, 1986: 31). It should come as no surprise, therefore, that most street children not only see nothing wrong with their lifestyle, but also generally endorse it (Taçon, 1991a, 1991b; Oliveira, Baizerman, and Pellet, 1992; Porio et al., 1994).

That certain people accept their lifestyle and might even enjoy it does not mean that others must accept it, even in today's postmodernist world. As Bebhabib (1992: 153) notes, interactive universalism, on which post-modernist thought is founded, "acknowledges the plurality of modes of being human, and differences among humans, without [necessarily] endorsing all these pluralities and differences as morally and politically valid." But should even part of the foregoing empirical evidence on street children be correct, that is, that child streetism is neither as personally nor as socially damaging as popularly thought, then one must ask why the phenomenon *in its entirety* is deemed so insufferable to justify the attention it receives.

Like most explanations of social phenomena, the answer to this question is complex. To simplify the discussion, some of the factors that might be involved include: (1) the troubled relations some adults have with children, especially with children who are poor; (2) the differences between the way people in the developed and undeveloped world perceive children and construct the idea of "childhood"; and (3) the misconceived use of Northern-informed developmental psychology to understand the reality of many children in the developing world.

Adults and Children: A Troubled Relationship

If we were to examine the average adult's perception of children, we would usually find that he or she holds children in one of two regards: as good scapegoats or bad. On the good scapegoat, adults project their ideals and hopes and so protect adoringly. Conversely, on the bad scapegoat, they project their guilt and consequently fear. As divergent as these perceptions might be, they have one thing in common: both are rooted in pathological constructs of childhood whose inherent response to bringing up children is to control their behavior.

The first of these outlooks, which might be called the protection model, derives primarily from an ideology that emphasizes the weaknesses and vulnerability of children, and so stresses the dangers that threaten them. For example, The Fourth World Movement (1986: 9) writes of "a street child or an exploited youngster" as though these are necessarily the same. Yet more importantly, this model is invariably ingrained with such emotionalism that it instinctively calls to "rescue" children before examining the alternatives; that is, it defies any semblance of rationale scrutiny. A typical example is the following quote from a report on street children in Kampala:

Through the city sewers, on a highway of slime, slide the street boys of Kampala. . . . For a creative or hardy few [these places] have become playground, transport system, hideout and sometimes bedroom. . . . They call it "Beirut," a nickname for any place were they feel safe. (Herbert, 1996b)

In contrast, the second outlook, which can be called the fear model, is grounded in judgments that regard children as a threat to society or to themselves. This position derives from the belief that moral thought and consequent behavior develop by constraint, and so children must be directed "properly" if they are to exert their energies harmlessly. It follows, therefore, that children must be controlled, as exemplified by the accelerating legislation in parts of the developed world that no child should be left unsupervised by a responsible adult at all times.

Within this last configuration, the children of the poor, especially in the Northern Hemisphere, tend to be regarded by the dominant elite as a particular danger. One of the earliest codifications of this view was the Elizabethan Poor Laws which separated "neglected" (that is, poor) children from their families, but its clearest manifestations came after the dawn of industrialization. With the introduction of mechanization, pauperism was declared first to be immoral and then criminal, as the bourgeoisie sought to command what little labor was available. This was done first by drafting religion to the cause of employment, making wage earning the definition of spirituality, and later by bringing in the law.

As Compton (1980: 153) observed, "Begging, movement, and vagrancy were [constructed as] essentially the same problem, a threat to the labor supply." Then, when a rapidly expanding population led to a glut in labor and unemployment set in, the fear of crime took over. In both cases, where children were concerned, and especially those "contaminated" by poverty (as if this in itself instilled in them some wired-in destructiveness), the usual strategy was to detain the "idle." In the nineteenth century this entailed the indenture of poor children. In the twentieth century it entailed schooling, which served not only to integrate children into mainstream society, but also to keep them from competing with adults for employment and from intruding on the adult world in general.

These fear and protection perceptions of children are, of course, only differences in emphasis. People who subscribe to the protection model recognize that children need control, just as those who subscribe to the fear model accept that they need protection. However, when applied to street children, these models are generally used in their extremity, with the result that researchers and persons who work directly with street children are prone to overlook their real lives in favor of predetermined prejudices.

Different Constructs of Childhood

A second factor that propels writers to regard the situation of street children so insufferable as to divert their attention from their own findings is these writers' adoption of Northern Hemisphere constructs of childhood. However, many of these constructs derive from developments that have not been part of the experience of most people in the developing countries.

The most critical of these dissimilar developments are demographics. Record-low fertility rates and increasing longevity in the developed world have fundamentally changed its age-structure at the expense of children. For example, in Europe, children 15 years of age and under made up only 20 percent of the population in 1991, and their number is expected to decrease by a further 10 percent before stabilizing (UN, 1992). Tackling society's growing dependency on an increasingly older labor force, not to mention ensuring its sheer existence, is thus a top Northern priority, with alternate strategies focusing largely on child care. In contrast, in much of the undeveloped world, especially in Africa, the fertility rate is more than three times as high as in Europe and the average longevity considerably lower. Consequently, 45 percent of the population in 1991 was 15 years of age and under. This figure dictates that the South has different priorities than the North—for example, that its people need to pay less attention to children's safety.

A second development is economic. Changes in the means of production, coupled with generous social security systems, have created conditions in the developed countries such that the instrumental value of children has been replaced entirely by their expressive value. As Scheper-Hughes (1980: 2) notes, "children [in the Northern Hemisphere] have become relatively worthless to their parents, but priceless in terms of their psychological worth." In contrast, for most families in the South, this situation is almost reversed. With physical labor at a premium, absolute poverty all pervasive, and collective expenditure on personal welfare almost nonexistent, the rational response is to put children to use as rapidly as possible in helping with the household's economic survival.

Lastly, the North is currently adopting ever stricter definitions of what are considered acceptable private conducts, which are moving it to accept an ever widening social policy designed to anticipate presumed deviance. In an insightful observation, Kaminer (1994: 34) calls this "[the belief] that there is a political solution for every interpersonal problem." Northern judgments about children's behavior and lifestyles that do not conform to these standards are therefore becoming increasingly harsher, which the people of the South, with other, more pressing agendas, simply accept or have come to tolerate as hazards rather than solvable problems. This is particularly noticeable around issues of child sexual abuse and physical safety.

Taken together, the major effect of these different developments is that childhood in the North has become such a clearly differentiated construct from adulthood that, with an expanding interim period of adolescence, is expected to be dedicated purely to growing up. From this it follows that children should live totally aloof from the worries of adult life, chief among which is their separation from the economic arena. Consequently, child streetism, whose major component *is* economic, is perceived by Northern observers as antithetical to proper childhood and in the light of its emotive force an anathema as well.

Cultural Biases in Developmental Psychology

The final factor that disposes researchers against street children relates to the fact that most of our knowledge of human maturation is grounded in the Western-informed developmental psychology, whose explanations of childhood—regardless of their theoretical orientation—are predicated on two fundamental assumptions. The first of these assumptions is that childhood is epigenetic. This means that it is believed that all children undergo the same physiologically programmed schedule in developing their social, physical, and emotional capacities and that any disturbance in this sequence leads to pathology. The second assumption is that within this schedule, the caring role of adults, and especially of mothers, is critical, separation from whom has adverse consequences in later life.

This latter "fact" is commonly called "attachment gone wrong" (De Zulueta, 1993) or what Sgroi (1982) refers to as neglected children being "damaged goods." It follows, therefore, that not only should society treat children well (especially, if as Holmes [1995] suggests, children who grow up insecurely adopt, in later life, strategies that chime with their experiences, such as extreme political disaffection), but it is the *duty* of children *to remain children*. That is to say, they must not have the same traits as adults. Hence, many of the qualities admired in adults, such as independence or wariness, are generally frowned upon in children, or as M. D. Hill (1855, in Hendrick, 1990: 43) argued long ago: "the delinquent . . . knows much and a great deal too much of what is called life. He can take care of his own immediate interests . . . [and] asks for no protection. He has consequently much to unlearn—*he has to be turned again into a child*" (emphasis added).

These two assumptions of developmental psychology currently play such a critical role in popular thought that they are generally accepted as "undeniably objective." In fact, most of the evidence that supports them owes more to the ideological status of children in the Northern Hemisphere than to firm data.

Maturation: Biological or Social?

Developmental psychology, simply by being "developmental," is based on the notion that children are in some way "incomplete human beings," and so it searches for laws that explain how they grow into an adult culture and when this might happen. This search usually involves treating certain social phenomena as natural facts and natural facts as biological facts, and consequently ends up "biologizing maturation" (Morss, 1990). It is then up to professionals, such as social workers and psychologists, to use such "laws" to guide society in the proper way to raise children, unadulterated by nonscientific social or cultural, influences (Rosenfeld, Schon, and Sykes, 1995).

Yet the truth is there is little agreement either on the definition of childhood or on what is proper for children. For example, the age at which children graduate into adulthood differs radically not only between different societies but within the same society, and is usually further differentiated by gender. Thus, one might be eligible for a driving license at 16, drink beer at 18, and vote at 21, and females can usually get married at an earlier age than males. Similarly, whereas some societies regard children as dependent into their teens (and often beyond), others expect children 6 or 7 years of age to look after their younger siblings and tend to the goats. Whether or not such practices are desirable is a moral issue, which is unconnected with whether they are either possible or practically "good" or "bad" (Chaput, 1991). Thus, the fact that certain societies do not socialize females to bear children at 15 does not mean 15-year-old females cannot bear children and remain psychologically undamaged. To see the negative implications in such practices—offensive as they may be to present-day Northern mores (which by definition can only reflect the North's history and its specific contexts)—does not drive them out of the existence of feasible alternatives in child socialization.

In the same vein, there is little to support the notion that adults are the necessary primary agents of child socialization or that children require particular kinds of adult contact. Clearly, as in much of Africa, multi-adult and sibling-care can socialize children to patterns other than monotropism or to its day care equivalents. Similarly, as an increasing number of both parents in two-partner families go out to work, we find that more children spend longer hours out of the sight of adults with no apparent harm (Solberg, 1990). Also, although some findings show that adult support can protect children from the negative effects of stressful experiences (Sandler et al., 1989), an equal body of evidence shows no such buffering effect (Treadwell and Johnson, 1980). Indeed, some research shows that adult support might even be associated with *higher* distress in children (McLoyd and Wilson, 1991). Creating laws and standards from contradictory positions such as these, and applying them universally, are, to say the least, problematic.

Disregard of Reality

A separate difficulty associated with developmental psychology is that it is insensitive to the social context of maturation (except as a facilitator for micro development), and it neglects people's feasible contexts of choice.

Other than physical growth, the primary task of children is to adapt to their environment and to master it (Meyer, 1991). When translated into research, this implies asking how children come to resemble the people of whom they are part and how they are prepared to interact with their surroundings (Chaput, 1991). In these respects, the daily reality of many people in the developing world differs radically from what people in the Northern Hemisphere have grown to accept. Most social and psychological "scientific" proofs seem to derive and feed back into this reality. Life in many developing countries chiefly involves living in or on the fringes of absolute poverty where a critical element is the fusion of public and private. In particular, those who are born into, and live in, these circumstances, are apt to make private use of "free" public resources, which in urban areas are found mainly in the streets. The streets, in effect, are their living rooms, recreational facilities, and places of business, as opposed to the middle class and its emulators who orient themselves around the home, the school, and the office (Lieber, 1981). Hence, as in India, whole families might live on the street, whereas in other places this is where people make a living and interact.

It is within this context, deplorable as it might be (but also, as we must remember, ineradicable for years to come, particularly in Africa whose economy is not expected to improve in the foreseeable future), that child streetism must be assessed because street children have no other context in which to develop. To single them out and, by this act, in effect to condemn them for adapting to their circumstances, as well as to divorce them from their context in favor of presumed universal principles, makes little sense. This is especially so when many of their parents endorse their activities, not because they like them but, because they realize that concepts stemming from the bourgeois modes of regulation are not salient to their situation. It is equally inane to fail to accept the notion that only rich societies can afford to treat increasingly older people as children and to sustain them for increasingly longer periods of time.

SO WHAT'S TO BE DONE?

One of the dominant features of present-day social life is the expansion of social equality, that is, the increasing categories of persons who have obtained the right to regulate their own lives and to be treated with respect on their own accord. Topping this list of people (though still battling to achieve many of their demands) are the inhabitants of former colonies, women, ethnic minorities, the physically disabled, and people with different sexual orientations. More recently, it has also been recognized that within these categories, different people fit into different molds. Hence, for example, separate advocacy groups of women with different backgrounds have been established.

To respect others as autonomous is to treat them as "capable of agency." This, at a minimum, demands that we allow them, in some situations, to make the choices that will determine how they conduct their lives, and that our responses to them are responses that respect their choices (Tännsjö, 1992). To date, however, no country has extended such treatment to children, not even informally.

Article 27 of the United Nations Convention on the Rights of the Child states that every child has the right to a standard of living adequate for his or her physical, mental, spiritual, moral, and social development. It also stipulates that parents have the primary responsibility to ensure that their children have this standard of living and that it is up to the state to ensure that this responsibility can be fulfilled and is.

Yet, conditions in much of the developing world are such that many parents are unable to meet this responsibility and governments are unable (or in some places unwilling) to play their part. Consequently, certain children in the South have taken to pursuing their own standard of living by appropriating what we commonly call "adulthood." They have, in effect, empowered themselves by refusing to accept the definitions of childhood and the powerless role that mainstream culture reserves for them simply because they are young and, more importantly, poor. More-over, as the first part of this chapter has tried to show, this self-empowerment does not seem to critically effect either them or society negatively.

Members of the caring professions and persons otherwise concerned about street children are entitled to object to this "liberation movement." They need to be aware, however, that the grounds for their objection are primarily moral, not empirical, and, hence, that their only recourse to combat the phenomenon is to preach. They are likely, therefore, to exert much greater leverage if they can change the circumstances that lead to child streetism. Since such changes are unlikely to occur in the foresee-able future, the professions might do better by helping street children in their liberation—which is to say, protect their right to better their posi-tion *as* street children.

To engage in this endeavor meaningfully, it is necessary to reexamine first our construction of childhood, especially as it pertains in much of the developing world and, second, what we deem proper activities for children. Concerning the construct of childhood, most people would agree that children are capable of more than what most adults give them credit for. For example, research has shown that already at 7 years of age children can be considered responsible and know when they do wrong (Bronfenbrenner, 1989; Collins, 1991). Indeed, for most children in the developing countries maturation is probably accelerated since they are socialized toward early independence (Apteker, 1990).

As to what is proper for children, the issue is not so much in which activities they take part and where, but whether their energies are em-ployed so that they benefit their well-being. What is required, therefore, is to ensure that when children engage in different activities, their op-portunities for development are optimized, which when related to street children pertains primarily to their work, to their education, and to their relations with the state.

What mainly distinguishes street children from other young people is that they spend much of their time working outside their homes for material gain, as opposed to working at school and at home without financial remuneration. There is no evidence, however, that this is dam-aging. Even in Northern societies, 40 to 70 percent of children age 11 to 16 work part-time (Moorehead, 1987), and in most countries, the legal minimum age of employment is between 14 and 16 years. Rather, it is the conditions of this work that may be problematic, that is, if they jeop-ardize a child's health or are exploitative. Hence what we require is not to ban all children from work but to accord those who must work the same protection from poor, dangerous, and exploitative working conditions that is extended to other segments of the labor force.

Interconnected with the extension of labor legislation to children is the question of education. In today's market, schooling is the primary avenue to gaining an adequate income. Consequently, any activity that adversely affects attaining an education, such as work, threatens a child's future. However for street children, conventional schooling, where available, is inappropriate: not only do its time frames clash with their schedule, but most of these children abandon school precisely because it fails to meet their needs. To this end, most of the alternatives developed to date, such as "street schools," are of little use. In part, this is because these so-called schools engage more in advice giving than in education (Gigengach, 1994), but it is mainly because these schools' ultimate goal is to get street children *off* the street. Alternative educational arrangements must be found, therefore, whose aim, in effect, will be to help street children function better *as street children*. For example, they could be taught how to be more productive in what they do, in a manner akin to the programs currently run for many rural women in some developing countries.

Yet the biggest challenge to social policy to ensure the well-being of street children is to decriminalize the street. By placing a premium on life organized in and around formal frameworks and private property, the middle class equates the street with idleness and delinquency, and therefore constructs street-life in its entirety as illegitimate. Two of the oldest measures to effect this construct are the prohibition of street trading and of loitering, which were exported to some countries by its then colonial masters to "protect" them from "the natives." Today, long after the demise of colonialism, these same measures are still being used and for much the same reason. The only difference is that the persons the current ruling class fears have replaced "the natives": the urban young and poor. Child streetism is thus criminalized automatically, with the result that its subjects are handled (or more often mishandled) mainly by the criminal justice system. Hence, as all street children agree, their major concern by far is not hunger, education, or ill health but the police and the harassment and violence this institution directs against them simply for doing their best to survive (Dewees and Klees, 1995).

CONCLUSION

Throughout history, the claims of any disadvantaged group of people for greater autonomy have been objected to as contradicting "the natural order of things." One such objection to child streetism is ideological. According to this view, if children are to grow properly into culture, then they must mature slowly, which is to say that they must remain children until they are admitted officially into adulthood. From this notion it is then derived that every child has *a right* to be a child, and so liberal theory has come to identify social progress with the formal exemption of children from the adult world (Lees and Mellor, 1986), if not their forced expulsion from this world.

Another possible objection to street child liberation is political. For example, child advocacy groups might fear that the acceptance of children as potentially independent might be used to justify spending cuts on child welfare. Also, such acceptance might anger some members of the caring professions, such as social workers, who believe that they are the custodians of empowerment. For these workers, the idea that certain people can determine their own destiny, without their input, may be professionally offensive. This is exemplified by the following slogan of a charitable organization spotted by this author in South Africa: "Help our street children to help themselves by donating directly to the fund and NOT the children."

Some of these objections are more telling than others, and none can be dismissed out of hand. However, to negatively regard child streetism, which is a predominantly Southern phenomenon, mainly because of Northern, middle-class perceptions is grossly inappropriate, especially before eradicating its causes. Well-wishers, who insist on their ideal image borrowed from afar instead of accepting local reality and confronting it feasibly, might well end up doing more harm than good.

REFERENCES

Agnelli, S. (1986). *Street Children.* London: Weidenfeld and Nicolson.

Apteker, L. (1989). "Characteristics of the Street Children of Colombia." *Child Abuse and Neglect,* 13(3), 427–437.

———. (1990). "Family Structure and Adolescence: The Case of Colombian Street Children." *Journal of Adolescent Research,* 5(1), 67–81.

———. (1991). "Are Colombian Street Children Neglected? The Contribution of Ethnographic and Ethnohistorical Approaches to the Study of Children." *Anthropology and Education Quarterly,* 22(4), 326–349.

Bebhabib, S. (1992). *Situating the Self.* Cambridge, MA: Polity Press.

Blanc, C. S. (1991). *Street and Working Children—Field Perspectives.* Florence, Italy: UNICEF.

———. (1994). *Urban Children in Distress: Global Predicaments and Innovative Strategies.* Yverdon, Switzerland: Gordon and Breach.

Bronfenbrenner, U. (1989). *Who Cares for Children?* Paris: Unit for Cooperating with UNICEF and the World Food Program (WFP).

Burling, K. (1990a). "Two Small Boys Tell of a Life of Hustling, Hunger." *The Namibian,* November 11.

———. (1990b). "Lord of the Flies: Life for Windhoek Street Survivors." *The Namibian,* November 23.

Chaput, W. F. (ed.). (1991). *Studying the Social Worlds of Children: Sociological Readings*. London: Falmer Press.

Chatterjee, A. (1992). *India: The Forgotten Children of the Cities*. Florence, Italy: UNICEF.

Collins, W. A. (1991). "Development During Middle Childhood." In C. Landers (ed.), *Development of Children from Infancy through Adolescence*. New York: UNICEF.

Compton, B. (1980). *Introduction to Social Welfare and Social Work: Structure, Function, and Process*. Homewood, IL: Dorsey Press.

Dewees, A. and Klees, S. J. (1995). "Social Movements and the Transformation of National Policy: Street and Working Children in Brazil." *Comparative Education Review*, 39(1), 76–100.

De Zulueta, F. (1993). *From Pain to Violence*. London: Whurr.

Donnison, D. (1995). "Ethics and Policy Analysis." In J. Baldock and M. May (eds.), *Social Policy Review 7*. Canterbury, England: Social Policy Association.

Dorfman, A. (1984). "Arraz Quemada y Pan; Cultura y Supervivencia Económica en America Latina." *Desarrollo de Base* 8(2), 9–20, quoted by J. Boyden (1990), "Childhood and the Policy Makers: A Comparative Perspective on the Globalization of Childhood," in A. James and A. Prout (eds.), *Constructing and Reconstructing Childhood: Contemporary Issues in the Sociological Study of Childhood*. London: Falmer Press.

The Fourth World Movement. (1986). "Position Paper on Street Children." *Action for Children*, 1(5).

Ghana National Commission on Children. (1991). *Annual Report*. Accra: Ghana National Commission.

Gigengach, R. (1994). "Social Practices of Juvenile Survival and Mortality: Child Care Arrangements in Mexico City." *Community Development Journal*, 29(4), 380–393.

Glauser, B. (1990). "Street Children: Deconstructing a Construct." In A. James and A. Prout (eds.), *Constructing and Reconstructing Childhood: Contemporary Issues in the Sociological Study of Childhood*. London: Falmer Press.

Hendrick, H. (1990). "Constructions and Reconstructions of British Childhood: An Interpretive Survey, 1800 to the Present." In A. James and A. Prout (eds.), *Constructing and Reconstructing Childhood: Contemporary Issues in the Sociological Study of Childhood*. London: Falmer Press.

Herbert, R. (1996a). "Children Play the Leading Role in Nigeria's Culture of Begging." *The Sunday Independent*, August 8.

———. (1996b). "Boom Economy Spawns a Tide of Street Children." *The Sunday Independent*, October 13.

Hill, M. D. (1855). "Practical Suggestions to the Founders of Reformatory Schools." In J. C. Symonns, *On the Reformation of Young Offenders*. London: Routledge.

Holmes, J. (1995). "Psychotherapy, Attachment and Society: Connecting the Inner and Outer Worlds." In J. Baldock and M. May (eds.), *Social Policy Review 7*. Canterbury, England: Social Policy Association.

International Fund for Agricultural Development (IFAD). (1993). *The State of World Rural Poverty*. Rome: IFAD.

Kaminer, W. (April 1994). "The Privacy Problem." *Mirabella*, 34–36.

Kotlowitz, A. (1991). *There Are No Children Here*. New York: Doubleday.

Lees, S. and Mellor, J. (1986). "Girls' Rights." In B. Franklin (ed.), *The Rights of Children*. Oxford: Basil Blackwell.

Lewnes, A. (1994). "Learning to Dream at Projecto Axè." *First Call for Children*, 2.

Lieber, M. (1981). *Street Life: Afro-American Culture in Urban Trinidad*. Boston: G. K. Hall and Co.

Lusk, M. W. (1992). "Street Children of Rio de Janeiro." *International Social Work*, 35(4), 293–305.

McLoyd, V. C. and Wilson, L. (1991). "The Strain of Living Poor: Parenting, Social Support and Child Mental Health." In A. C. Huston (ed.), *Children in Poverty: Child Development and Public Policy*. Cambridge: Cambridge University Press.

Meyer, W. E. (ed.). (1991). *Protecting Working Children*. London: Zed Books and UNICEF.

Mishra, R. (1995). "Social Policy after Socialism." In J. Baldock and M. May (eds.), *Social Policy Review 7*. Canterbury, England: Social Policy Association.

Moorehead, A. (1987). *School Age Workers in Britain Today*. London: Anti-Slavery Society.

Morss, J. R. (1990). *The Biologising of Childhood: Developmental Psychology and the Darwinian Myth*. Hove, England: Lawrence Erlbaum Associates.

Munyakho, D. (1992). *Kenya: Child Newcomers in the Urban Jungle*. Florence, Italy: UNICEF.

Natale, B. G. (1992). "Street Children." Paper presented in Workshop on Children in Especially Difficult Circumstances. Francistown, Botswana, June 8–12.

Okello-Wengi, S. (1994). *Profile of Street Children in Gaborone City*. Research Report Submitted in Partial Fulfillment of Bachelor of Social Work Degree, Department of Social Work, University of Botswana.

Oliveira, W., Baizerman, M., and Pellet, L. (1992). "Street Children in Brazil and Their Helpers: Comparative Views on Aspirations and the Future." *International Social Work*, 35(2), 163–176.

Oloko, B. A. (1991). "Children's Work in Urban Nigeria: A Case Study of Young Lagos Street Traders." In W. E. Meyers (ed.), *Protecting Working Children*. London: Zed Books and UNICEF.

Palaparti, P. (1995). "Editorial." *Botswana Today*, 4(5), February 10–16.

Porio, E., Moselina, L., and Swift, A. (1994). "Philippines: Urban Communities and Their Fight for Survival." In C. S. Blanc, *Urban Children in Distress: Global Predicaments and Innovative Strategies*. Yverdon: Gordon and Breach.

Rizzini, I. and Lusk, M. W. (1995). "Children in the Streets: Latin America's Lost Generation." *Children and Youth Services Review*, 17(3), 391–400.

Rizzini, I., Rizzimin, I., Munoz-Vargas, M., and Galeano, L. (1994). "Brazil: A New Concept of Childhood." In C. S. Blanc, *Urban Children in Distress: Global Predicaments and Innovative Strategies*. Yverdon: Gordon and Breach.

Rosenfeld, J. M., Schon, D. A., and Sykes, I. J. (1995). *Out from Under: Lessons from Projects for Inaptly Served Children and Families*. Jerusalem: JDC-Israel, Children at Risk and Brooksdale Institute for Gerontology and Human Development.

Sandler, I., Miller, P., Short, J., and Wolchik, S. (1989). "Social Support as a Protective Factor for Children in Stress." In D. Belle (ed.), *Children's Social Networks and Social Support*. New York: John Wiley.

Scheper-Hughes, N. (1989). *Child Survival: Anthropological Perspectives on the Treatment and Maltreatment of Children*. Dordrecht: Reidel.

Sgroi, S. (ed.). (1982). *Handbook of Clinical Intervention in Child Sexual Abuse*. Lexington, MA: Lexington Books.

Solberg, A. (1990). "Negotiating Childhood: Changing Constructions of Age for Norwegian Children." In A. James and A. Prout (eds.), *Constructing and Reconstructing Childhood: Contemporary Issues in the Sociological Study of Childhood*. London: Falmer Press.

Tacon, P. (1991a). *Reap a Hundred Harvests: A Study on Street Children in Three Urban Centres of Zambia*. Unpublished.

————. (1991b). *Survey on Street Children in Three Urban Centers of Namibia*. Unpublished.

————. (1992). *Marco Jemuse and the Malevolent Monsters: A Program for Children in Especially Difficult Circumstances in Africa 1993–2000*. Paper presented at the Organization of African Unity and Its International Partners, November 25–27.

Tännsjö, T. (1992). *Populist Democracy: A Defense*. London: Routldge.

Treadwell, M. and Johnson, J. (1980). "Correlates of Adolescent Life Stress as Related to Race, SES, and Levels of Perceived Social Support." *Journal of Clinical Child Psychology*, 9, 13–16.

United Nations. (1992). *Demographic Yearbook 1991*. New York: United Nations Organization.

Van Ham, N. A., Blavo, E. Q., and Opoku, S. K. (1992). *Street Children in Acrra: A Survey Report*. Legon: Social Work and Administration Program, Department of Sociology, University of Ghana.

Vittachi, A. (1989). *Stolen Childhood: In Search of the Rights of the Child*. Cambridge, MA: Polity Press.

Werner, E. and Smith, R. (1982). *Vulnerable But Invincible: A Study of Resilient Children*. New York: McGraw-Hill.

Chapter 11

Housing Delivery Systems in Botswana: The Inadequacy of Gender-Neutral Policies

Faustin Kalabamu

INTRODUCTION

The last 100 or so years have witnessed the rise of feminism and gender planning as one of the liberation struggles. As Mannathoko (1992: 71) notes, feminism questions and challenges the origins of oppressive and discriminatory gender relations and attempts to change the relations for the better. Gender is defined as socially, psychologically, and historically constructed beliefs, roles, values, symbols, and perceptions that are associated with or assigned to women and men in a given community and time (Hombergh, 1993: 15–16; Meena, 1992: 1–2; and Buswell, 1989: 5–20). Unlike the body parts and functions that distinguish men and women all over the world, gender roles, relations, and perceptions vary from community and over time in the same community. Gender is learned through a process of socialization and culturalization—through toys given to children, the kind of discipline meted out to boys and girls, job and career orientations, and the portrayal of men and women in the arts and by the media (Brett, 1991: 3–4). Gender planning includes all approaches to development planning that recognizes the unequal gender and power relations between women and men in a given society and attempts to address women's concerns in development processes (Wieringa, 1994: 829–830).

APPROACHES TO GENDER PLANNING

Early feminists challenged the then commonly held chauvinist views of women as submissive, married, and dependent on men. Questioning the stereotyping of women as being inferior to men, the feminists argued that "the defects in reason that were manifest in women at that time were due to lack of proper education and the sheltered environments within which [women] were brought up" (Gaidzanwa, 1992: 95). Early feminists did not question the structural inequities between women and men, and, as such, their efforts did not lead to gender planning (Mannathoko, 1992: 73). Their work was, however, instrumental in raising gender awareness.

Although several conventions and declarations called for an end to all forms of discrimination and for the equality of women and men after the Second World War, it was not until the 1970s that the need for gender planning and the role of women in social and economic development was fully acknowledged (Wieringa, 1994; Moser, 1993; Brett, 1991; Meena, 1992). The acknowledgment culminated in the declaration of 1975 as International Women's Year and 1975–1985 as the UN Decade for Women. Moser (1993: 55–79) has grouped subsequent gender planning initiatives in Third World countries under five broad categories, as described below.

Welfare Approach

Initiatives under this category are designed to meet the practical needs of women, children, and the family in general without challenging structural gender inequities. Examples include mother-child health programs and services, family planning, food handouts, and similar programs aimed at improving family welfare. It is the oldest and most popular approach dating back to the 1950s.

Equity Approach

This approach recognizes women's productive role and challenges structures that tend to restrict women to domestic and child-bearing activities. It calls for direct state intervention to eliminate institutionalized gender inequities; and for political and economic autonomy to women. Examples of equity programs have included increasing the number of women in political posts (notably in parliaments and cabinets); amendment of legislation that discriminates against women; and increased female enrollment in educational institutions. It was most popular among feminists during the UN Decade for Women but was not fully accepted by governments in developing countries.

Anti-Poverty Approach

According to Moser, the anti-poverty approach is a "toned down" version of the equity approach in that it seeks to increase women's ability to earn income through improved access to private ownership of land and capital, and to the elimination of sexual discrimination in the labor market without challenging male supremacy. Most programs under this approach have centered on launching small-scale income-generating projects for women such as sewing, poultry, vegetable gardening and retailing. Most projects focus on low-income women. The approach is most popular among nongovernmental organizations and aid agencies.

Efficiency Approach

The efficiency approach is based on the assumption that increased participation by women in economic activities will lead to accelerated socioeconomic development, which will result in equity for all (men and women). It seeks to meet practical gender needs, and it is in step with structural adjustment policies advocated and imposed on Third World countries by the International Monetary Fund and the World Bank. It is currently the most popular approach among governments and multinational agencies probably because it promises economic development with least resource inputs from governments, investors, and donors.

Empowerment Approach

The empowerment approach acknowledges the right of each individual within a household, family, community, and nation, and it challenges oppressive structures, customs, laws, and practices at various levels and at all times. It seeks to enhance women's own self-reliance and internal strength through the right to determine their choices in life and the redistribution of power within each sociopolitical grouping. It is also aimed at increasing women's decision-making powers over household, local, and national resources. All these are to be achieved not by reversing existing power hierarchies but by transforming structures that have been used to subordinate and discriminate against women, including changes in law, civil codes, property rights, personal rights, and privileges. It also calls for political mobilization, consciousness raising on gender issues by both men and women, and women's participation in project planning and implementation.

Ann Schlyter (1995) suggests a sixth approach: market adaptation, which she describes as a blend of efficiency and empowerment approaches. The market approach supports only market solutions and is aggressively negative to public solutions. The approach seeks to minimize central government financing of projects and relies on the private sector, local authorities, and cost recovery principles.

There is a great deal of overlap between the above approaches (Moser, 1993; Schlyter, 1995: 20–27). The empowerment approach, for example, contains elements of equity, whereas the distinction between equity and equality approaches is very thin. The major difference, however, is the extent to which each approach meets both practical and strategic gender needs—that is, whether it accepts or challenges the status quo. Only two approaches, equity and empowerment, meet strategic gender needs. The equity approach is dependent on government initiatives (top-down), whereas the empowerment approach is grassroots based (bottom-up). Most countries have pursued a mixture of approaches over time (without discarding preceding initiatives), with varying degrees of success. Within Africa, the majority of states have applied "a bit of each" approach depending mostly on political imperatives, external donor requirements, and activities of nongovernmental organizations. During liberation wars, nationalist parties mobilized women to gain political independence and thereafter to win mass support. Many governments have since created women departments or units and "ensured participation of some women in parliament and in the party organs" (Mannathoko, 1992: 74). Most governments have also introduced gender-neutral laws, policies, and civil codes; paid maternity leave for women; and mother-child health care centers and several welfare programs targeting women and the children. Planners in some countries, such as Botswana, have constantly adhered to a mixture of welfare and gender-neutral policies and programs. The present chapter evaluates the effectiveness of Botswana's postcolonial gender-neutral housing policies, taking the town of Lobatse as a case study.

TRADITIONAL HOUSING DELIVERY SYSTEMS IN BOTSWANA

Similar to most African countries, Botswana's traditional communities were characterized by patriarchal structures and attitudes. Women controlled domestic and household activities and resources, while men enjoyed exclusive control of the public sphere and private wealth, including community leadership, cattle, and land. Every married man was entitled to three free pieces of land—one each for a homestead, cultivation, and grazing (Schapera, 1943: 44). When a man died, his male children inherited his land. Women were never given land on which to build their homes; they had to live with their parents or husbands (Schapera, 1943: 100).

Although women were denied desired land rights, they played a major role in the production of subsistence crops as well as house construction and maintenance. In fact, traditionally, each house in Botswana was usually known by the name of the wife occupying it, even though the husband habitually shared it with her (Schapera, 1943: 86). According to Anita Larsson and Viera Larsson (1984: 94–128), women were responsible for most activities in the house-building process. They collected clay and water, mixed them with sand, and molded bricks. They then pegged the house layout and erected walls. Women were also responsible for collecting grass and thatching roofs, constructing floors, as well as plastering and decorating walls. Women of the household performed these tasks collectively assisted by young sons and female relatives and friends.

Traditionally, men were responsible only for collecting poles and erecting roof trusses. They, too, often received assistance from male friends and relatives. Whenever a husband or wife sought assistance, women brewed beer to be drunk by all who worked on the house. Thus, house building has traditionally been a "do-it-yourself" activity, with some mutual assistance from other members of the community on a reciprocal basis. Houses were built from locally available materials obtained at no monetary cost and were designed for owner-occupation.

EMERGING GENDER ROLES AND RELATIONS

Patriarchal structures were retained during the colonial period except that, while the majority of women continued to reside and work in rural areas, a substantial proportion of men migrated into urban and mining centers and commercial farming areas within Botswana and South Africa. Most African male migrants were assigned professional and technical jobs such as mining and construction engineering; driving and operation of machinery and equipment; and administrative and managerial work. The few female migrants were streamlined into employment related to labor reproduction (e.g., domestic and personal services, nursing, and education). In 1971 (five years after Botswana's independence), almost three-quarters of female cash earners were employed in the provision of services compared to about one-third of male earners in the same sector (Table 11.1). At the same time, more men than women were offered formal education and vocational training, thereby reinforcing male supremacy. The majority of laws and institutions on ownership and control of wealth introduced by the colonial administration also reinforced the marginalization of women by denying them the right to acquire property or financial loans without the assistance of men—fathers, husbands, or sons.

Since the 1980s, the government of Botswana has initiated several programs to uplift the status of women. First, the government established national machinery known as the Women's Affairs Unit under the Ministry of Labor and Home Affairs to facilitate the full involvement and integration of women in the development process. The unit was recently elevated to a department with the expectation that the upgrading would enable the unit to carry out its functions in a timely and effective manner.

Table 11.1
Population Working for Cash by Sex and Major Industry, 1971–1991 (Percent)

Industry	1971		1981		1991	
	Female	Male	Female	Male	Female	Male
Agriculture	9.5	26.6	2.6	9.4	4.5	13.6
Mining	0.5	7.2	1.6	11.5	0.7	6.6
Manufacturing	5.4	6.6	2.4	3.7	11.4	7.1
Utilities	0.2	1.1	0.4	2.4	0.7	2.9
Construction	0.9	10.6	1.9	17.7	6.6	26.2
Trade	9.0	5.5	15.0	6.3	17.9	7.0
Communications	0.9	5.2	0.7	3.1	1.6	5.0
Finance	0.7	0.8	1.6	0.9	4.0	4.6
Services (all)	72.3	35.8	73.7	44.4	50.6	25.5
Government			16.8	21.4	6.9	13.9
Education			14.6	2.9	13.1	4.2
Health			2.5	1.2	3.9	1.6
Personnel			39.6	18.4	24.5	1.9
Other			0.2	0.5	2.2	3.9
Not Stated	0.6	0.6	0.1	0.6	2.0	1.5
All Industries %	100.0	100.0	100.0	100.0	100.0	100.0
(number)	(12,352)	(39,056)	(41,483)	(91,410)	(114,098)	(190,469)

Source: Kalabamu (1996b): 5.

Other initiatives have included some revision of laws and regulations that impact on women's access to land, property, credit finance, employment, and education. Government's efforts have been complemented by self-empowering initiatives undertaken by women and nongovernmental organizations. As a result of these and other progressive forces, women's participation in political, social, and economic activities has increased considerably. As indicated in Table 11.1, over the last two decades, the number of women employed in the cash economy has grown at an annual rate of 12 percent. In 1991 women accounted for almost 38 percent of the total population employed in the cash economy compared to 24 percent in 1971.

Employment of women in hitherto male-dominated sectors such as manufacturing, construction, and finance has also increased considerably. According to the 1991 census, female students constituted the majority (at 57%) in educational institutions at both primary and junior secondary schools. However, this figure dropped to 42 percent for senior secondary schools. The national teaching force at the primary school level was 78 percent female. At the secondary school level, 40 percent of the teachers were female, but in vocational/technical training centers only 19 percent of the teachers were female. In the health sector, 96 percent of all nurses and health educators were female, whereas 78 percent of all doctors and dentists were male. As elsewhere in developing countries, women in Botswana are employed mainly in fields which do not require high technical qualifications (e.g., nursing and education). Such work is "considered an extension of the essentially female role which has its origin in the household—the mother care offered to the family" (ICPE, 1986: 29)

Other significant changes relate to house ownership and construction as documented by Larsson (1988, 1989, 1990, 1996) and Datta (1993, 1994) among others. First, due to the proliferation of exogenous building materials and techniques, the role of women in the construction industry has been downgraded from that of principal player to that of passive participant or unskilled laborer (Kalabamu, 1996). Mud bricks have been replaced by cement blocks; thatch grass by metal sheets; firewood by paraffin and electricity; and so on. Second, the introduction of a cash economy and different lifestyles have transformed houses into marketable commodities. Since women are employed in less remunerative jobs, they are the most negatively affected by the transformation. Third, patriarchal structures have weakened in the form of widespread and socially accepted female-headed households.

According to the 1991 census, the proportion of de jure households headed by women stood at 47 percent for the whole of Botswana, and at 34 percent and 52 percent for urban and rural areas, respectively. Of the seven gazetted towns, Lobatse had the second highest proportion of female-headed households. Ingstad (1994: 214) estimates that the de facto proportion of female-headed households may be as high as 75 percent of total households in some rural settlements. The increase in female heads of households has been largely attributed to prolonged male absence from home while employed in the mines and towns.

Related to the increase of female-headed households has been the rapid growth of the number of women who have never married or who marry late in life. In 1971, only 23 percent of women aged 15 years and above had never been married compared to almost 45 percent in 1981 and 50 percent in 1991. The proportion of men who had never married increased less dramatically during the same period—from 44 percent in 1971 to 55 percent in 1991. The 1991 census showed that only 39 percent of women were married or living with men. The proportions of never-

Table 11.2
Proportions of Never-Married Women in Botswana, 1981 and 1991

Age Groups	1981 Census	1991 Census	% Change
20–24	68.9%	88.1%	19
25–29	46.9%	71.6%	25
30–34	32.4%	56.5%	24
35–39	25.2%	47.2%	22

Sources: Central Statistics Office (1983): Table 9; Central Statistics Office (1994): 1.

married women by five-year groups in 1981 and 1991 are shown in Table 11.2.

These data show that the proportion of never-married women in each cohort group increased by 19 to 25 percent between 1981 and 1991. As a result of never marrying or delaying marriage, there exists a large number of children and grandchildren born to unmarried mothers which has given rise to families consisting of up to three generations headed by women (Larsson, 1989: 50). Members of such families focus on maternal linkages, often talking of mother, sister, and grandmother and hardly of male relatives. Thus, the gendered myth that men are the persons who can head, provide, and raise families has been summarily deconstructed in Botswana.

GENDER-NEUTRAL HOUSING DELIVERY SYSTEMS IN BOTSWANA

Since independence in 1966, the government of Botswana has consistently upheld gender neutrality in all its national policies and programs in conformity with the country's constitution, which provides for non-racial democracy and freedom of speech, press, and association; affords equal rights for all citizens; and forbids all forms of discrimination. A gender-neutral approach may be defined as planning which—while aware of the existing structures, practices, and institutions that subordinate women—designs policies, projects, and programs that neither address women's disadvantaged positions nor appears to favor men. Gender-neutral planning uses terminology and phrases (such as households, low-income earners, beneficiaries, target group, and first-come-first-served) that seek to portray gender equity and social justice.

These policies and programs, as Kellet and Garnham note, are a "reflection of academic interpretations which stress economic and political factors and ignore or underplay cultural and social variations," which is the way groups and individuals make decisions on economic changes and opportunities (Kellet and Garnham, 1994: 1). The use of "low-income group," for example, does not reflect differences in opportunities available to women, men, single parents, the disabled, migrants, and the landless. A low-income earner who is landless and a single-parent mother has less opportunity to access a self-help housing program than an unmarried low-income man who owns a piece of land in the same settlement. Brett (1991), Meena (1992), Moser (1993), Varley (1994), and Molapo (1994) attribute the inability of policy makers to fully address gender issues to patriarchal attitudes and perceptions which assume that every household is headed by a man and, therefore, that policies designed to uplift low-income households will naturally benefit women.

Moreover, as Wieringa (1994: 835) observes, development planners want to fix problems with easy schedules, quantifiable targets, and simplicity. Feminist theories (e.g., on empowerment) are considered too complicated and not directly relevant to their everyday work. Gender-neutral policies and programs in Botswana may also have been informed by the changing gender roles and relation discussed above.

Gender-Neutral Land and Housing Policies

The Botswana National Assembly approved the operative National Policy on Land Tenure in April 1985 and the National Policy on Housing in 1982. To avoid all forms of discrimination, documents containing both policies do not refer to women, men, or any terminology insinuating race, sex, or gender, nor do they have a single line or paragraph on gender issues and women in particular.

In order to provide for equal access to land by all urban residents, the land policy advocated:

1. The use of public lotteries in the choice of successful applicants whenever the number of applications exceeds the number of plots to be disposed.
2. The reintroduction of tenant purchase schemes "to enable citizens who cannot afford to make down-payments to purchase houses" (Central Statistics Office, 1985: 8).

Throughout its length and breadth, the document avoids the use of such words as men, women, girls, boys, father, and mother. It also sticks to the term "farm citizens."

In a similar manner, the housing policy document uses gender-neutral phrases—notably households, citizens, lower/middle/high-income households, their staff, and government officers—and paraphrases sentences in the same spirit. Examples of gender-neutral housing policy statements include:

1. "Housing subsidies should be reduced over a period of time. Remaining subsidies should be directed to middle and lower income housing, from urban and rural areas."
2. "The commercial banks and the building society should adapt to the nation's needs by lending to lower income and rural households."
3. "Local Authorities should be allowed to build housing for their staff."
4. "The right to receive free institutional housing should be determined on an individual basis rather than given to entire departments" (Government of Botswana, 1982: 3–7).

Recent statements redefining or clarifying land and housing policies also lack a gender focus. The National Development Plan: 1991 to 1997, for example, emphasizes "promoting social justice and equity by enabling Batswana to participate more fully and effectively in the development of housing and settlements and, therefore, the benefits arising from that development" and "ensuring that all Batswana have access to adequate shelter, with explicit, targeted subsidies to those in need, to cover the cost of basic services and housing" (Central Statistics Office, 1991: 421).

Housing Delivery Systems

Housing delivery systems in Botswana may be divided into two broad categories: owner-occupied and rented. Owner-occupied houses may be self-built, inherited, or bought. Houses may also be rented from private landlords, employers, central/local government, or private/parastatal companies. The following sub-sections discuss general principles that govern access to owner-occupied and rented housing.

Owner-Occupied Housing

The most common way to own a house in Botswana's urban areas is through self-help initiatives. The first and most critical step in self-help housing is to acquire land from the state. Almost every piece of land in each town is state owned. State land is currently available at cost on a first-come-first-served basis (Central Statistics Office, 1990). All applications are kept on computerized waiting lists for various plot categories—low, medium, and high-income residential plots. Previously, plots were allocated through lottery systems for medium and high-income plots and on a first-come-first-served basis for low-income plots. Any citizen of Botswana over 21 years of age, regardless of sex or marital status, may apply for an urban plot on state land.

Rental Housing

The Botswana Housing Corporation, a state-owned company and major supplier of rental accommodation, lets its houses and flats on a first-come-first-served basis. Any company or individual regardless of age, employment, sex, or marital status may apply for a low, medium, and/or high-cost house. The corporation keeps computerized application lists for the various house categories. Employer housing (including central/ local government housing and parastatal housing) is available to respective employees according to entitlement, eligibility, and seniority. Priority is given to chief officers in each institution, or company, regardless of family size, sex of household head, homelessness, and the like.

To date, Botswana has not spelled out formal rules or regulations governing relationships between private landlords and tenants probably because this is considered to be a purely private transaction. In principle, landlords and ladies let houses or rooms to whoever can pay the rent.

OUTCOME OF GENDER-NEUTRAL STRATEGIES: EVIDENCE FROM LOBATSE

Lobatse, with a population of 26,052 inhabitants in 1991, is located 70 km south of Botswana's capital city of Gaborone and is currently the fourth largest urban center, although it was the second town to be established (1909) in the country. During the 1991 census, women headed 2,477 households, or 37 percent of the total households enumerated in Lobatse. About 75 percent of the female heads were single-parents compared to 42 percent single-parent male heads of households. Close to 32 percent of the male-headed households were one-person households, while only 23 percent were one-person households among female-headed ones. Up to 50 percent of male-headed households had no more than two persons each compared to 39 percent among female-headed households. Thus, female-headed households in Lobatse were generally larger than the male-headed ones.

Data from the same 1991 census indicate that, although female heads of households in Lobatse had relatively better basic education than male heads, more male heads of households had attained higher education (ordinary level examinations and above) than female heads. Thus, more male than female heads were better placed to assume the top managerial positions. Furthermore, although women constituted 51 percent of the total labor force in Lobatse, they accounted for only 41 percent of the economically active population (Central Statistics Office, 1994: 25–26). About 42 percent of the economically active women were employed in nonskilled (elementary) jobs compared to 29 percent among men. Only 4.5 percent of gainfully employed women occupied top administrative and professional positions compared to 6.8 percent among males.

Table 11.3

Percentage Distribution of Housing Tenure by Sex of Household Head, 1981–1991

Tenure	Male (1991)	Female (1991)	Both Sexes (1981)	Both Sexes (1991)
Owner-Occupied Dwelling Unit				
Allocated by Tribal Authority	3.3	5.6	12.4	4.2
Purchased	2.8	3.5	8.2	3.1
Inherited	0.9	1.6	2.4	1.1
Self-Help Housing Land	15.4	22.0	—	17.8
(Sub-total)	*(22.4)*	*(32.7)*	*(23.0)*	*(26.2)*
Rented Dwelling Unit				
Botswana Housing Corporation	5.5	7.8	10.2	6.3
Central Government	2.2	1.9	—	2.1
Local Government	2.0	2.8	21.4	2.3
Individual	43.6	43.9	20.3	43.7
Company	14.8	3.5	13.2	10.6
(Sub-total)	*(68.1)*	*(59.9)*	*(65.1)*	*(65.0)*
Rent-Free	8.9	7.3	7.0	8.3
Self-Allocation	0.4	0.0	3.9	0.3
Not Stated	0.2	0.1	1.0	0.2
Total				
Percent	100.0	100.0	100.0	100.0
Number	(10,280)	(6,509)	(4,389)	(16,789)

Source: Central Statistics Office (1982): 429.

Housing Conditions of Female- and Male-Headed Households in Lobatse

According to the 1981 and the 1991 census, more than two-thirds of households in Lobatse live in rented accommodations (Table 11.3). A quarter of all households live in owner-occupied houses, while 7 to 8 percent live in rent-free dwelling units (inclusive of servant quarters, watchmen houses, and construction site camps). In 1991, individual landlords dominated the housing rental market.

Data in Table 11.3 also reveals substantial differences in types of houses occupied by male and female-headed households. First, the pro-

Table 11.4
Type of Infrastructure Services by Sex of Head of Household, 1991, in
Percent

	Service	Male	Female	Both Sexes
Sanitation	Flush Toilet	31.4	20.3	27.3
	Pit Latrine	55.5	65.0	59.0
	Others	10.4	11.8	10.9
	Not Stated	2.7	2.9	2.8
	Total	**100.0**	**100.0**	**100.0**
Water Supply	Within Plot	37.8	28.4	34.3
	Public Stand Pipe	62.2	71.6	65.7
	Total	**100.0**	**100.0**	**100.0**
Fuel for Lighting	Electricity	16.6	10.8	14.5
	Gas	0.9	1.1	1.0
	Paraffin	55.3	60.4	57.2
	Candle	26.4	27.3	26.7
	Others	0.8	0.4	0.6
	Total	**100.0**	**100.0**	**100.0**

Source: Central Statistics Office (1991).

portion of female heads living in owner-occupied houses is higher (at about 33%) than male heads, which are only 26 percent of their total. Second, the proportion of female-headed households living on self-help housing plots and tribal land (both of which are not accepted for registration by the Registrar of Deeds) is higher (at almost 28%) than among male heads (which are about 19% of the total). Third, there are relatively fewer female-headed households who rent company houses than their male counterparts. About 15 percent of households headed by men live in dwelling units rented from companies, compared to only 3.5 percent among female-headed households.

Furthermore, examination of infrastructure services available to households by sex of head of household indicates that female-headed households have relatively lower quality services, as depicted in Table 11.4. Only 20 percent of female-headed households have access to flush toilets compared to 31 percent among male-headed households. About 39 percent of male-headed households obtain water from within their plots compared to 28 percent among female-headed households. Eighteen percent of male-headed households depend on electricity and gas as their main fuel for lighting compared to 13 percent among female-headed households.

From the above information, it can be concluded that (1) more female-than male-headed households live in owner-occupied houses—notably self housing; (2) fewer female heads than male heads live in company rented housing; and (3) male-headed households live in relatively better quality housing than their counterparts. Although the differences are not enormous, they are consistent. And this has happened in spite of strict observance of gender-neutral policies. The better services and housing conditions under which male-headed households live accords them many advantages over female-headed ones. For example, it is easier for more male-headed households to attain proper domestic hygiene than female-headed households. It also means that more male-headed households can generate more income for themselves because they are physically healthier, have fewer mental worries, and spend less time drawing water, fuel-wood, or digging pit latrines. They also spend less money on medication and hospital expenses. As Tipple (1994) demonstrates, quality housing promotes income-generating activities such as baking, sewing, shops, and printing which are undertaken from homes: Such "economic activities enable housing improvements and the latter improve employment prospects and productivity from which residents are able to undertake all types of improvements to their living conditions" (Tipple, 1994: 3). It follows, therefore, that those who are born and/or raised in quality housing have an advantage over those whose housing conditions are poorer. In other words, male-headed household members are better off in many ways than the dependents of female household heads.

CAUSES OF THE GENDERED HOUSING INEQUALITY

The formulation of gender-neutral policies and programs appears to be based on three refutable presumptions. First, as seen earlier, is the hidden/unsaid presumption that a man heads each household or family. Second is the assumption that provision of gender equality before the law automatically makes men and women equal, which ignores the long history of patriarchy that, generation after generation, has created enormous disparities between men and women. The third presumption, which emanates from the second, is that given equal opportunities, each man and woman has a 50–50 chance of emerging as the winner, forgetting that women have the triple responsibilities of reproduction, production, and community management while men have only two (production and community management). Gender-neutral policies tend to ignore the various ways in which society expects men and women to act. "Women (and men, for that matter) are engaged in a constant struggle of negotiating the different interests with which they are faced: ambivalence, contradictions, clashes with the interests of other individuals or groups are central in these processes," (Wieringa, 1994: 835). Because of such presumptions, planners and project designers fail to recognize policy implementation bottlenecks and world realities. In the case of Botswana, the following have been identified as the major factors contributing to gendered differences in housing.

Laws and Regulations

Gender-neutral laws and regulations have not accompanied gender-neutral policies. To date, Batswana women married under customary or common law automatically become minors under the guardianship of their husbands—unless they explicitly marry under out-of-community-of-property as provided for by the Married Persons Act of 1971. Otherwise, the husband becomes the sole administrator of the joint estate, which is a merger of any properties held by either party before and after marriage. Women, regardless of their marital status may, however, acquire usufruct land rights for the purpose of housing, cultivation or commerce. Certificates denoting usufruct rights (such as the Certificate of Rights [COR]) given to low-income urban plot holders are not registrable and are not accepted as collateral by money-lending institutions. Many women opt for land under COR, which does not require registration. Holders of CORs may only obtain loans in the form of building materials from the appropriate local authority.

Lack of Access to Credit Finance

Only single women and women married under the out-of-community-of-property regime may readily obtain loans from financial institutions. Women married in-community-of-property must obtain their husbands' consent, which may not be obtained for a number of reasons, including simple denial or difficulty in reaching the man when he has traveled or during separation. Consequently, very few women apply for loans. Between 1990 and 1994, only 6 women (out of 16 applicants from Lobatse) applied for housing loans from the Botswana Building Society. In Francistown, only 18 out of 117 loan applicants were women. In Lobatse, all the female applicants were not married, while 2 (or 11%) of all female applicants in Francistown were married. Thus, the majority of women in Botswana do not qualify for formal housing loans because they either lack a registered land title or are married in community of property or fail to obtain the husband's consent.

Lack of Access to Rural Resources

Women in Botswana, as in all patriarchal societies, have traditionally been denied access to property and wealth. In Botswana, as Dow and Kidd (1994: 84–85) note, the most valued wealth is livestock, notably cattle which, as observed earlier, has always been in the public sphere of men. It may be acquired through inheritance, donation, or as bride price (*lobola*) for daughters, yet only men (as fathers, husbands, uncles, or sons) can make decisions to buy, sell, or slaughter the cattle. Thus, women have no wealth to fall back on when confronted with the need to raise funds. At the same time, many men sell family cattle to raise money for housing, investment, and social/cultural activities.

Abject Poverty

The number and proportion of women employed in the Botswana cash economy has increased considerably since independence—from 24 percent of the economically active population in 1971 to 38 percent in 1991. Nevertheless, the majority of women continue to be employed in the provision of services (notably domestic work) and other low-paying jobs. Consequently, women's average incomes are half those of men as revealed by the 1985–1986 and 1993–1994 Household Income Expenditure Surveys (Central Statistics Office, 1987, 1995). Most women's financial position, especially single mothers, is worsened further by having large households, "insufficient access to male labor and little support from spouses" (Larsson, 1989: 48). Poverty aggravates women's housing conditions and impedes their ability to participate in projects and activities aimed at housing, social, and environmental upliftment.

Low Status of Women at Work

As mentioned earlier, very few women occupy senior and top management posts in companies, parastatals, and government departments. It follows, therefore, that fewer women than men are entitled and/or eligible to apply for company and institutional housing; this explains why fewer women than men live in company and local or central government houses in Lobatse. Although men are allocated bungalows and houses of similar quality as senior officers, women (as junior ranking officers) are allocated semidetached and one-bedroom units regardless of their marital status, family size, or composition.

Lack of Modern House Construction Skills

Women who, under Botswana culture and society, are acknowledged architects and builders of traditional houses find their skills inapplicable

in urban areas where mud-and-thatch houses are excluded by town planning rules and regulations in favor of exogenous structures in which very
few women are employed during their construction. In 1991, only 2.2
percent of the economically active female labor force was employed in
the construction industry, and these, mostly as cleaners, painters, or, at
best, "clerk of works" (Kalabamu, 1996a). Women have to rely on male
labor during the construction of their self-help housing because the modern society has transformed them from builders to unskilled laborers and
domestic servants.

CONCLUSION

The government of Botswana has been exemplary in its commitment
to promote equality and to integrate women into development processes.
It has been responsive to women's demands as exemplified by the establishment of the Women's Affairs Unit (soon to become a department)
within the Ministry of Labor and Home Affairs. It also signed the instrument of Accession to the UN Convention on the Elimination of All
Forms of Discrimination Against Women in July 1996. In addition, it
identified over 20 pieces of legislation that discriminate against women
with a view to amending them.

Having pursued gender-neutral policies for over 30 years and having
complied with international and national demands to integrate women
into mainstream socioeconomic development, planners in Botswana generally believe that nothing more needs to be undertaken in respect of
housing, gender, and environmental management. The involvement of
women in environmental management is one of the six critical areas of
concern excluded in the Botswana Platform of Action as priority national
issues. The terms of reference recently issued for the long overdue review
of the National Housing Policy do not include examination of gender
issues. The two national programs are indicative of the current wave of
complacency—the feeling that enough has already been done in this regard.

To be sure, there is room for improvement. First, there is a need to
actively involve women in decision making at all levels—the household,
the community, subnational, and national levels. Of the four, the household level is the most critical as it affects everyday life. Second, there is
a need to integrate gender, and women's perspectives in particular, in
the formulation of policies and programs. Third, there is a need to conduct research and be informed on gender constraints and various impacts of projects on women groups. Fourth, there is a need to take
affirmative actions and positively discriminate in favor of women—for
example, by giving priority to single mothers with large households and
allocating free land to teenage mothers. It is essential that women be

mentioned in policy and project documents. Being gender blind will not eliminate subordination and prejudices against women. Fifth, the role of advancing gender equality should not be confined to the Women's Affairs Unit and nongovernmental organizations (NGOs). It should be everyone's and every department's duty to promote gender equality in both word and deed.

This chapter has attempted to show that gender-neutral policies do not necessarily bring about gender equality, however consistently pursued, unless equally gender-neutral rules, regulations, beliefs, and affirmative actions accompany the policies. Indeed, it may be necessary to practice positive discrimination in order to rectify historically constructed gender imbalances so as to level the playing field whereby women and men can then be at par. Hiding behind gender neutrality serves the existing patriarchal structures adequately because it sustains the status quo and places the blame squarely on women, who are said to fail to take the opportunities availed to them. Further research is required to unearth gender constraints buried under gender neutrality.

REFERENCES

Brett, A. (1991). "Why Gender Is a Development Issue in Wallace." In T. March and C. March (eds.), *Changing Perceptions*. Oxford: Oxford University Press.

Buswell, C. (1989). *Women in Contemporary Society*. Hampshire: Macmillan.

Central Statistics Office (CSO). (1982). *Summary Statistics on Small Areas*. Gaborone: Government Printers.

———. (1983). *Census Administrative/Technical Report and National Statistical Tables*. Gaborone: Government Printers.

———. (1985). *National Policy on Land Tenure*. Gaborone: Government Printers.

———. (1987). *Household Income and Expenditure Survey: 1985/86*. Gaborone: Government Printers.

———. (1990). *Allocation of State Land: New Policy*. Gaborone: Ministry of Local Government and Lands.

———. (1991). *National Development Plan 7: 1991–1997*. Gaborone: Government Printers.

———. (1994). *Census 1991: Employment Indicators*. Gaborone: Government Printers.

———. (1995). *Household Income and Expenditure Survey: 1993/94*. Gaborone: Government Printers.

Datta, K. (1993). *Research on Women in Economy and Its Impacts on Policy Making in Botswana*. Gaborone: National Institute of Research.

———. (1994). "Strategies for Urban Survival? Women Landlords in Gaborone, Botswana." *Habitat International*, 19(1), 1–12.

Dow, U. and Kidd, P. (1994). *Women, Marriage and Inheritance*. Gaborone: Women and Law in Southern Africa.

Gaidzanwa, R. (1992). "Bourgeois Theories of Gender and Feminism and Their

Shortcomings with Reference to Southern Africa Countries." In R. Meena (ed.), *Gender in Southern Africa: Conceptual and Theoretical Issues*. Harare: Sapes Books.

Government of Botswana (GOB). (1982). *National Policy on Housing*. Gaborone: Government Printers.

Hombergh, H. (1993). *Gender and Environment in Development*. Amsterdam: Institute for Development Research.

Ingstad, B. (1994). "The Grandmother and Household Viability in Botswana." In A. Adepoju and C. Oppong (eds.), *Gender, Work & Population in Sub-Saharan Africa*. London: International Labor Organization and Heinemann.

International Centre for Public Enterprises in Developing Countries (ICPE). (1986). *The Role of Women in Developing Countries*. Ljubljana: ICPE.

Kalabamu, Faustin T. (1996a). "Women Labour in the Construction Industry in Lobatse Botswana." *African Urban Quarterly*, 11(1, 2).

———. (1996b). *Access to Urban Housing by Women in Botswana*. Gaborone: National Institute of Research.

Kellet, P. and Garnham, A. (1994). "Contrasting Value Systems in Self-Help Housing Process." Paper presented at the Second Symposium on Housing for the Urban Poor held at the International Convention Centre, Birmingham, England, April 11–14.

Larsson, A. (1988). *From Outdoor to Indoor Living*. Lund, Sweden: University of Lund.

———. (1989). *Women Householders and Housing Strategies: The Case of Gaborone, Botswana*. Lund, Sweden: National Swedish Institute for Lund, Building Research.

———. (1990). *Modern Houses for Modern Life*. Lund, Sweden: University of Lund.

———. (1996). *Modernisation of Traditional Tswana Housing*. Lund, Sweden: University of Lund.

Larsson, A. and Larsson, V. (1984). *Traditional Tswana Housing*. Stockholm: Swedish Council of Building Research.

Mannathoko, C. (1992). "Feminist Theories and the Study of Gender Issues in Southern Africa." In R. Meena (ed.), *Gender in Southern Africa: Conceptual and Theoretical Issues*. Harare, Zimbabwe: Sapes Books.

Meena, R. (ed.). (1992). *Gender in Southern Africa: Conceptual and Theoretical Issues*. Harare, Zimbabwe: Sapes Books.

Molapo, M. (1994). "Women and Shelter Development." Paper presented at the Second Symposium on Housing for the Urban Poor held at the International Convention Centre, Birmingham, England, April 11–14.

Moser, C. (1993). *Gender Planning and Development: Theory, Practice and Training*. London: Routledge.

Schapera, I. (1943). *Native Land Tenure in the Bechuanaland Protectorate*. Cape Town: Lovedale Press.

Schlyter, A. (1995). "Approaches to Women and Housing in Development Policy." In S. Sithole-Fundire et al., *Gender Research on Urbanisation. Planning, Housing and Everyday Life*. Harare, Zimbabwe: Women's Research Center and Network.

Sithole-Fundire, S. et al. (1995). *Gender Research on Urbanisation. Planning, Housing and Everyday Life*. Harare, Zimbabwe: Women's Research Center and Network.

Tipple, A. Graham. (1994). "Employment from Housing." Paper presented at the Second Symposium on Housing for the Urban Poor held at the International Convention Centre, Birmingham, England, April 11–14.

Varley, A. (1993). "Gender and Housing." *Habitat International* 17(4), 13–30.

Wieringa, S. (1994). "Women's Interests and Empowerment: Gender Planning Reconsidered." *Development and Change* (25), 829–848.

Chapter 12

Women, Knowledge, and Power in Environmental and Social Change

Mark Chingono

INTRODUCTION

Considering only the last three decades, especially since the time of the 1972 Stockholm United Nations (UN) conference on the environment, a massive literature on women and the environment has accumulated. The increasing number of national, regional, and international meetings being held on the subject is evidence enough of the importance of this issue. There are indeed differing accounts of the nature of key issues, and hence different priorities and strategic positioning by the activists concerned. Nonetheless, what comes shining through is the fact that the discourses on the environment and women, or ecofeminism as it is currently called, have managed to arrive at some far-reaching and important conclusions about our relationship to the environment.

   This analysis critically reevaluates the case and claims of ecofeminists who contend that ecological destruction is, at its base, misogynist and the inevitable result of the masculine drive to control and dominate the female. At its core, ecofeminism, as a discourse on environmental history, critiques perceived male degradation of the environment and celebrates a more sustainable vision of human interaction with nature. Merchant (1995) contributed tremendously to the redefinition of this discourse and provided "important ideas for ecofeminism as a distinct strand of environmental thinking" (Beinart, 1998: 776). Today ecofeminists posit that women are intrinsically connected to the environment, and should therefore be seen as "the managers of the rural areas . . . rather than as mere consumers and destroyers of rural resources" (Sow, 1997: 253). This discussion challenges as biased and banal some of the ecofeminist assertions.

An underlying subtheme will be the operation of the dialectic of resistance and reinvention. In this context, the role of knowledge and power in defining the women/environment nexus and in transforming it receives particular attention. The question that arises is, what forms of knowledge and power are adequate for women to overcome obstacles to their emancipation and to transform society and the environment in ways that promote egalitarianism and equality between the sexes, races, and classes? And, finally, do women in general really have similar needs and wants individually and collectively? This analysis does not offer definitive answers to such fundamental questions; instead, the objective is to invite critical conversation and to contribute to new ways of thinking about these issues. As a preliminary attempt, the discussion suggests alternative strategies for transcending some of the divisive ideological "isms and schisms" that present the major obstacle to realizing a more humane society for both women and men.

Conceptual Framework and Context

Ecofeminist critiques of male bias and hegemony in social sciences in particular and society in general state that "women's different kinds of interactions with nature and social life . . . provide women with distinctive and privileged scientific and epistemological standpoints" (Harding, 1987: 295). Women are depicted as intrinsically connected to the environment and as "the managers of the rural areas . . . rather than as mere consumers and destroyers of rural resources" (Sow, 1997: 253). By virtue of their supposed predominance in natural resource management, women become key actors, "first and foremost the very source of the solutions to be found" (Sow, 1997: 253). This conviction is the cornerstone of the research network on Women, Environment and Development (WEDNET).

Indeed, some African and Asian cultures establish specific relations between women and nature. In these cultures women and the environment, especially land, are considered the sacred sources of life and its nourishment. Land is perceived as a female entity, especially in India where "women are closely associated with nature both in their daily gestures and in their imagery" (Sow, 1997: 255). This perceived women–environment relationship is imbued with moral, religious, and spiritual connotations. Indeed, it is considered sacred, for both are the sources of life. In the nine months between June 5, World Environment Day, and March 8, International Women's Day, a woman can conceive and deliver new life; and in the next three months (between Women's Day and Environment Day), that life may be in jeopardy if we do not look after the *environment* and *women*. Thus, from this perspective, the relationship between women and the environment is seen as a question of life and death.

With respect to Africa, the gender-specific character of imperialism as well as scientific progress is said to have resulted in the displacement of "organic metaphors associated with women's approaches to nature" and their substitution with "mechanical images and male rationalism" (Beinart, 1998: 776). Is it really true, however, that, as a variation of this doctrine claims, "women's different kinds of interactions with nature and social life . . . provide women with distinctive and privileged scientific and epistemological standpoints?" (Harding, 1987: 295). Which women in class, race, profession, and organizational terms? A poor peasant woman's environment and that of a baroness in, say, England are totally different.

In particular, on closer scrutiny the supposed innocuous relationship between women and the environment turns out to be no more than a form of wishful thinking. Similarly, the assumption that men (poor and rich, black and white) are solely responsible for ecological destruction seems to be based on hatred of men, or rather on a misconception of the problem; indeed, it ignores African men's traditional approaches to the environment. These claims not only excuse women from their complicity in destroying the environment, but more seriously, they blur the nature of class exploitation and struggle. Second, the discussion argues that, although beneath the surface of socially constructed gender differences, women's ideas and praxis with respect to the environment are not substantially different from those of men. Third, it concludes that the marginalization of women in the production and dissemination of knowledge makes them susceptible to becoming accomplices in their own subjugation. Indeed, given this reality, the limited achievements of ecofeminists are inevitable, as is the flimsy foundation on which their case rests. Telling poor women that the cause of their miseries are their poor men is miseducation and undermines their potential to transform repressive statist and capitalist structures.

In order to transcend the limits of this kind of miseducation, which is perpetrated through the dissemination of gender and race-prejudiced knowledge, oppressed women—and men—need to effectively participate in the production of philosophical and scientific knowledge. Such knowledge constitutes an indispensable weapon in the struggle to protect the environment and to bring forth a new emancipatory vision. Possession of useful knowledge can translate into empowerment for its holder. Women's complicity in environmental degradation and in their own subjugation through, for instance, accepting patriarchal domination in the name of tradition, is due to their marginalization in the production of knowledge. Ignorance can be bliss. As McFadden (1999: 11) aptly notes: "Women must become knowers, they must participate in the definition and creation of knowledge. A lot hinges on the ability of African women to conceptualise themselves and to articulate theoretical positions."

No doubt, in the information age, it is through the ability to conceptualize and articulate theoretical positions, as well as to use information technology, that women can empower themselves. Since the production and dissemination of knowledge is implicated in power relations, women have to empower themselves; power cannot be given but instead has to be nurtured and developed. Power and knowledge, as is implicit in Foucault's (1972) insightful contribution on the subject, are two sides of the same coin that shapes social life. Neither is given or static, and neither can be taken away. Manifesting themselves in many different forms, knowledge and power are constantly being contested and redefined.

Since knowledge lies at the core of various systems of control and domination, accumulation, and distribution, the challenge then is to discover how women can become knowers. In particular, how can they increase their ability to engage in abstract and theoretical analysis and to manipulate information technology without at the same time becoming victims of their own power? What forms of knowledge are adequate for women to resist oppressing themselves by rivalling men's masculinity and evil? How can women—and all other oppressed social groups—move beyond resisting to reinventing the future? How can power and knowledge be mobilized to produce a new emancipatory vision? These are some of the questions tentatively addressed in this discursive analysis.

THE NATURAL VERSUS SOCIAL ENVIRONMENT: A FALSE DICHOTOMY?

In 1972 the United Nations declared June 5 World Environment Day to mark the opening of the Stockholm Conference on the Human Environment. The same conference adapted a resolution that led to the creation of the United Nations Environment Program (UNEP), the agency that coordinates the UN's environmental activities. The environment was conceived of as a "physical concept"—as water, land, forest, geosphere, biosphere. As used conventionally, the term has gradually taken on an economic, political, and social connotation (Sow, 1997: 251). The intensifying degradation of the physical environment through human activity, such as farming, grazing, and building, has pointed up the close connection between the natural and social environment. Indeed, in most of West and Central Africa, "people realised quite early the economic and social impact of the erosion of land used for intensive cash crop production (in groundnuts, coffee, cocoa, tea, pineapple, cotton, etc." (Sow,

1997: 251). In short, specific forms of accumulation, production, and organization have specific ramifications for the relationship between human beings and the natural environment.

At a global level, industrial pollution, through carbonic gas emissions from human activity (automobiles, airplanes, factories, and coal-driven power stations), has led to increasing global warming, an issue that was highlighted at the Earth Summit in Rio de Janeiro, Brazil, in 1992. The recent work of U.S., French, and Russian scientists at Russia's Vostok research station—the coldest spot on earth—is revealing. The scientists laboriously drilled out a 3-kilometer-long ice core/cube, which shows that the levels of heating greenhouse gases are higher now than at any time in the past 420,000 years. They also discovered that certain gases—carbon dioxide and methane—play a big role in warming the planet when the ice age ends. As one of the scientists puts it: "It is clear that greenhouse gas levels are unprecedented compared with the previous 400,000 years. . . . What this says is we're going well beyond the bounds of nature's variation" (Sapa-AP, 1999: 10).

Such interaction between human beings and their environment, and the unintended consequences of this interaction, are inevitable in a global consumer and industrial society. In their different ways, both women and men participate in ecological and environmental degradation, and this fact is conditioned by the mode of production and economic organization within their particular society.

The social environment, that is, economic and political relations, shapes the individual's relationship with the natural environment, just as the natural environment defines the range of possible human activities. Therefore, it is perhaps useful to dispense with the false dichotomy between "natural" and "social" environments, and instead focus on the dialectic between them. Similarly, it is important to stress that, although men may dominate women in certain forms, with respect to environmental degradation perhaps the most decisive form of domination is that between the poor and the rich. As the research network on Women, Environment and Development (WEDNET) recognizes, the present environmental crisis in Africa and the recurrent poverty of women are not unrelated but are "the simultaneous consequence of global and regional policies which lead women to unwittingly project their own poverty on African basic natural resources" (Sow, 1997: 253). Exploited women have little choice but to exploit the natural environment in turn in order to survive.

WOMEN AND THE ENVIRONMENT

The relationship between women and the natural environment, as should be clear from the foregoing, is primarily a function of the balance of social, political, and economic forces. In some respects, women's sociopolitical and economic environment may be far more distinct from that of men than their interaction with the natural environment. For instance, issues such as marriage, pregnancy, child bearing, work, rape, customary inheritance laws, and patriarchal ideology in general affect women's lives, choices, and destiny in more distinctive ways than their interaction with the natural environment—which for urban women is not that different. The case of rape, which is on the rise in South Africa, where a woman is raped every 26 seconds (Fenster, 1999: 57), is a typical example of how the social environment can affect women's lives in more fundamental, if not traumatic, ways than their mythologized interaction with the biophysical environment.

The irony is that the celebrated "organic metaphors associated with women's approaches to nature" may actually be a myth that justifies a submissive and subordinate role for women. Through a combination of poverty and ignorance, poor rural women are forced to destroy the environment by, for instance, cutting down trees for firewood and building, gathering grass for thatching and grazing, creating soil erosion through ploughing, and so on. In short, the human environment seems more decisive in the first and last instance, precisely because hitherto men have subjugated women and abused the environment through their dominance in economics, politics, and social life.

Through capitalist-patriarchal hegemony, characterized by a macho and masculine culture of grabbing and raping women and the environment, men risk irreversibly destroying the environment and life on earth. Whether or not women can reverse men's destructive propensity and restore respect for Mother Nature—the environment—thereby preserving life on earth, there certainly is some hope. One purpose of the present discussion is to give positive shape to this hope by subjecting beliefs in patriarchal hegemony to critical scrutiny. In exploring the weaknesses of the ecofeminist movement, it highlights its possible role in creating a new emancipatory vision.

ECOFEMINIST PHILOSOPHY AND PRAXIS

Since Simone de Beauvoir (1964) published her groundbreaking *The Second Sex* almost half a century ago, feminist debate has moved beyond her analysis. Her shocking suggestions that "one is not born, but rather becomes a woman, and that biology is not destiny" "have atrophied into truisms of equal opportunity laws" (Muir, 1999: 22). The distinction she made between sex and gender is now commonly recognized and so will not be discussed here at length. While sex refers to the natural human physiology, biology, chromosomes, genitals, and hormones, gender is socially and historically constructed. It refers to socially ascribed values of feminine and masculine roles, behaviors, attributes, and ideologies, which are arbitrarily linked to biological sex (Imam, 1997: 2).

Described as the mother of modern feminism, de Bouvoir was the forerunner of the women's revolution of the 1960s and 1970s. Although her followers have splintered into different schools, her concept of woman as "The Other" is still viable. "When we abolish the slavery of half of humanity, together with the whole system of hypocrisy it implies, then the 'division' of humanity will reveal its genuine significance and the human couple will find its true form" (Muir, 1999: 22).

Today, feminism has become a label that names the kaleidoscopic, "many-faceted responses of a multitude of women wrestling with the question of self-determination, seeking social changes that will give greater justice, power, and dignity to women" (Keen, 1996: 195). There are now many variants of feminism. However, a broad distinction can be made between feminism as prophetic protest—a model for the changes men are beginning to experience—and feminism as an ideology—a continuation of a pattern of gender enmity and scapegoating that men have traditionally practiced against women (Keen, 1996: 195).

According to Keen (1996: 196), prophetic feminism is based on the following premises: women culture has been dominated by patriarchy which in turn is rooted in hierarchy, power, control, and violence; ecological destruction is rooted in patriarchal attitudes and behavior; men tend to devalue all things considered "feminine"; and women can liberate themselves through their own struggle.

Based on the assumption that women are the innocent victims of a male conspiracy, ideological feminism, in contrast, is characterized by the tendency of women to resent and denounce patriarchal domination and to seek vindictive triumph over men. Accordingly, problems such as poverty, injustice, warfare, and environmental degradation are blamed on the so-called masculine conspiracy. As Betty Reardon (cited in Keen, 1996: 197), the ideology's foremost representative, has put it, "Ecological destruction is, at its base misogynist. . . . It is simply another result of the masculine drive to control and dominate the feminine."

Without disputing these claims, one wonders whether or not the threat of the desecration of the earth is too immediate an agony to be used in partisan warfare between the sexes? In the final analysis, the issue of gender remains a mystery. It is an artificial separation of masculine and feminine qualities, an act of intellectual fascism that forces the complex beauty of actual men and women into the two-column goose-step of "masculine" and "feminine" attributes. However, as Keen (1996: 218) argues, underneath the stereotypes lies the mystery: "Peel away the layers of the social conditioning and there remains the prime fact of the duality of men and women. . . . Each sex is one side of Mobius strip, a fragment necessary to create a whole."

The mystery of our sexual being is not something that can be settled by science. It is about who we are, where we come from and where we are going. It is deeper than our ability to abstract and objectify. The problem is compounded by the effects of globalization, as manifested by many people's exhausting wrestling with multiple identities that emerge as a result of bombardment by information and choice. Gender warfare, mudslinging, and assigning blame do not guarantee answers to our contemporary environmental predicament. Instead, and as globalization picks up momentum, development of environmentally sound technologies and appropriate information systems seems increasingly the most vital asset in environmental sustainability.

Therefore, in the struggle to reduce socioeconomic inequality, especially gender inequality, the vital question becomes: Who owns, controls, and disseminates information? The monopolization of information technology and of the production and dissemination of knowledge by a few presents formidable difficulties for the democratization of politics, economics, and society. The proliferation of environmentally oriented nongovernmental organizations (NGOs) seems to provide a needed antidote against the monopolization of information control by private and public media giants.

ENVIRONMENTAL ORGANIZATIONS

Worldwide, there are hundreds of environmental organizations. These range from local nongovernmental organizations like Campfire in Zimbabwe and the Chipko movement in India to more sophisticated international organizations such as Greenpeace. Many governments have also joined the bandwagon of environmentalism, though often in not unambiguous ways. Notwithstanding the proliferation of statutory and nongovernmental organizations that have been established to deal with environmental issues, without addressing important questions of power, profit, and knowledge, such initiatives may not be successful. Any fruitful discussion and attempt to save the environment should proceed by way of a number of steps in which various theoretical and political positions are appraised and subjected to critique. The objective should be to expose the myths that undergird the status quo and hopefully to arrive at a critical and emancipatory synthesis of the diverse and opposite, the universal and the local.

WOMEN, KNOWLEDGE, AND POWER

At the core of women's subjugation is their marginalization in the complex process by which new knowledge is created, consolidated, and transformed into power. Foucault (1995: 182–183) defined knowledge as that which one can speak in a discursive practice, and which is specified by that fact: the domain constituted by the different objects that will or will not acquire a scientific status. . . . ; knowledge is also the space in which the subject may take up a position and speak of the objects with which he deals in his discourse. . . . ; knowledge is also the field of coordination and subordination of statements in which concepts appear, and are defined, applied and transformed. . . . ; lastly, knowledge is defined by the possibilities of use and appropriation offered by discourse.

These forms and bodies of knowledge are interdependent, and each of them has "a particular discursive practice; and any discursive practice may be defined by the knowledge it forms" (Foucault, 1995: 183).

Historically, hegemonic discursive practices have been a male-dominated enterprise. Women have not been centrally involved in the ways in which new discursive practices and ideas are developed, nurtured, and translated into action and the production of knowledge and power. Consequently, ideas and ideologies about appropriation, control, and destruction or protection of the environment are implicated in gender power relations. In order to effectively control and transform their environment, woman would therefore be wise to struggle to acquire knowledge and power. Such a struggle should not only unveil the destructive impact of men's appropriation of the right to manage natural resources over women, but should also reveal the processes by which such dominant power relations are constructed and legitimated, as well as how they can be subverted and overthrown.

Although marginalized from the power center, dialectically, women's ideas and actions can also alter and change reality. By participating in the dialectic of control, women in particular and the weak in general can alter the overall distribution of power and carve up a political space for themselves by mobilizing resources at their disposal (Giddens, 1982). This is possible precisely because the powerful depend on the weak in many ways, and vice versa, which is why power relations are relations of autonomy and dependence.

Knowledge, in its many forms including religious, scientific, and practical survival skills, is simultaneously the glue that binds societies together and the powder keg that explodes them. Naturally, the history of knowledge and power is littered with remarkable horrors, many of which are, of course, inevitable consequences of the ignorance of the time. Even so, they are among the most momentous horrors in the history of humankind, and many of them have had devastating enduring legacies. These horrors, include, among others, the backwash epochs of slavery, the catastrophe of colonialism, the persistent violence of war, the destruction of the environment, the continued abuse and rape of women, and the exploitation of labor. All these are partly a result of the celebration of powerful forms of patriarchal, racial, and class domination. As Vandana Shiva points out in her assessment of the impact of science and technology on rural women in the "Third World," "development thinking and policy, dominated by a patriarchal, scientific perspective, has facilitated a project of 'domination and destruction, of violence and subjugation, of dispossession and the dispensability of both women and nature" (cited in Beinart, 1998: 776). She adds, "the period of the scientific revolution itself was full of alternatives to the masculine project of mechanistic, reductionist science, and it was also full of struggles between gendered and non-gendered science" (p. 776). But patriarchal approaches were victorious against those who were defined into nature and made passive and powerless: Mother Earth, women, and colonized cultures.

In other words, the process of technical and industrial revolution smothered women through "compulsive masculinity" and the competitive quest for scientific innovation and control; as a consequence, women are socially disadvantaged (Beinart, 1998: 776). Beinert further argues:

European expansion was, in its initial phases in many areas of the world, often a male endeavour. This was the case not only in respect of military, naval, commercial and bureaucratic activity but also of scientific exploration that accompanied and facilitated expansion. Insofar as analysis of the gender-specific character of imperialism has been pursued, it has been seen as the font of particularly powerful forms of patriarchal and racial domination. The European masculinities associated with empire, formerly judged heroic and self-sacrificing, are now often presented as harsh and uncompromising, roughened by long absences from women at home, and steeled by conquest and arrogation of racial superiority. (p. 775)

Within the context of Southern Africa, Pratt (1992: 38) convincingly argues that "natural history asserted an urban, lettered, male authority over the whole of the planet; it celebrated a rationalising, extractive, dissociative understanding which overlaid functional, experiential relations among people, plants and animals" (Beinart, 1998: 776).

If knowledge can be translated into power, then women and other oppressed groups need education in order to acquire knowledge, a necessary weapon for challenging myths that celebrate male authority and masculinity. Indeed, over the last half of the twentieth century, women, through their participation in the dialectic of control, shifted and reconfigured the overall distribution of knowledge and power. With remarkable ingenuity and skill, they exploited the resources of a dependence relationship, which are astutely fabricated as much as predetermined. For those who aspire to a free, social, and unpolluted natural environment, the challenge is to explore further the possibilities of giving a more positive form to these enthusiastic engagements in the dialectic of control.

THE POVERTY OF ECOFEMINIST PHILOSOPHY AND PRAXIS

In spite of much ecofeminist activism, in many parts of the world, especially the developing countries, control and subjugation of women by men and brutality and violence against them remain the norm rather than the exception. Why? Unfortunately, there is no simple answer, let alone a way to delineate the often-contradictory perceptions and implications. With a degree of poetic license, it can be argued that the fact that patriarchal and racial forms of domination and masculinities are still hegemonic, albeit in more subtle forms, after decades of ecofeminist activism, is testimony to the limited achievements of the movement. More important, it makes understanding and deconstructing the myths that undergird these forms of domination particularly interesting and instructive.

In his compelling analysis of the operation and organization of the scientific enterprise in the eighteenth- and nineteenth-century Cape (South Africa), Beinart (1998) arrives at some interesting conclusions that are pertinent to this analysis. First, he concludes that by the mid-nineteenth century, men and women could at least share the scientific enterprise. Second, he points out that, "perhaps what is more noteworthy is the subordinate position of women in scientific work rather than the essential difference of their ideas" (776). Paradoxically, ecofeminist critiques of patriarchal hegemony and environmental degradation tend to operate within the same patriarchal praxis that they criticize vehemently. This constitutes the major weaknesses of ecofeminist discourse and practice.

The rationale for linking women and the environment in feminist critiques of male bias is rather flawed; it offers only a partial view of reality, and hence it is inadequate to meet the challenges at hand. As Sow (1997: 254) points out,

whatever the objective of this [rationale]—exploitation of women's labour, of women's scientific knowledge and technological know-how—and its impact on women (whether they suffer from it or they use it to acquire a higher status, more power, more control over the material and spiritual wealth of their community), a debate should be embarked on.

Both men and women, rich and poor are all accomplices in environmental degradation, but for different reasons. Rich men and women destroy the environment for profit or luxury, and poor men and women, for survival. Often it is lack of scientific knowledge necessary for coming up with environmentally sound alternative technologies that force many to partake in environmental degradation. Moreover, even if women's different kinds of interactions with nature and social life may provide them with "distinctive and privileged scientific and epistemological standpoints," ultimately it is the logic of capital expansion that dictates policy options that in turn shape women's relationship with the environment. Thus, poor rural men and women are forced to over-exploit natural resources precisely because they are marginalized within elite-dominated institutional structures. In addition, these discourses gloss over the fact that it is through male-dominated scientific and technological breakthroughs that the waste and inefficiency inherent in nature has been arrested, for instance by harnessing rivers that would otherwise "run to waste" (Coyle, 1994: 34).

A more serious problem is that ecofeminist discourses ignore the important fact that in many male-dominated traditional African societies, the relationship between human beings was almost religious, if not sacred. For example, in the central regions of Mozambique, before appropriating any of nature's resources by, for instance, hunting, farming virgin land, cutting grass, and many other activities, one has to perform certain rituals in order to appease and get permission from the ancestors. It is easy to dismiss such practices as mere superstition, but the point is these discursive practices ensured a balance between human beings and nature, and natural resources were used for survival, and not for profit as under capitalism. As Mazrui (1995) points out, in precolonial Africa animals were considered men's closest brother and were believed to have a soul. People killed animals in order to survive. But with the advent of colonial capitalism, the relationship between man and nature was commercialized, with men making money out of their brothers; Africans have been quick to catch up to that greed.

As Keen (1996: 203) has emphasized,

The injustices that go with class and race are too severe to be confused with gender. All upper classes are composed of equal numbers of men and women. The fruits of exploitation are enjoyed equally by men, women, and children of the upper classes as the outrages of exploitation are borne equally by men and women and children of the lower classes. Both class and ethnic minorities suffer real oppression.

In short, it is a deliberate distortion of history and an insult to the oppressed of the world to group rich and powerful women within the congregation of the downtrodden merely because they are female.

Apart from that, some women bully and inflict pain on their men as well as children. For example, Madeleine Albright (1998), the U.S. secretary of state, was clearly celebrating violence, and indeed playing the modern Goddess of War, when she threatened Saddam Hussein of Iraq thus: "If we have to use force (against Iraq), it is because we are America. We are the indispensable nation. We stand tall. We see further into the future."

Progressive men and women alike should object to such arrogant and inflammatory language, which celebrates violence and the nation-state. In fact, the idea of the nation-state, and its celebration of violence and boundaries, is one major obstacle to the unity of the women of the world and human progress in general.

It is because of such extremities in feminist praxis—a praxis that seeks to rival patriarchal vices—that there has been a massive backlash against feminism. In wartime Mozambique, for example, a significant number of divorces and separations were a result of men running away from bullying wives, who in some cases beat up their husbands and openly brought their boyfriends home (Chingono, 1996). This is perhaps a far more widespread phenomenon than is realized, but male victims do not publicly admit to this harassment because of the social conditioning that tells men to be, or appear to be, in charge and control. It would be interesting to find out whether or not the incidence of these abuses, especially for example, the rape of young boys by women is rising worldwide. Commenting on the rape of a 10-year-old schoolboy by a 16-year-old girl, Childline, a South African NGO that monitors child abuse, says there has been "a slight increase in the number of males raped by females" (Nkosi, 1999: 5); the country has the highest number of rape cases in the world.

A classical example of tyrannical mothers and bullying wives is the case of Backler, 52, from Durban, South Africa. Her 18-year-old daughter, a first-year Fine Arts student, made an unusual urgent application to the Court to be removed from the custody of her parents and instead be placed in the care of her confidante (Govender, 1999: 3). In papers before the Durban High Court, she said she was a virtual prisoner in her parents' home; her mother had on several occasions threatened to deregister her as a student and to keep her under lock and key until she turned 21. She continues:

Ours is not a happy family. We have existed together miserably for many years under the brutal dominance of my mother. [For] as long as I can remember, my mother has brutalised me and my siblings, both physically and verbally. I have been assaulted with sticks, a foot stool and fists, had my head bashed against the wall and was punched in the stomach a few weeks ago. At different times all of us have ran away from home as a result of her behaviour. (Govender, 1999: 3)

Although her father was the breadwinner, her mother ruled the family—with force if necessary—and bullied him: "My father also seems to have fairly low self-esteem. He will argue with my mother from time to time, but will not seriously oppose her, particularly in so far as her 'disciplining' of me is concerned" (Govender, 1999: 3). Unfortunately, as the increasing numbers of street children in major cities of the world suggest, poor Phillippa's case is not an exceptional one.

Furthermore, without denying the guilt of men and the type of thinking that has traditionally been designated as "masculine," are we to excuse womankind from complicity and active participation in the spoiling of the environment? Perhaps more so than men, women are compulsive and conspicuous consumers, as exhibited in their penchant for the latest fashions and food. Insofar as women (especially affluent women) also crave the latest technologies—cars, televisions, computers, and planes— they are just as responsible as men for despoiling the earth. The point is this: Women's supposed "distinctive and privileged" interaction with nature has not translated into an active, sensitive, and environment-friendly interaction with nature.

Apparently, women have not been an exception to the common disease that afflicts almost every revolution and revolutionaries. Is it not a remarkable paradox or historical irony that, almost invariably, the oppressed, including women, tend to adopt the strategies of their oppressors in their struggles for liberation? As is clear from the history of revolutions in the twentieth century, this is self-defeating in the long run. Worse still, as soon as they are in power, the women's first task is to become conservative revolutionaries—only theirs is a genuine revolution, and anything else is a reaction to being suppressed.

Emang Basadi (EB), Botswana's foremost women's pressure group, has adopted an interesting strategy since 1993—seven years after its birth. After realizing that advocating for change in laws takes time, effort, and money, EB decided that the best strategy would be to "put more women in political office where statutes are formulated. The idea was that in formulating these laws, if there are more women in those structures, the laws that come up will be gender sensitive" (Gaelesiwe, 1999: 23). The strategy is not very novel, and indeed today many governments and political parties have women in top executive leadership positions, but this has only served to entrench the status quo. Is it testimony to the difficulty of being creative that women have not been excepted to this human fallibility? Whatever it is, the point is that the cause of reclaiming female dignity and achieving greater economic justice for women will not be served by such sexist ideology, which mimics its enemy's tactics and strategy. In this case ideology tends to paralyze intelligent reasoning.

The task of reasonable men and women is to transcend the childish game of blame, for herein lies only a dead end. A switch in the dialectics toward reconciliation, collective responsibility, resistance, and reinvention seems the only way we can enjoy the joys of mature love and wisdom. Some men are in fact victims—exploited, oppressed, and forbidden to express their feminine side—of the system and are increasingly becoming aware of the feelings of wounds and victimhood. The social system we have all conspired to create is victimizing us all:

The surplus suffering of men and women of all colours comes from this system—a human construction. If we do not change our economic-political-social-genderal sytem, then the fault will lie "not in our stars but in ourselves, that we are underlings." The fault will not be with woman because she gave us the apple, nor with man because he created technology, but with all of us because we preferred the easy way of remaining victims and blaming others for our condition. (Keen, 1996: 207)

Thus, instead of articulating a new emancipatory vision, the majority of women seem content to compete with and rival men in their evil. This, too, is self-defeating.

"We are out of tune" with the needs of Mother Nature and the requirements of our times. What a "sordid boon" has developed: women draining their energies, exhausting their intellect, and killing their compassion in pursuit of a vain ego-trip to outsmart man in his masculinity. It should be clear that Western forms of industrialism and consumption, which are a product of the capitalist-driven enterprise, are not sustainable at a global level. Americans can afford to consume and deplete natural resources as much as they do precisely because the majority of the world's people are not doing the same. Yet everyone seems to cherish the American lifestyle as the ideal. This is a mind-boggling predicament.

In Mozambique where the average person consumes far less than American ecofeminists, some women believe that the feminist struggle, as articulated by the Organization of Mozambican Women (OMM), was both unnecessary and the main cause of current family problems. The traditional family collapsed when the OMM introduced new values and norms that undermined the old ones which had kept society stable.

For many women, the "equality" that the OMM promoted was the main cause for the collapse of the family: It allowed women to rival men in all their vices. This view is expressed and well articulated in Crittenden's first book, *What Our Mothers Didn't Tell Us*, with its provocative subtitle, *Why Happiness Eludes the Modern Woman*, which has "had traditional feminists spitting into their gazpacho" (Coles, 1999: 11).

Criticizing mainstream feminist discourses, Crittenden argues that modern woman's life is "upside down," and this is primarily because "those of us who grew up in the 70s and who are now in their late 20s and 30s were short-changed by our mothers when they groomed us to have it all" (Coles, 1999: 11). She is convinced that it is wrong to postpone having children and that the sooner we all get married and have families, the better. That way, women will end up being more productive in the workplace in the long run, as there will be "no need for day-care or maternity leave or guilt ridden farewells with children clinging to our ankles on the front door" (Coles, 1999: 11). Commenting on the material benefits of feminism, she says: "We have never been richer or more grasping. Our houses are bigger and we have more cars. But we have degraded the importance of what mothers did." For saying this, Crittenden has been caricaturized by feminists of all sorts; the feminist writer Erica Jong described her as "so ignorant," while the grande dame of feminism, Betty Friedan, dismissed her as "anti-women" (Coles, 1999: 11). Crittenden has also been accused of being anti-ambition. She argues that's a great irony because she has been trying to look at the issue "from an ambitious woman's point of view: . . . Having a kid at 42 is exhausting, and the older you are the harder it is to adjust. I don't think the women's movement has addressed this honestly" (Coles, 1999: 11).

It is not clear whether or not women want a stake in the status quo or want to change that status quo. Women's demands for equality and justice seem to suggest that *all* men are enjoying both, yet this is not entirely true. The truth, within the context of capitalism and stratified societies, seems to be that class more than gender tends to determine "who gets what, why and how." In many situations, wives and daughters of the elite, whether or not they are exploited within their households, enjoy more rights than working-class or unemployed husbands and sons.

In South Africa, for example, affirmative action for women seems to have created another layer of rich women in a hierarchical class society. Almorie Maule, the chief executive of the South African oil giant company, Engen, for example, "has gone all the way to prove she has what it takes to do what is perceived as a man job." The first woman to head a national oil company, "the ultimate macho domain . . . she does not lack the steely determination and rigid discipline needed for the job" (Blignaut, 1999: 11). Even though the number of women in such executive positions is still miniscule, many of them seem content with only getting a stake in the unjust system and do not try to change its injustices—economic exploitation and political oppression of both men and women.

Often when men go to war or enslave or colonize others, it is women who give them moral and physical support. Sometimes the desire to materially please women provides men with the motivation to engage in violence and warfare. The mother of Roy Welenski, who was born in Southern Rhodesia and later became a prominent colonial politician in Southern Africa, especially in Northern Rhodesia, is a typical example of these hawkish and exploiter women (see, e.g., Godwin, 1993). Mrs. Welenski was one of the few women among the early pioneers who took

dangerous risks—fighting the natives and surviving tropical disease—
and who was motivated by the quest for happiness in the "land of promise." Mrs. Welenski's trek was just one among many of the unfolding
Rhodes' dreams to conquer Africa. Did slavery and colonialism bring
benefits only to white men, and not white women? Women are neither
a hegemonic nor a homogeneous social group; instead, they are affected
by the dynamics of class and race politics.

   This means that different women have different relationships with the
human environment and experience patriarchal and racial domination
differently. Surely white upper class women's desires, wants (as opposed
to needs), and interests are a world apart from those of African peasant
women. It is precisely in recognition of this fact that a significant number
of women disdain the dichotomization of men and women and,
therefore, dissociate themselves from the label "feminist." Depending on
circumstances, women's immediate interests may well coincide more
with those of men than with those of other women. There are many
instances in which women, often in the name of tradition, voluntarily
partake in the abuse of other women. Typical examples include the prime
role played by older women in many African cultures in genital mutilation, circumcision, arranged marriages, marriage through rape as in
some parts of Ethiopia, and the general enforcement of norms and values
that keep young women under a tight grip. The essential role played by
white women during slavery and colonialism is another example of
women of the world not uniting, but instead fighting alongside their
men. Similarly, female freedom fighters fought alongside their men in
dislodging colonialism. Indeed, in colonial Africa, the major schism was
between black and white rather than between men and women. These
inevitable centrifugal tendencies present formidable difficulties for the
ecofeminist movement.

   Finally, in spite of the feminist critique of male dominance, women's
ideas are not that different from men's. Given the chance, as examples
of the likes of Margaret Thatcher suggest, women can also exhibit the
propensity to dominate, exploit, oppress, and be selfish, just as their male
counterparts do. Like men, women are historical products of their times,
and their ideas and actions are shaped by their reality. In addition,
women are not a homogeneous social group with common interests all
the time, in all places. Different identities based on class, race, age, and
religion all tend to simultaneously divide and unite women. For instance,
what do prostitutes and professors, models and nuns, urban young
women and rural grandmothers, Naomi Campbell and Mother Theresa,
have in common, if not biology? In short, there are as many issues that
unite and divide women, and in many instances women's interests tend
to coincide more with those of men who belong to their class and race—

husbands, fathers, brothers, relatives, friends, etc.—than with those of other women. Women have to face up to the challenges that this creates.

Instead of just resisting, women should reinvent as well. Do women want a piece of the rotting steak, or do they want to prepare their own fresh one or even a light salad? In particular, they need to address directly the question of capitalism and its implications for the community. Is a feminine capitalism possible? Is the market compatible with collective community needs? Do contemporary forms of governance fulfill people's quest for freedom and happiness? What forms should alternative socioeconomic arrangements take?

BEYOND PRESENT ANACHRONISMS

Remarking on the predicament of the contemporary world, Objectivist philosopher, Ayn Rand (1993: 1) notes: "It is not necessary to prove that something is wrong with today's world. Everybody—of any creed, colour or intellectual persuasion, old and young, rich and poor, conservative and liberal, foreign and domestic—senses that something monstrous is destroying the world. But no one knows what it is, and people keep blaming one another—with some justice."

With respect to environmental degradation, ecofeminists keep blaming men without examining the cause. If we do not know the causes of behavior that leads to environmental degradation, how can we be sure of discovering effective solutions to the crisis?

As should be clear from the preceding discussion, it is the construction of modernity that has produced environmental catastrophe and the untold misery that this has entailed for its victims, ranging from "the peasantry, proletariat and artisans oppressed by capitalist industrialization to the exclusion of women from the public sphere, to the genocide of imperialist colonization" (Best and Kellner, 1991). Modernity has also produced a set of disciplinary institutions, practices, and discourses that legitimate its mode of domination and control. It is not clear, however, whether its promise of liberation "masks forms of oppression and domination" (Best and Kellner, 1991) or constitutes "unfulfilled potential" (Habermas, 1987) for liberation. Undeniably, however, it is the dynamics of this modernity and the global capitalist mode of production that shape the nature of human beings' interaction with the natural environment; the latter defines the limits of the range of possible human activities.

More specifically, in the contemporary world the dynamics of the world capitalist system have forced certain groups of people to behave in ways that endanger the environment, and hence human life. Some of the accusations leveled against men by ecofeminists are inevitable by-products of the logic of capitalist production and distribution. Is not environmental degradation, for example, often an inevitable consequence of the commodification of the environment? Can this commercialization be arrested in a society addicted to the toxic ideology of capitalist consumerism? This is the catch-22 situation.

The point is that many men and women enjoy the material products of capitalism, but by consuming these products they contribute to environmental degradation. Yet ecofeminists find solace in scapegoating men as the sole culprits. This will not solve the problem. To find practical solutions, it may perhaps be necessary to go beyond contemporary thinking on economic and political arrangements. It may be necessary to deconstruct myths and ideologies that legitimate a system of production and consumption that is based on destruction, instead of enhancement, of the environment, a system that is self-defeating in the long run. Often, it is what we know that is the most serious obstacle in the process of discovering and building new knowledge and alternative socioeconomic arrangements.

Next is presented a tentative outline of possible ways of escaping from the old ideology of capitalist production and consumption that threaten the environment, and hence human life on earth. Instead of squabbling about who is to blame, it is perhaps useful to find ways of ameliorating some of the extreme features of capitalism, which in its contemporary vicious form has become a great impediment to a humane and environmentally sound society. It is precisely because of the marginalization of women in the production and dissemination of knowledge that such obsolete capitalist ideologies of social organization have remained unchallenged. To acquire this vital ability to deconstruct myths and construct new possibilities, women in particular and exploited people in general need education. They have to struggle to learn, and learn to struggle, in order to resist subjugation and to reinvent the future as they wish.

REINVENTING THE FUTURE

What, then, are the elements of new and appropriate forms of economic and political organization that will promote egalitarianism and sustainable environmental transformation? Perhaps the way forward consists in being able to identify elements of the solution in the problem, by dialectically distilling each problem to its basic essentials. As Coyle (1994: 33) aptly notes: "Environmental and land-use regulation can be complex, tedious, and dry. It can seem excessively technical and far removed from the great questions of social and political life. But the questions of how the earth shall be used, and who shall decide this, are inexorably tied up with issues about the nature of society and with issues of freedom and responsibility, community and democracy."

Environmental regulation is contentious not because the world is full of "aspiring soil and water engineers, but precisely because regulation directly affects the social choices of individuals. Ordering the uses of land orders the users" (Coyle 1994: 33). Indeed, the language of environmental disputes mirrors the debate over the comparative merits of social arrangements, or cultures based primarily on order, liberty, and equality. Those who stress order argue that a well-ordered society is predictable and desirable, and can be promoted by regulatory controls. Libertarians argue that regulation violates the basic freedoms of the individual, especially the right to own private property, while egalitarians contend that state power should be used to promote equality by redistributing power and wealth in society. Many participants in these debates are not rigidly or even consistently ideological, but everybody has ideas about how they wish to live.

The political and social conflicts embedded in environmental and land-use disputes are inevitable given the logic and values of capitalist production and distribution. Central to capitalist production is the profit motive, and it is this quest for profits that explains why many goods produced and consumed within the capitalist context tend to be both unhealthy and environmentally destructive. First, in order to cut costs of production and raise profits, many corporate enterprises dump their industrial waste in ways that directly affect the environment, causing, for instance, air and water pollution. Second, and also for the same profit motivation, manufactured goods are packaged in material that endangers the environment when disposed of by the unknowing consumer. Third, when profit is celebrated above all else, community values, especially those involving protection of community "commons" will be the first casualty. In its quest for profit, private enterprise tends to destroy the environment. An alternative system should therefore seek to transcend the idea of profit as the main motivation for engaging in business and should instead inculcate ethical enterprising and appropriate moral and material incentives.

Such an alternative economic system could be based on a flex-time working system in which employees work a maximum of four hours a day, and the total working time could be increased from eight to twelve hours per day. The three-shift-day system (6:00 A.M.–10:00 A.M., 10:00 A.M.–2:00 P.M., and 2:00 P.M.–6:00 P.M.) has many advantages over the current one eight-hour day. Simple mathematics shows that, overall, employment will rise by about three times, thereby removing the unemployed from the streets. The consequent increase in buying power will have overall ripple effects of increasing total demand, thereby creating more employment in order to meet this demand. Physiologically, working only a four-hour day can result in a rise in productivity as workers are dismissed while they are still at their productive peak instead of when diminishing returns set in. Absenteeism, which is quite prevalent in many African countries, especially after payday, could also be curbed as the extremes of capitalism that necessitate that kind of "resistance" would have been eliminated. Moreover, working parents will not be separated from their children for too long, and there will be no need for long maternity leaves. Finally, every worker will be left with enough time to learn and practice reforestation, instead of discovering innovative ways of "going-slow" at work as another form of resistance to capitalist alienation. *Ceteris paribus*, profits could also rise as a result of increased productivity and better morale.

Such an innovative approach, once the modalities are worked out, can not only breathe fresh life into many ailing economies by increasing productivity, but also make it possible to realize most human rights while maintaining the integrity of the community. In fact, historically the current eight-hour day was achieved after long political agitation for its reduction from the initial 16-hour, and then 12-hour day. Of course, technology played a decisive role in these changes by making it possible to produce far more goods within a short space of time than was ever possible. If the revolutionary breakthroughs in technology over the century have shrunk distances, making cyberspace and cyberculture a reality, surely they can make it possible for workers to work fewer hours, without compromising standards and quality. Working for fewer hours, in addition to boosting worker morale and productivity, will also afford workers an opportunity to be creative and recreational and to reflect on their relationship to the environment. Surely, this should be a healthy antidote to the burdensome nature and drudgery of most urban and rural women's work. The proliferation of NGOs is an expression of the desire for, as well as the possibility of, such an ethical enterprising system. It only needs to be given a more positive form by, for instance, putting in place appropriate incentives and penalties to change people's attitudes and behaviors.

Politically, such an ethical enterprising economic system could be complemented by a system that transcends the current anachronisms of the party, the tyranny of the elite, and the intoxication of ideology. These anachronisms are the major obstacle to the unity of the oppressed, lack of which in turn undermines their ability to resist the logic of capitalist environmental degradation. None of the presently hegemonic ideological "isms and schisms" seems capable of dealing with the challenges of global ecological destruction. Liberal democracy appears to be fatally wounded, as demonstrated by the rise in political apathy among ordinary people in the West, where party electioneering has proven inadequate to give substance to democracy. For example, in the United States, the so-called greatest democracy in the world, only 55 percent of whites who were eligible to vote for the president did so in 1996 and only 45 percent of African-American registered voters actually went to the polls

(Mkhondo, 1999: 13). Yet these low figures represent the highest voter-turnout percentages for presidential election since 1972. The reasons non-voters give for not voting are insightful: "The system is corrupt, and I don't want to be part of it; my vote ain't gonna make no much difference; and I forgot all about" (Mkhondo, 1999: 13).

In many African countries, with the exception of South Africa where some excitement over the idea of voting continues, the situation is even worse. Given the high illiteracy rates of the country, voting along party lines seems a waste of resources, for many of those who vote have no adequate understanding of the intricacy of the issues at stake. For example, few understand the arguments for or against, say, fiscal versus monetary policy, protectionism versus free trade, the agendas of the IMF and the World Bank, multinationals, as well as local politicians' ulterior motives. It would therefore make more sense if people could vote solely on issues they understand and that concern them directly—as suggested below. In much of Africa, as in South Africa, neo-liberalism is considered an attack on workers (Hlatshwayo, 1999: 15) and hence is unsustainable and undesirable.

Frustrated with such ostentatious politics, Muammar Gaddaffi has suggested a "people's democracy" that dispenses with party politics, while Yoweri Museveni has experimented with a "no party-system." As with most of the contemporary hegemonic ideological "isms and schisms," none of these alternatives seems fruitful and emancipatory. This is partly because, although they denounce the party system for only representing a part (Gaddaffi), their systems operate like blameless superparties. Notwithstanding these weaknesses, their attempts underscore an important point made by C.L.R. James (1991). Tracing and documenting the daily struggles of ordinary people to be happy, James showed beyond any doubt that the era of the party system is past and that the main challenge of the twenty-first century is to give form to an alternative political arrangement. His ideas provide a basis for not joining the political dinosaurs in the twenty-first century.

Recent research by political scientists actually points to the demise of party politics—as in the United States—and a corresponding ascendancy of interest and nongovernmental groups. In many countries, such as Botswana and Zimbabwe, women have managed to achieve significant rights by mobilizing as women, and not through political parties. In other words, issue-centered, rather than party or ideology-centered, politics has a greater promise of delivery. Institutionally, this means that instead of people voting for or according to parties, they will elect their leaders individually and on the basis of their specific interests.

For instance, with respect to education, everyone concerned—parents, teachers, students, employers—will come together to elect their leader on the basis of merit alone, who will represent them in the cabinet. The same people may also vote and elect another leader in a different context, for instance, a health or culture minister who will represent them in government. The leader of the cabinet could either be elected directly by all the people or from these elected leaders by the elected. The modalities of this alternative arrangement could be worked out, but the guiding principle should be meritocracy and avoidance of the divisions along party or ideological lines that undermine poor men and women's ability to resist the excesses of capitalist ecological genocide.

In addition, this arrangement is far cheaper and simpler to run than the current bureaucratic quagmires we have to contend with. To counter tendencies of electing leaders on the basis of ethnic, religious, and other affiliation, the masses must arm themselves with the weapon of critical theory that can help them see through these myths. They could also set up structures to ensure transparency and accountability. Thus, by abolishing both the party and parliament, much time and resources will be saved and directed toward the promotion of environmental sustainability, and by enabling people to choose the ablest leaders possible, direct democracy may become real rather than illusory as it is now. Real democracy in economics, politics, race, and gender relations is the fundamental condition for sustainable environmental transformation.

It is a testimony to the intellectual laziness of the time that the marginalized, instead of being prepared to take risks and participate in the creation of alternative economic and sociopolitical arrangements, are scrambling for a stake in the crumbling edifice. Is there fear of taking calculated risks or of getting it wrong? As Youngson (1998: xii) points out with respect to scientific knowledge, "Getting it wrong is very often the way that science advances. Provisional, but wrong, ideas give way to better—but still wrong—ideas. Every stage in this process may involve a blunder."

Political blunders and their consequent horrors that result from the subversion of power should add to knowledge insofar as they demonstrate what is wrong with that approach. Effectively harnessing science and technology for environmentally sustainable development requires a preparedness to undertake risk experiments in social engineering.

SUMMARY AND CONCLUSION

The late twentieth century alone witnessed a number of fascinating intellectual, economic, political, and social developments that are directly pertinent to the subject under consideration here. First, on March 8, 1911, a group of women organized the first ever demonstration for women's rights in America. That demonstration, which is now celebrated worldwide as International Women's Day, set in motion a process that has profoundly shifted the tectonic plates of the modern world. The first women suffrage movement set in motion a process, if not an earthquake, that is shaking men and women, transforming their roles and interrelationships. The inevitable and remarkable consequences of that struggle include, among others, the United Nations' declaration of the 1980s as the Women Development Decade, the proliferation of gender and development studies in the social sciences, and the change in women's economic status, in both the public and private sector. These are certainly the indirect products of that struggle.

Certainly, the communications revolution, brought about by breakthroughs in information technology since the Second World War, also played an important role in this development. Information technology in particular, and new environmentally sound technologies in general, are a double-edged sword for women. On the one hand, if they seize the opportunity, technology can facilitate their emancipation and hopefully bring about a better life for all (see Mottin-Sylla, 1998). On the other hand, if they content themselves with playing second fiddle, present gender inequities could be further entrenched by the same technology. In fact, in spite of this, discourses on women and the environment are not only as diverse as they are confusing, but also patriarchal and masculine ideas are still dominant. This chapter has proposed to explain the limited achievements of women's liberation struggle as follows.

First, women have followed their oppressor's strategies in trying to emancipate themselves from him. This strategy has obvious limitations; it is easier for the enemy to develop counterstrategies. This weakness also has an obvious cause, namely, the difficulty of being creative and, sometimes, outright intellectual laziness. Second, women, having been unable to offer an alternative vision, seem content to rival men in their evil. This again has obvious negative consequences. As Keen aptly notes (1996: 7), "the modern rites of passage for men, violence, wealth and sex, impoverish and alienate men." There perhaps have already been more than enough women casualties of this hackneyed strategy.

Just as Africans are oppressing themselves by uncritically copying everything from the West, women are oppressing themselves by copying men. One trivial example of this mistake is the fact that they judge themselves, their success and lives, by male standards. Yet, many men spend most of their time thinking about women, how to get them, how to please them, how to enjoy them. Perhaps the real problem is that women do not realize the power they wield over men. Because of this blissful ignorance, women impoverish and alienate themselves in trying to rival men in their vice. The marginalization of women in the production of power and knowledge has therefore reduced them into, at best, beautiful slaves (e.g., prostitutes) and, at worst, accomplices in their own subjugation. The point, however, is that women cannot emancipate themselves or change their environment without gaining power and knowledge, which they can achieve only through struggle.

As we have seen, the rhetoric that pronounces men responsible and women innocent belies the findings of psychological dynamics on the interactions among persons in a system; power, responsibility, action, and blame are shared by all participants within a system. Our hope lies in dismantling the system that has made men the way they are and women the way they are. We are free. Whether we exercise this freedom or wallow in blame and victimhood is also a matter of choice (Keen, 1996: 207). In a globalizing world, scientific and technical knowledge are among the most vital forms of knowledge that we need in order to empower ourselves and achieve equitable development and sustainable environmental change.

To recapitulate, the twentieth century witnessed an enormous expansion of the knowledge base of society in general, and gender and the environment in particular. This constitutes a real revolution, which ecofeminists should be proud of. They have "gone a long way toward articulating a systematic critique of modern society, redefining female identity, and securing equal rights" (Keen, 1996: 5). They have correctly "re-evaluated the Western Scientific revolution as an essentially male enterprise which classified and exploited nature, as well as facilitating the domination of women and colonized peoples" (Beinart, 1998: 775). In spite of enormous obstacles and problems, the movement has made remarkable progress. More important, this quest shows that the present system is unjust, that the desirable ideal may be possible, and that elements of the solution may be present in the problem.

In conclusion, those who aspire to freedom have to participate in the production and dissemination of knowledge, for the ways in which new ideas are developed, nurtured and translated into action has important implications for power relations. As the work of feminist philosophers, theologians, poets, and social activists shows, knowledge is an indispensable theoretical weapon in the struggle for change and equality. Youth, the inheritors of present successes or failures, in particular need to be equipped with the weapon of theory so that they can effectively engage the exigencies of globalization. Women—and all oppressed groups—can realize equal access to and control of the environment, not by rivalling men in their vices, but by creating new forms of knowledge and ethics. And in order to do so, they need to participate actively in the production of scientific and technological knowledge rather than be mere consumers of the products of male-controlled science and technology.

REFERENCES

Albright, M. (1998). *The Guardian*, London, February 24.

Beinart, W. (1998). "Men, Science, Travel and Nature in the Eighteenth and Nineteenth-century Cape." *Journal of Southern African Studies*, 24(4), 775–799.

Best, S. and Kellner, D. (1991). *Postmodern Theory: Critical Interrogations*. London: Macmillan.

Blignaut, C. (1999). "Oil Baroness Driven to Succeed, Is Engen CEO." *Saturday Star*, Johannesburg, June 26.

Chingono, M. (1996). *The State, Violence and Development: The Political Economy of War in Mozambique*. Aldershot, England: Avebury.

Coles, J. (1999). "Moms' Duel with Babes and Their Bosses." *Saturday Star*, Johannesburg, June 26.

Coyle, D. J. (1994). "This Land Is Your Land, This Land Is My Land." In D. J. Coyle and R. J. Ellis (eds.), *Politics, Policy and Culture*. Oxford: Westview Press.

Crittenden, D. (1999). *What Our Mothers Didn't Tell Us: Why Happiness Eludes the Modern Woman*. Johannesburg: HarperCollins.

de Beauvoir, S. (1964). *The Second Sex*. London: HarperCollins.

Fenster, P. (June 1999). "Rape Victims Are People Too." *Marie Claire*, Johannesburg, pp. 56–58.

Foucault, M. (1972). *The Archeology of Knowledge*. London: Tavistock.

Gaelesiwe, L. (1999). "Women Review Political Strategy." *Mmegi/The Reporter*, Gaborone, June 4–10.

Giddens, A. (1982). *Profiles and Critiques in Social Theory*. London: Macmillan.

Godwin, P. (1993). *Rhodesians Never Die: The Impact of War and Political Change on White Rhodesians*. Oxford: Oxford University Press.

Goldenberg, S. (1999). "Killed in the Name of Honour." *Mail and Guardian*, Johannesburg, June 4–10.

Govender, R. (1999). "Free Me from My Tyrant Mom: Desperate Fine Arts Student Pleads with the High Court to Release Her from Her Parents' Care." *Sunday Times*, Johannesburg, June 20.

Habermas, J. (1987). *Lectures on the Philosophical Discourse of Modernity*. Cambridge, MA: MIT Press.

Harding, J. (1987). *Perspectives on Gender and Science*. London: Falmer Press.

Hearn, J. (1987). *The Gender Oppression: Men-Masculinity and the Critique of Marxism*. Brighton: John Spiers.

Hlatshwayo, M. (1999). "Neo-liberalism Is an Attack on Workers." *Sowetan*, Johannesburg, June 17.

Imam, A. M., Mama, A. and Sow, F. (eds.). (1997). *Engendering African Social Sciences*. Dakar, Senegal: Council for the Development of Economic and Social Research in Africa (CODESRIA).

James, C.L.R. (1991). *American Civilization*. Oxford: Basil Blackwell.

Keen, S. (1996). *Fire in the Belly: On Being a Man*. London: Piatkus Publishers.

Krost, P. (1999). "Warped Ideas about Women Persist." *Saturday Star*, Johannesburg, May 29.

Matlhaku, S. (1999). "World Environment Day." *Sowetan*, Johannesburg, June 4.

Mazrui, A. (1995). *The Africans: The Nature of a Continent*. London: BBC Educational Video-Films.

McFadden, P. (1999). Interview by M. Sayagues, "Feminist Doc Turned on by Controversy." *Mail and Guardian*, Johannesburg, June 11–17.

Merchant, C. (1990). *The Death of Nature: Women, Ecology and the Scientific Revolution*. San Francisco: Harper and Row.

———. (1995). *Earthcare: Women and the Environment*. New York: Routledge.

Mkhondo, R. (1999). "The Precious Right Is on the Table, But Half of the US Chooses to Ignore It." *The Star*, Johannesburg, June 14.

Mottin-Sylla, M-H. (1998). "African Women Turn unto the Inform@tion Super-highw@y." *Women's World* (ISIS), No. 32. Dakar.

Muir, K. (1999). "While America and Britain Have Learnt, Slowly, to Appreciate the Grown-up Feminism of de Beauvoir, France Is Still in Its Infantile, Kneejerk Stage." *The Times*, London, May 22, p. 22.

Nkosi, P. (1999). "Girl Accused of Raping 10-Year-Old Schoolboy." *Sunday World*, Johannesburg, November 21.

Pratt, M. C. (1992). *Imperial Eyes: Travel Writing and Transculturation*. London: Routledge and Kegan Paul.

Rand, A. (1993). "Introduction." In L. Peikoff, *The Ominous Parallels*. New York: Meridian.

Rantao, J. "The Men and Women Who Govern SA." *The Star*, Johannesburg, June 18.

Sapa-AP. (1999). "Huge Ice Cube Shows Worst Global Heat in 420,000 Years." *The Star*, Johannesburg, June 28.

Shiva, V. (1988). *Staying Alive: Women, Ecology and Development*. London: Zed Books Ltd.

———. (1994). *Close to Home: Women Reconnect, Ecology, Health and Development*. London: Earthscan.

Smith, C. (1999). "SA Rape Gets More Violent." *Mail and Guardian*, Johannesburg, June 11–17.

Sow, F. (1997). "Gender Relations in the African Environment." In A. Imam, A. Mama, and F. Sow (eds.), *Engendering African Social Sciences* (pp. 251–270). Dakar, Senegal: CODESRIA.

Wordsworth, W. (1989). *Poems: 1815*. Oxford: Woodstock.

Youngson, R. M. (1998). *Scientific Blunders: A Brief History of How Wrong Scientists Can Sometimes Be*. New York: Macmillan.

Appendix

Status of Women in the ERNESA Region: Statistical Summary

	Botswana	Ethiopia	Kenya	Lesotho	Malawi	Mozambique	Namibia	Swaziland	Tanzania
Population (millions)	1.3	53.1	25	2.7	10.3	15.1	1.5	0.8	27.9
Purchasing power parity per capita (international $)	4,650	380	1,310	1,800	780	380	3,930	1,690	100*
Primary enrollment (% of age group)	98	39	95	70	48	64	119	88	69
Literacy (% population over 17 years)	75	50	71	78	45	34	40	71	55
Life expectancy	70	50	55	63	45	45	60	NA	52
Infant mortality	35	123	67	46	134	148	71	108	103
Human Development Index	67	25	43	48	26	25	43	51	31
Ranking in Africa (51 countries)	5	41	18	13	38	40	19	12	30
Human Rights Rating	79%	13#	46%	Poor#	33%	53%	Good	Mediocre	41%
Freedom for or Rights to									
Political and legal equality for women	yes	no	no	NA	yes	no	NA	NA	no
Social and economic equality for women	no	no	no	NA	no	no	NA	NA	no
Personal Rights									
Equality of sexes during marriage/divorce proceedings	no	no	yes	NA	no	NA	NA	no	no

Key: * = GDP per head ($U.S.); # = 1985 rating; NA = data not available.

Sources: data abstracted from R. Dallas, *The Economist: Pocket Africa: Profiles, Facts, and Figures about Africa Today* (London: Penguin Books, 1995); C. Humana, *World Human Rights Guide* (London: Pan Books, 1986); C. Humana, *World Human Rights Guide* (3rd ed.) (Oxford: Oxford University Press, 1992); The Economist, *The Economist: Pocket World in Figures* (London: Penguin Books, 1994).

Index

About the Editor and Contributors

ARNON BAR-ON, a citizen of Israel, is an Associate Professor in Social Work at the University of Botswana. He has previously taught at universities in Israel and Hong Kong. His broad teaching and research interests are in the theory of Social Work and Social Policy. Dr. Bar-On has authored books and numerous articles in these areas. He has served as African editor for the *British Journal of Social Policy*.

ABAYIE B. BOATEN is Associate Professor and Deputy Director of the Institute of African Studies, University of Ghana, Legon. He is also the Chief of Asonomaso–Kwagyanson, Ashante Region, Ghana. From 1975 to 1984 he was Chief Economics Officer in the Ministry of Finance, Budget Division, and Chief Rural Planing Officer, Ministry of Rural Development and Co-operatives. He is the author of *The Adae-Kese Festival of the Asante and Chieftaincy Institution*, among other publications.

DOROTHY BRANDON is a Lecturer in the Department of Home Economics Education at the University of Botswana. Prior to her current position she taught Home Economics at Ohio State University. She has also served as a Peace Corps Volunteer in Botswana. Dr. Brandon's research and teaching interests include Computer Applications in Home Economics, Theory and Practice of Teaching Home Economics, Foundations of Teaching Home Economics, and Home Economics for Productivity. She is the author or co-author of several textbooks and articles in these areas.

MARK CHINGONO is a Lecturer in the Department of Political and Administrative Studies, University of Botswana. He has also taught and/or conducted research at the British universities of Cambridge and Oxford. His research interests encompass politics of change, conflict, and cooperation; global political economy and democratization; social movements and the quest for happiness; and science, society, and progress. His major publications include *The State, Violence and Development* (1996) and *The Quest for Development and Happiness* (forthcoming).

ANTHONY G. HOPKIN, a British citizen, is an Associate Professor in the Faculty of Education, University of Botswana, where he is Director of Affiliated Institutions. He previously taught at the University of South Pacific and at the University of Wales, Cardiff. He has also held visiting professorships in South and North America, Southeast Asia, West Africa, Australasia, and Europe, which has enabled him to maintain a comparative dimension in his teaching, writing and research. Professor Hopkin has taught and conducted research *inter alia* in the areas of educational development and teacher education, broadly defined. He has published extensively in these areas.

FAUSTIN KALABAMU, a Tanzanian, is a Senior Lecturer in Environmental Science at the University of Botswana. Previously, he worked and taught in Tanzania, Bangladesh, and Zimbabwe. His current research focuses on gender, and housing and land development. He has published widely within the field of Urban Planning—especially on transportation, land management, and housing—in various international journals such as *Habitat International, Geoforum,* and *Journal of Urban Affairs*. He has also edited and contributed chapters in several books.

GWEN N. LESETEDI is a Lecturer in Sociology at the University of Botswana. She is currently a doctoral student at the University of Cape Town. Her teaching and research interests include Sociological Research Methods, Gender and Health, and Migration. She has written and published papers in these areas. Gwen is also a Research Associate of Women and Law in Southern Africa (WLSA), an action research organization attempting to improve the legal status of women in Southern Africa.

ISHMAEL MAGAISA, a Zimbabwean, is a Lecturer in Sociology at the University of Zimbabwe, where he has taught courses in Sociological Theory, Crime and Deviance, Urbanization, and Development. Dr. Magaisa's research interests and publications are mainly in the areas of human sexuality and social deviance.

TAPOLOGO MAUNDENI, a citizen of Botswana, is a Lecturer in Social Work at the University of Botswana. Dr. Maundeni's teaching and research interests revolve around child welfare, gender relations, social work supervision, and community-based social services. She is the author of several scholarly articles in these fields.

ROSELINE C. ONAH, a citizen of Nigeria, is a Lecturer in Public Administration and Local Government at the University of Nigeria, Nsukka. Her research and teaching interests have spanned gender inequality and political empowerment of women, and local government. Dr. Onah has published several articles and chapters dealing with these subjects. She has served as a consultant to UNDP.

BERTHA Z. OSEI-HWEDIE is a Lecturer in Political Science in the Department of Political and Administrative Studies, University of Botswana. Her teaching and research interests are in the areas of political economy, international relations, gender, African politics, and democracy. Dr. Osei-Hwedie has published in such journals as *Journal of African Studies, Journal of Social Development in Africa, Lesotho Social Science Review, Journal of Contemporary African Studies,* and *Politikon.* She has also published chapters in many books.

NORMA ROMM served as Associate Professor of Sociology at the University of South Africa in the 1980s. More recently, she was Associate Professor of Sociology at the University of Swaziland, where she also was the Dean of the Faculty of Social Sciences. She is currently a Senior Researcher in Systems Studies at the University of Hull, England. Her scholarship has focused mainly on social science methodology. Professor Romm has authored and co-authored at least 5 highly regarded books and more than 50 journal articles.

APOLLO RWOMIRE is currently Associate Professor of Social Work at the University of Botswana. He previously taught Social Work and Sociology at Makerere University, the University of Nairobi, the University of Jos, and the University of Swaziland. He has authored or co-authored many books and book chapters, as well as many journal articles.

ABDUL-MUMIN SA'AD is a Senior Lecturer in Criminology and Head of the Department of Sociology and Anthropology at the University of Maiduguri, Nigeria. His teaching and research interests include Criminology and Criminal Justice in developing countries, Human Rights, Women and Social-Legal Regulation, and Social Change and Development. Dr. Sa'ad has published widely in these areas.